S0-BMS-718

SUPER MARIO

JEFF RYAN

SUPER MARIO

HOW NINTENDO
CONQUERED AMERICA

PORTFOLIO / PENGUIN

PORTFOLIO / PENGUIN
Published by the Penguin Group
Penguin Group (USA) Inc., 375 Hudson Street, New York, New York 10014, U.S.A. • Penguin
Group (Canada), 90 Eglinton Avenue East, Suite 700, Toronto, Ontario, Canada M4P 2Y3
(a division of Pearson Penguin Canada Inc.) • Penguin Books Ltd, 80 Strand, London WC2R
0RL, England • Penguin Ireland, 25 St. Stephen's Green, Dublin 2, Ireland (a division of Penguin Books Ltd) • Penguin Books Australia Ltd, 250 Camberwell Road, Camberwell, Victoria
3124, Australia (a division of Pearson Australia Group Pty Ltd) • Penguin Books India Pvt Ltd,
11 Community Centre, Panchsheel Park, New Delhi – 110 017, India • Penguin Group (NZ),
67 Apollo Drive, Rosedale, Auckland 0632, New Zealand (a division of Pearson New Zealand
Ltd) • Penguin Books (South Africa) (Pty) Ltd, 24 Sturdee Avenue, Rosebank, Johannesburg
2196, South Africa

Penguin Books Ltd, Registered Offices:
80 Strand, London WC2R 0RL, England

First published in 2011 by Portfolio / Penguin,
a member of Penguin Group (USA) Inc.

10 9 8 7 6 5 4 3 2 1

LIBRARY OF CONGRESS CATALOGING IN PUBLICATION DATA
Ryan, Jeff, 1976–
Super Mario : how Nintendo conquered America / Jeff Ryan.
p.   cm.
Includes bibliographical references and index.
ISBN 978-1-59184-405-1
1. Nintendo Kabushiki Kaisha. 2. Video games industry—United States. 3. Nintendo video
games. I. Title.
HD9993.E454N5767 2011
338.7'6179480973—dc22   2011004054

Printed in the United States of America
Designed by Daniel Lagin

TO BILL RUDOWSKI

I'MMA GONNA WIN!

CONTENTS

CONTENTS

SUPER MARIO

INTRODUCTION

MARIO'S INSIDE STORY

While Super Mario is a plumber by profession, exploration is at the heart of his stories. As with other distinguished explorers of Italian descent, such as Christopher Columbus, the place he discovered was already inhabited. It was the world of play, a world to which all of us are born holding passports. (As one Royal Geographical Society wag presciently put it more than a hundred years ago, "Explorers become explorers precisely because they have a streak of unsociability and a need to remove themselves at regular intervals as far as possible from their fellow men." He could have been yelling it down the stairs into a modern rec room.) Most of us let that passport expire, but Mario gives us a way to renew it, and revisit our homeland.

There are 240 million Super Mario games out there. Just one game, the original *Super Mario Bros.*, has more than forty million copies in print, not counting releases on other platforms or the uncountable emulators that let you play samizdat versions on your computer.

Broken down by hour, it's an extremely economical buy: few will spend twenty-five hours watching a single twenty-five-dollar DVD, but most everyone who purchases a fifty-dollar Mario game can put in fifty hours or more to explore its nooks and crannies.

Let's talk about economy some more. Do a quick back-of-the-envelope calculation: the number of Mario games sold times fifty bucks each, the average price of a game. This number is going to be off, since it doesn't account for games being bundled with consoles, which are discounted. But it also doesn't account for merchandise and tie-in games like *Dr. Mario*, or for anything else Nintendo sells: Mario games are only one or two of its hundreds of titles a year, and that's all just the software. Hopefully you used a commercial-size envelope: the ballpark figure of Nintendo's Mario's sales is $12 billion. If each one of Mario's gold coins was worth a million dollars, to collect that much moola he would have to knock his head on a coin block for almost three and a half hours.

Mario is unique in that he seems to offer so little appeal. What person who had been living in a cave the last few decades would have picked *Super Mario* as the dominant game franchise, over the *Halo* (30 million sold), *Tomb Raider* (35 million), *Guitar Hero* (40 million), *Resident Evil* (43 million), and *Madden* (85 million) game franchises *combined*? And that doesn't even count Mario's other appearances, such as *Mario Kart* (12 million) and *Mario Party* (5 million). The other top franchises let you experience the adrenaline and horrors of war, or deep fantasy worlds, or pro sports. A Mario game lets you pretend to be a middle-aged chubster hopping onto a turtle shell. Huh? No superheroes? No soldiers? No wizards? What sort of cut-rate wish fulfillment is this?

There's something to Mario more than just looks. Games are different from all other entertainment due to their interactivity: they light up totally different parts of the brain than watching a movie or reading a book does. And Mario's bland persona is part of his appeal: he's a one-size-fits-all hero. For twenty years everyone tried to create distinct memorable avatars for us to control: Sonic, Lara Croft, Mega Man. That trend has reversed, and popular games now feature silent, unknown characters such as *Halo*'s Master Chief and the faceless grunts from *Call of Duty* and *SOCOM*. Yet they're still copying Mario, who is both wackily specific (an overalled plumber) and vague as fog (anyone ever see him unclog a drain?).

My own Mario memories probably aren't too different from anyone else's. My first experience was with the cardboard box the NES came in, rather than any game. A schoolmate brought it on the bus every day to show off, and we crowded around to look at the screen shots on its obverse side. A few months later our parents bought us a NES, and my brothers and I put it through usage that would put a Miami air conditioner to shame. We traded games with neighbors, kids older and younger than us, even traded out of the middle-school caste system with the cool kids. We started a neighborhood fan club: to get in, you had to beat a game and find a secret. Most everyone's secrets were from *Super Mario Bros.*, which had them in spades.

Then high school and college and life happened, and I stopped gaming, save for a PC shooter once a year or so. I never chose to quit gaming—it just fell off my priorities list. Then about ten years ago, I landed a copyediting job at a dot-com. No one had any copy for me to proof before noon, yet I was coming in at 8:30 A.M. I asked my managing editor if there was anything I could write, to help out.

There was. She gave me a press release about a *Pokémon* tournament. The company had been using a freelancer for its irregular reporting of video game news and reviews. Having me write for this section of the site would bolster that coverage—and for free, since I was salaried. I typed up the piece, handed it in, and a few minutes later heard my editor on the phone firing the freelancer. She said they had just hired a new video game expert. Gulp.

In the months that followed I studied video games in a way very few others have. I wasn't actually playing them, since I was at work. I wasn't designing them, either, so I didn't need to know alias coding or texture mapping. I needed to know why they were popular, what made one title better or "cooler" than the next. I made myself an expert in all things Sega, Sony, and Nintendo.

And just about all things Nintendo, I found out, were connected to Mario. He was everywhere: in sports games, fighting games, role-playing games, puzzle games, racing games, and every bit of branding imaginable. He had become a one-word shortcut for Nintendo, for gaming itself, and (I'm sure Nintendo hoped) for the concept of fun. Streets were named after him. There was even an unofficial holiday for him, on March 10 (MAR 10, get it?).

"Super Mario" has become the default nickname for any Mario. Formula One champion Mario Andretti (born in 1940) sometimes gets asked if he's named after Super Mario. (He says he is, to the delight of the seven-year-olds who ask.) Chef Mario Batali is called Super Mario as well. If you're good at a professional sport, and your name is Mario, you know what your nickname will be. Just ask hockey's Mario Lemieux, football's Mario Williams, ultimate fighting's Mario Miranda, cycling's Mario Cipollini, and soccer's Mario Basler, Mario Gomez, and Mario Balotelli. They are, respectively, Canadian, American, Brazilian, Italian, German, Spanish, and Ghanaese. The nickname cannot be avoided wherever on the globe you are a Mario.

At some point I realized that the "life story" of Super Mario is the history of gaming itself. Yes, it's a history of Nintendo and its creators: designer Shigeru Miyamoto, billionaire Hiroshi Yamauchi, and his underestimated son-in-law Minoru Arakawa. But at its core, it's the biography of a man who's not real, but has a Q rating up there with Mickey Mouse. A figure whose specific tale of the tape—pudgy Italian plumber from Brooklyn—merely serves to make him as perpetual an underdog as that undertall Italian boxer from Philadelphia, Rocky Balboa. A world-beloved character with roots across three continents: Asian invention, American setting, European name. A character almost totally blank, yet beloved. A hero who is at once us, more than us, and so much less than us. A guy with a brother named Luigi, and a princess to save.

Super Mario.

PART 1

ARCADE FIRE

1 - BABY MARIO

THE BIRTH OF NINTENDO OF AMERICA

n 1980, starting an arcade game took a quarter. Starting an arcade-game company took a lot more. But the rewards were more than getting your initials up on the high score. Companies in the arcade-game business tapped into a gold mine by updating their old electro-mechanical games, which had been collecting first pennies and nickels and now dimes and quarters for nearly a hundred years. One by one they were replacing the solenoids and miniature puppet shows and blinking lights with fancy new "TV thrillers" and "video skill games." These games, shown on sideways television screens, used solid-state electronics to lure players into a web of lighting-fast reflexes, sweaty palms, and cramped fingers, all in an attempt to defeat computer opponents. They were bits of science fiction dropped out of the twenty-third century into the polyester-plaid laps of the 1970s.

And the biggest game maker by far was Atari, the company that put out the first rock-star megahit game, *Pong*, in 1972. Atari followed

Pong with hit after hit—*Asteroids, Tank, Lunar Lander*. In 1980, it introduced two big crazes: *Battlezone*, a wireframe game of tank combat, and *Missile Command*, a Cold War nightmare where players had to see how long they could keep civilization alive while shooting down nukes raining in from the USSR. Everyone else merely treaded in Atari's wake. It brought in untold millions every year, it was run by a hippie, and it flat-out didn't exist ten years ago. Everyone wanted a piece of Atari's success: it spurred the game industry for a 5 percent *monthly* expansion rate.

No one dreamed of *beating* Atari.

A six-person start-up called Nintendo of America was ahead of the pack of wannabes in one crucial way: it was already a success. Too bad that was only in Japan. A Kyoto-based playing card manufacturer since 1894, Nintendo had craftily shifted over to the toy market to capitalize on its existing distribution route for cards. Lots of other Japanese firms were selling arcade games: *Pac-Man*'s Namco, *Frogger*'s Konami, *Bomberman*'s Hudson Soft, and *Space Invaders*'s Taito. Japan's specialty, as journalist Chris Kohler has pointed out, was personality: its good guys and bad guys were characters, of a very crude sort, instead of abstract art come to life, like Atari's *Breakout* or *Tempest*. If everyone else could make games, so could Nintendo.

Nintendo's most skilled inventor was Gunpei Yokoi, who had started his lifelong career with Nintendo repairing its playing-card machinery. He made a telescoping fake hand as a gag, and company president Hiroshi Yamauchi decided to market it as a toy. The "Ultra Hand" sold over 1.2 million copies in 1970, and was soon followed by novelties such as the "Ten Billion Barrel" maze, the "Love Tester" device, and a Roomba-like remote-control vacuum.

Yokoi's most recent success was in portable electronic games. After watching a salaryman playing with an electronic calculator on a train one day, Yokoi had the idea of making small games that could run off of watch batteries. (As with the Ultra Hand, Yokoi only told the imperious Yamauchi about his game idea because he was desperate for conversation. In this case he was stuck as the boss's chauffeur for the day.) The inventor taught himself about segment display, which let the pieces of an LCD "8," when lit up separately, represent all ten digits. By designing a man with many hands, and only lighting up two at a time, segment display could animate a cartoon character for a game. And thanks to the pocket calculator boom, LCD was cheap to acquire. Games people were paying a hundred yen each to play on machines weighing five hundred pounds could be engineered to fit into a shirt pocket. The resulting device was called Game & Watch.

The first Game & Watch game, 1980's *Ball*, was a juggling game. Players watched a ball tick back and forth from one hand to another, and pressed either the left or right button to keep it airborne. Game A was two balls, Game B three. There were five games like this for the "Silver" collection, named after the shiny color of the case. Five more "Gold" games followed in 1981. All flew off the shelves, and lots more were in the works.

This was on top of Nintendo's other game successes. It had joined the home-*Pong* clones, releasing its undistinguished but popular Color TV Game 6, with a fifteen-game follow-up the following year. It had found success with 1974's EM game *Wild Gunman*, tanked with the malfunctioning horseracing title *EVR Race*, and rebounded with its first true video arcade game, *Computer Othello*. Now it had a team of designers (including Yokoi) cranking out new titles every few months, cresting the faddish wave of whatever was currently gobbling up hundred-yen pieces in smoky arcades. How hard could it be to duplicate Japan's success overseas?

Hiroshi Yamauchi, Nintendo's president, ached to be a major

player not just in Japan but in the world. He had his eyes opened during a mid-fifties trip to America, where he had met with Walt Disney executives about licensing its characters on cards. The experience had walloped him with the scope of the global market for entertainment, showing him just how rinky-dink his Japanese-only, family owned playing card business truly was. A small, intense man with prematurely silver hair, he had worked hard to keep it going in the postwar years and beyond. But true success in the era of global *zaibatsus* and international corporations meant making money all around the world.

Hiroshi's great-grandfather Fusajiro Yamauchi opened a Kyoto card shop in 1894 manufacturing colorful flower cards called *hanafuda*, and named the shop Nintendo Koppai. (The word "Nintendo" means "leave luck to heaven" or "We do what we can," which suggests the chance inherent in card games.) He sold to gamblers, who used a new deck every hand. The company hung on through thick and thin over the years, following Japan's economic roller-coaster as it crashed after World War II, rebounded, then crashed again after the 1964 Summer Olympics in Tokyo.

Hiroshi Yamauchi, who at age twenty-one took over from his grandfather in 1949 after the older man suffered a stroke, was at the forefront of Nintendo's changes. Yamauchi tried out various new business models—rice, taxicabs, "love hotels" rentable by the hour. None clicked, until he decided to utilize his network of card and toy shops. His single-minded dedication to running *his* company *his* way made him few friends. Even his family was distant: his children were virtual strangers who feared him the rare times he was home. Like so many family businesses, the business became more important than the family it was supposed to enrich.

A family member would be needed to run the new American branch of Nintendo, Yamauchi knew. But who? Yamauchi's son,

Katsuhito, was too young to take over an American division, despite being older than Hiroshi was when he assumed control of the whole company. His other two kids were girls, Yoko and Fujiko. But the Yamauchis had a history of bringing sons-in-law into the family business. So his eldest daughter Yoko's husband would run the U.S. branch.

If only the son-in-law wanted the job. Minoru "Mino" Arakawa, Yoko's husband, was the second son of a wealthy Kyoto textile family. Mino had Western experience—he and Yoko were living in Canada for his real estate development job with the *zaibatsu* Marubeni. He spoke English, had a graduate degree from MIT, and had driven across the United States in a VW bus. He was a far cry from Yamauchi, a man so callous he took his daughter to one of his favorite geisha clubs for her twentieth birthday—and stayed there after she went home.

Arakawa turned down Nintendo jobs before, but Yamauchi was bred by his grandparents to be persistent. (Hiroshi's father had abandoned his family, and a probable Nintendo presidency, for another woman.) In the end, Arakawa accepted the role as president of a new subsidiary, Nintendo of America. Taking the job meant going against his wife's wishes—Yoko had a distant relationship with both her father and his company—but Yamauchi was just that convincing about the expansion opportunities. At least Arakawa didn't have to change his last name to Yamauchi, like the two previous sons-in-law.

Nevertheless, Yoko's bad premonitions were seemingly confirmed the day they left on a road trip from Vancouver to New York. They had set up a Seattle-based "distribution channel"—really just two truckers named Ron Judy and Al Stone, who had been importing used Nintendo arcade cabinets from Hawaii, and reselling them locally. Before heading out to the East Coast, Arakawa hired them, on commission, to set up distribution channels for the North American market. Then it was time to drive cross country to set up the New York headquarters of Nintendo of America. What was the bad omen? The day the couple crossed over from Canada into Washington State, May 18, 1980, Mount St. Helens erupted.

HAVING SURVIVED THE VOLCANO, THE ARAKAWAS SET UP shop an ash-free three thousand miles away in New York City, with a rented warehouse across the Hudson River in Elizabeth, New Jersey. The Arakawas were in the Big Apple because it was, and still is, the toy capital of the world. Visiting three buyers in a day took a dollar's worth of subway tokens, not a week of airports and hotel lounges.

But it wasn't a good fit. Kyoto was fourteen hours ahead of Manhattan, and any conversation with the home office required one party to stay up very late or wake up very early. Yoko didn't know as much English as her husband, and New York's cesspool vibe—this was the year of the transit strike, Studio 54 being shuttered, and John Lennon's murder—was hardly the Asian-friendly Pacific Northwest of Vancouver. They were unhappy in the city, yet supposed to figure out what sort of games these American foreigners wanted to play. In the vigilante atmosphere of the Guardian Angels, they decided on a game about shooting.

The success of *Space Invaders* had started a worldwide rage for shooters. (Since its release in June 1978, *Space Invaders* was also responsible for a shortage of hundred-yen coins in Japan, and for giving the Japanese something to be as proud of as Brazil was of Pelé.) Namco released a color sequel, *Space Invaders, Part II*, in 1980: it was a worldwide hit as well. Taito responded with *Galaxian* in 1979, which was basically *Space Invaders* with some swooping attacks: it was a hit too. Its sequel, *Galaga*, came out in 1981, with minor upgrades: yet another global hit.

In Japan, Nintendo tried its hand at its own space shooter game in 1980, *Radar Scope*. *Radar Scope*'s twist was that the enemies flew down, but then retreated back to the safety at the top of the screen. There were no shields for players to hide behind, and the more blasts a player let fly, the slower the "rapid-fire laser blaster" would become. Finally, some wireframe buildings in the background made for the illusion you were standing among skyscrapers, looking up at the alien horde.

Radar Scope was Nintendo's biggest game of the year. Its catalog also boasted *Space Firebird,* a top-down dogfight game. There was also *Space Fever*, a straight-up replica of *Space Invaders*, from a year or two back. *Space Launcher* (sensing a theme to the names?) was a *Frogger*-style obstacle course game. *Monkey Magic* was a *Breakout* rip-off. *Head-on-N* was a maze game with race cars, except nowhere near as good as *Pac-Man*. Finally there was *Sheriff*, a Western-themed shooting game, which would seem perfect for America. But it had odd and frustrating controls, with two joysticks instead of one.

So, a few out-of-date knockoffs, a game that had players fuming over the lousy control scheme, and one proven hit. Yamauchi went all in on *Radar Scope*, telling Arakawa it had the best chance for American success. Nintendo started manufacturing three thousand cabinets, shipping them from Kyoto to the New Jersey warehouse. Arakawa's job was to get them all sold. If he succeeded, Nintendo would have a toehold in the American market.

It would take a few months to assemble that many *Radar Scope* cabinets, so Arakawa starting preselling them. His first solo decision for the company was to focus almost exclusively on *Radar Scope*, and cut bait on the others: its success and Nintendo's success would be one. Nintendo farmed out the distribution of *Space Firebird* to Gremlin, a company that worked with other Japanese companies such as Nichibutsu, Namco, and Konami. *Space Fever* never saw U.S. shores. *Sheriff* was released by Exidy as *Bandido*. None were big hits, which must have been a relief to all concerned.

But this wasn't *Let's Make a Deal*: just because all the other doors had donkeys behind them didn't mean that the one Yamauchi and Arakawa chose had a new car. Arcade vendors found *Radar Scope*'s beeping annoying. (Presumably they knew their beeps, working among a hundred machines all set to "migraine.") The news that the game was big in Japan didn't impress. And did arcade vendors need yet another cloned *Space Invaders*, an expensive one at that, from a company with next to no track record?

Arakawa was able to wheel and deal about a thousand of the *Radar Scope* units, breaking even on production and shipping costs. But Yamauchi had sent him three thousand. Now two thousand of them were collecting dust in a warehouse in New Jersey, aging about as well as unrefrigerated milk. This was exactly why Yoko, who was now a three-pack-a-day smoker, hadn't wanted her husband to go into business with her father.

It hardly seemed a success. Certainly not to Ron and Al back in Seattle, who were getting killed by their commission-based deal on an expensive game. What could Arakawa do to prove himself to his father-in-law? Keep selling it, to even more diminishing returns? Or write off the loss and move on to next year's models? Yamauchi might fire him for either decision. He had plenty of experience canning his own relatives: back in 1949, Yamauchi fired first his relatives, then every last executive, to remove all institutional memory of anyone but himself in charge. To avoid their fate, what should Arakawa choose?

There was a third option: Arakawa could preemptively resign, to keep his dignity intact. But this wasn't Japan, where the samurai's *wakizashi* sword was a constant metaphor for reclaiming one's honor after a loss. This was America, the land where the breakfast flake, the ice cream cone, the microwave, and the Post-it note were all botched engineering projects salvaged into worldwide sensations. Failure, not necessity, was the mother of invention. Arakawa had an idea, a cavalier and audacious one—something that would never fly in Japan. Even if the new plan didn't work, though, it would be a game changer.

2 - MARIO'S ARTIST

SHIGERU MIYAMOTO AND
THE CREATION OF DONKEY KONG

inoru Arakawa, a little Mino in a big pond, can't be blamed for failing to break into the arcade game market. It was tough enough for American companies such as Exidy or Cinematronics to compete with the Atari juggernaut, especially since Atari had huge crews of employees churning out hit game after hit game, thousands of cabinets at a time. And Atari was now owned by Warner Communications, meaning it had pockets $100 million deep. Arakawa had no way of knowing he would defeat Nintendo's eight-hundred-pound gorilla of a competitor with his own eight-hundred-pound gorilla.

One of Arakawa's stumbling blocks was in trying to sell games himself. The way most Japanese game makers got their games into American arcades was by licensing them to U.S. firms. Both Namco's *Pac-Man* and Taito's *Space Invaders* were released in America by the same company: Midway. (Midway's name came from the carnival midway, not the Battle of Midway, presumably a sore spot for Japan.) Nintendo had grown profitable in Japan by controlling distribution, and Yamauchi wanted to be his own distributor in America as well. That gave Arakawa two different challenges to overcome: come up with a game to sell, and keep the middlemen out of it.

Neither challenge looked surmountable at present. Nintendo could only deliver cabinets to arcades if it sold them first. The arcade business was entirely cash based, run by vendors so sleazy that towns regularly tried to chase them out adult bookstore–style. Arcades were considered one step away from circus life, and not a step up. It was no stretch to suppose that games made their way into arcades on something other than merit.

Japanese game makers were used to this—they dealt with Yakuza knockoffs of their games often enough, after all. This was yet another reason for Yamauchi to want a distribution network: if he had the power, no one else could touch Nintendo for fear of reprisals. So he was willing to hear out Arakawa, who called up, laid out the facts, then proposed his game-changing solution.

Fact: *Radar Scope* wasn't going to sell any more units. Fact: To keep Ron and Al from walking away, Arakawa had promised them that the next Nintendo game would be a smash. Fact: They needed a new game to sell. Fact: despite adding words such as "explosive," "pulsating," and "ecstasy" next to the hot chicks in their trade-magazine ads, Nintendo had little up its sleeve, sexy or not. (All game ads of the time featured such big-haired Spandexed women, perhaps on break from leaning suggestively next to sports cars.) Fact: There were two thousand cabinets wasting away in Jersey. Conclusion: The new game had to arrive soon. It had to sell well. And the game changer? Change the game.

Arakawa's gamble was to create not a new game, but a conversion kit for *Radar Scope*, to freshen it up with something new. It would save

Nintendo the cost of the two thousand cabinets, plus it would be a whole lot quicker than making two thousand cabinets in Kyoto and shipping them halfway around the globe. Conversion kits were a form of aftermarket sales for arcades, which let arcade owners squeeze more life out of their older machines such as *Asteroids* by juicing them up with new elements. But they were for older hit games, not brand-new duds.

It was certainly a bold idea, trying to reheat yesterday's blue plate special into a new entrée. And cracking the American market—or at this point merely minimizing the loss—was worth one last half-hearted try. Yamauchi agreed; he'd get a new game made to try to move the two thousand *Radar Scopes*. But he hedged his bet. Yamauchi's top designers were all busy on their own games, and he wasn't going to pull any of them off their projects for this rush job. So he announced an internal competition for conversion ideas. He received several ideas from a surprising source, a boyish, shaggy-haired staff artist with an industrial design degree but no previous game experience. The kid had designed the casings for some Nintendo products: maybe he'd be good designing their guts as well.

That staff artist was Shigeru Miyamoto, then twenty-nine. Miyamoto hadn't been a fan of the first video games he played, such as Taito's *Western Gun*. He was raised on puppets and manga and baseball in the Kyoto suburb of Sonobo, and was much more into music (he loved the Beatles and bluegrass) than electronics. While he preferred his left hand, Shigeru was cross-dominant, which put him in the rarefied company of some of the world's great thinkers: Nikola Tesla, Albert Einstein, Ben Franklin, Michelangelo, Ludwig van Beethoven, Leonardo da Vinci, and Mohandus Gandhi.

Despite all this potential, Miyamoto took five years to get his four-year engineering degree. His father had to get him the job with

Nintendo, helping design toys and sometimes painting the cabinets. He hadn't even been interested in video games until *Space Invaders* came along, with its high-concept plot and ever-increasing game-play speed. But Yamauchi saw something beyond the slacker haircut, and decided to give him a shot.

Yamauchi wasn't crazy, so he assigned Gunpei Yokoi to help translate Miyamoto's vision for the new game—whatever it would be—into reality. Yokoi was ten years older and wiser than Miyamoto, and would show him the gaming ropes. Yokoi was the optimist, focusing on what could be done. Miyamoto worked negatively, always aware of limitations. Yin and yang. Miyamoto and Yokoi then contracted the services of Ikegami Tsushinki, a company that had designed many of Nintendo's arcade games, so the two wouldn't be flying blind hammering out a solid-state motherboard. Ikegami Tsushinki had built *Radar Scope*, so it knew what its own components could do.

Inside *Radar Scope* was a Sanyo monitor turned sideways, displaying pixel-based raster graphics. (A fancy way of saying it couldn't display the bouncing geometric shapes of a *Tron* or a *Tempest*.) It had a DAC (digital-to-analog) converter, so it could turn electronic semaphore from the game board into sounds. It was running the Zilog Z80 8-bit microprocessor, an inexpensive alternative to Intel's 8080 microprocessor. The Z80's affordability and utility quickly made it the generic drug of computer chips: just as good, at a fraction of the cost. So far so good.

Radar Scope had a control panel with one joystick and one button. This was perfectly normal for a shooting game; multiple buttons were a few years away. So whatever the game would do, it would have one primary mode of interaction. Which was usually shooting: what else would you do?

Yamauchi wanted the replacement game to be based on the cartoon *Popeye*, since a live-action movie starring Robin Williams as the titular sailor was in the works. Twenty years ago Nintendo, in a bout of corporate identity confusion, had tried to be a food manufacturer: one of its products was Popeye Ramen. Thus, it had an in for the rights, and Yokoi was designing a Game & Watch Popeye title. Whatever that turned out to be might be good enough for an arcade game. Yokoi and Miyamoto would figure out the details. Even if the game stunk, what great marketing!

But Yamauchi found out it would take years for Nintendo to acquire the rights to a global property such as Popeye for the arcades. If he wanted to play with the big boys, he had to follow their rules. So no Popeye. It was probably for the best: anyone who knew arcades knew that game play was more important than the often laughable story. Sega's *Motocross* didn't do any better when it was renamed *Fonz*, after the *Happy Days* character, did it?

Miyamoto, though, was committed not so much to the story of Popeye as to its goal: defeat the villain to save the girl. The main characters were the barrel-chested hero ("I just made a vague set of characteristics for him as a middle-aged man with a strong sense of justice who is not handsome," he would later say), the enormous hairy opponent, and the tall, willowy heroine who needed rescuing. These storytelling archetypes made the hero an underdog, gave him a noble reason to fight, and even gave some sympathy to the villain. No hero named Popeye? Fine, Miyamoto wouldn't call him Popeye. No boulder-size Bluto? Fine, "Bluto" would be someone else. Popeye by any other name would play the same. And Miyamoto liked the idea of naming a video game after the bad guy, as in *Space Invaders* or *Sinistar*. It'd be easy to come up with a good name for a big gorilla of a villain.

A big, angry gorilla. What a perfect antagonist. A big, angry, dumb gorilla won't let Olive Oyl—er, some other lady—go free. Miyamoto decided to use King Kong, a Japanese synonym for ape. King Kong, after all, had scaled the Empire State Building *and* fought Godzilla: a shared cultural foil for a Japanese American game.

Miyamoto then took a stab at translating. He understood English pretty well since his dad taught it in school, but never could get his tongue around speaking it correctly. He wanted the English word for "stubborn," since a stubborn gorilla was the heart of the game he envisioned. And what animal was more stubborn than a donkey? Thus, a game about an ape was named after a pack animal. (Miyamoto, like many true artists, has since told this story a few different ways.)

Miyamoto now had both a name and a villain in *Donkey Kong*. The story would be a brave man fighting the big dumb ape to get his girl back. A love triangle. Recognizing that actions and motivations were more important than mere names, the damsel in distress would just be "Lady"—a generic MacGuffin of a character. Even the hero lacked a true name: he was "Jumpman." (Miyamoto originally thought of him as "Mr. Video," or just *ossan*—"middle-aged man.") Borrowing the *mukokuseki* concept of ethnically generic people from the manga comics he loved, Miyamoto set about building his digital hero, pixel by pixel.

And as his name would suggest, Jumpman jumped. Quite a phenomenal gravity-defying leap at that: from a standing position, he could spring his full body height. While walking or running, Jumpman could clear an obstacle the relative size of a trash bin. In bold defiance of the one-button controls, Miyamoto came up with a second activity for the athletic Jumpman. He scattered hammers throughout the level that Jumpman could acquire by touching them. With a hammer he was unable to jump, presumably because of its weight. But he could pound away on obstacles with a well-timed wallop of the (now dual-) action button.

Jumpman, like most every movable "sprite" in early video games, was limited to three colors. (Designers fudged black by leaving some spaces blank, and having their sprite move on a black background.) Peach was Miyamoto's first color, for Jumpman's face, ear (just a square block of four pixels), and hand (another four pixels, plus a fifth on the side for a thumb). Blue served two purposes. On his boots (seven pixels each), his shirt, and his single-pixel eye, it was true blue. But on his hair it doubled for black, just as Superman's spit curl was tinged with blue in comic books to show shininess. Miyamoto gave Jumpman a bushy mustache, mostly so players could tell where the nose ended and the mouth began. Two superfluous blue pixels by the sideburns and nape gave Jumpman a bushy, early eighties hairdo—not unlike Miyamoto's own.

Making video game hair look realistic was (and still is) a problem—especially blue hair. So Jumpman got a hat—a red one. And because red fulfilled the three-color quota, that meant Jumpman's pants would have to be red as well. By adding more and more pixels, and crucially placing a single peach pixel to suggest a button, Miyamoto was able to make Jumpman a credible pair of overalls. And quite a paunch, especially for a high jumper. (Author Steven Poole has hypothesized that game characters' bodies are so squat because it gives more proportional room for their head and eyes, which allows the gamer to connect with them better.)

The Lady was designed differently. She was more than a head taller than Jumpman, a Barbie next to a troll doll. She had flowing orange hair, a cinched pink dress with white trim on the bottom, and skin as white as the font flashing the game's high score. Hotter than Olive Oyl, Miyamoto joked.

Donkey Kong (nicknamed DK) himself was built bigger still, to fulfill Miyamoto's idea of having three characters of different sizes mixing it up. DK used up about six times as many pixels as Jumpman, as befitted a true heavy, and was technically multiple sprites Voltroned together into one body. Dark and light brown did most of the color work, showing a thickly muscled, nippled chest; big, hairy arms; legs that ended in wide-splayed simian feet; and ears that would have looked comically big if they hadn't bookended a mouth the size of an August watermelon. His teeth and eyes alone were white, which made them stand out that much more.

Who wore overalls? People in construction jobs such as carpentry and plumbing. So Jumpman gained an occupation: he would be . . . a carpenter. His plumbing years were to come, but he wasn't the first video game plumber. That honor goes to 1973's forgotten safecracking arcade game *Watergate Caper*, where gamers played as one of the leak-plugging "plumbers" who broke into Democratic National Committee headquarters.

If Jumpman died, he would return at the bottom of the screen, ready to take on the challenge of the level again. Each game created three Jumpmen (three lives were standard in gaming), with more earned for high scores. There was something quite spiritual about the concept of a man returning from the dead again and again to complete a task left undone. Facing the monster was a ritual of purity for Jumpman, with impurity of form (i.e., getting clobbered) punished by death. This game of Miyamoto's, and most every video game since, could be seen as a digital Shinto purification ceremony.

It was all coalescing. Donkey Kong would be situated at the top of the screen, with Jumpman fighting his way up: gamers were used to enemies up top. What better setting than a construction site? Donkey Kong could roll barrels down the bare I beams, and Jumpman would have to jump to avoid them. The "sloping" girders were progressively tiered, since angling them wasn't possible with mere raster graphics.

Miyamoto gave Jumpman a choice of ladders to ascend. (Yokoi had suggested seesaws instead, but that would have strained the Z80 processor more than angled girders.) The farther ladder was safer, but it took longer to reach. This gave players a true choice right away: take the quick and difficult path, or the slow and easy one? Crushing barrels and jumping over them was worth some points, but finishing early was worth a lot too. Another choice: go for the high score with the barrels, or try to beat the clock?

Miyamoto wanted his story to progress like a chase, and chases needed multiple locations. The four-person Ikegami Tsushinki development team was baffled; variations on a theme were what sequels were for. Why put all this work into level 2 (with five stories of conveyor belts) when 90 percent of players won't ever see it? Not to mention level 3, with elevators and springs. And now a level 4, with Jumpman smashing rivets to finally bring down Donkey Kong?

Miyamoto couldn't program, but he could play the piano, and he knew that *Radar Scope* had a solid DAC converter. He composed a brief score to go with the game, not just beeps and blasts. There was an intro, a breezy, sad affair that established Jumpman and the Lady's moods. When Jumpman died, there was a four-note dirge. And when Jumpman grabbed a hammer, the soundtrack celebrated with a zippy little march. In true Zen fashion, the happy music was tinged with sadness, and the sad music was tinged with happiness.

What's more, instead of just an introductory screen leading into the game, Miyamoto wanted an animated story to appear after each quarter was plunked. Donkey Kong, with the Lady in hand, would climb to the top of the (not yet slanted) construction site. When he stomped his feet, the screen would tilt into its now-familiar jackstraws shape. After the first level, Miyamoto wanted another cut scene, in which Jumpman and the Lady would be reunited briefly, before Donkey Kong would grab her again and climb higher up the I beams.

Start to finish, *Donkey Kong* was twenty thousand lines of code, way more than usual. Some extra sound equipment had to be added to get the audio to work. But since Miyamoto had composed his music digitally, it took up a fraction of the space of a much shorter clip of true digitized sound, such as a speech sample.

While Miyamoto and Yokoi were designing the new chip in Japan, Minoru Arakawa was moving his American team cross-country again. New York may be Toy Central, but it was too far from Japan. Moving the warehouse from New Jersey to Tukwila, Washington, would save two weeks per shipment, and let the Arakawas return to the Pacific Northwest. The small Nintendo of America staff (including Mino and Yoko Arakawa, Ron Judy, Al Stone, and a gofer they hired named Howard Phillips) would work out of the new warehouse.

At first, *Donkey Kong* was no picnic to sell. Arcade vendors and sales crews were as comfortable with shooting games as the kids dropping quarters into them were. This game was quite literally a different animal. How do you sell a title about a carpenter fighting a monkey who throws barrels at him? With a name that makes no sense in English? Jumpman never once attacks Donkey Kong: the worst he does is destabilize a platform he's on. Some hero. It didn't fit into any recognizable category—not a sports game, not a shooter, not even a driving game. Couldn't Miyamoto have just let you shoot the gorilla with a gun?

At least it was hard: most gamers killed off their allotted three Jumpmen after a minute or so. Nothing dropped a game's profit margins like making a quarter last half an hour. The secret was, like the tiny basketball hoop in carnivals, to make it only *seem* easy. And if somehow a gamer got past all four levels, the game started over again in an even tougher mode.

The first conversion kits were readied. Arakawa had the name Donkey Kong trademarked. (All attempts by Nintendo of America to change the name failed. An urban legend has it the name was originally Monkey Kong, and was changed due to a misheard phone call or garbled fax.) Out of the two thousand dusty *Radar Scope* cabinets, fresh from Jersey, two were chosen for test subjects.

The old game board had to be removed and the new one put in. The wiring harness had to be perfectly connected. One incorrect wire could fry the game board, or overload the monitor so it would smoke out. The wires weren't labeled (this was not a Dell computer), so it wasn't clear which wire went where. And the team assembling the games—including Mino and Yoko—was not brimming with electrical engineering know-how. Next, the old art from the red-colored cabinets—the marquee overlay in front of the screen, the control panel, the instructions along the side—had to be slid out from its protective plastic and replaced with the *Donkey Kong* art and text. And they had to do this during unseasonably hot summer months: it hit a record 107 degrees in nearby Shelton in August.

The rebranding was important for the game, and not just to remove evidence of its previous life as *Radar Scope*. Good cabinet art set an atmosphere for the game that its limited graphics couldn't meet. It was too bad most games were lined up between other cabinets like so many Laundromat washers. Arakawa lost a fight to rename both *Donkey Kong* the game and Donkey Kong the character, but he received permission to rechristen Jumpman and Lady.

The warehouse where the *Radar Scopes* had been gathering dust was run by Don James, whose wife was named Polly. As a way of thanking the warehouse manager, who received a lot of heat from the landlord over Nintendo's uncollected rent, they decided to rename "Lady" after his wife. Lady became Pauline, close enough to Polly.

Around this time, the Tukwila warehouse's owner showed up in person to angrily remind Arakawa about the rent. As the legend goes, the owner, Mario Segale, interrupted a conversation over what to call Jumpman. Segale said his piece, and he grew so incensed he almost jumped up and down himself. After the landlord left, eviction threat delivered, someone suggested the name Mario. It was a joke, since both men had mustaches. But everyone liked the name.

To the Japanese, the name has a familiar consonant-vowel pattern—Yukio, Hanako, Hiroto, Mario. Just one letter away from the Japanese girl's name Mariko, in fact. No troubling Ls that could cause lallation errors, not so commonplace as to be heard regularly in America, not already associated with anyone too famous (*Godfather* author Mario Puzo was about it), and yet not so unusual that it drew undue attention. Although most people think of it as an exclusively Italian name, it's also Spanish and Portuguese. Mario is a variant of the Latin Marius or Marcus—both of which are believed to derive from Mars, the Roman god of war. Sometimes it's used as a masculine version of Mary, which means "star of the sea." For the past thirty years, it's made the list of the two hundred most popular boys' names in America, peaking at 111 in the 1980s.

Yes, Mario would be a super name for Jumpman. If Mr. Segale had only shaved that morning, who can say what name the character on the screen might have been given. Super Carlos? Super Ivan? Super Stavros? Would that alternate-universe name have made a difference in Nintendo's success? Under any other name, would Mario play as sweet?

With the two cabinet conversions done, Nintendo then needed a guinea pig. Ron and Al placed the *Donkey Kong* games in two bars in the Seattle area that already had *Radar Scope* machines: the Spot Tavern and Goldies. They visited every day, mostly because the few quarters in the machines were their business's sole source of income. The bars therefore served as an ersatz product testing ground for arriviste games. *Donkey Kong* immediately started to deliver more than thirty dollars a day in quarters, much more than *Radar Scope* was pulling in. Ron and Al added more cabinets, and each game pulled in more than two hundred dollars a week. That's close to ten pounds in change.

Converting the rest of the two thousand cabinets took months, but each was a guaranteed sale. As they were being completed, new *Donkey Kong* games arrived from Japan, this time with blue cabinets. (The red-cabinet conversions eventually became collector's items.) Demand seemed to increase exponentially, with every arcade-game venue needing a cabinet, then two, then three. At one point, there were sixty thousand *Donkey Kong* machines in simultaneous use worldwide. You were sixty times more likely to find a *Donkey Kong* machine than a theater playing *Raiders of the Lost Ark*, 1981's most popular film, on opening week.

Modern pinball offered basically no correlation between what you do (pull a plunger) and the "reward" of a hundred buzzers and doodads making a racket. Its addiction quotient was low. *Space Invaders* offered a regular reward schedule: ten, twenty, or forty points per ship hit. Its addiction quotient was high. *Donkey Kong* had an irregular reward schedule, since what earned you points changed each level, and you could also score points by speed. Like a slot machine with the slightest house advantage, this was a formula for a stratospherically addicting game, one in which either your skill or your luck may make all the difference next game. That is, until you were out of quarters.

And Mario's abiogenesis would never have happened if *Radar Scope* was a bit more popular, if Arakawa had swallowed the financial loss, if Yamauchi had given the reconfiguration project to experienced designers, if Yokoi hadn't given Miyamoto free rein to design, or if Miyamoto had decided to just make a game—instead of tell a story.

3 — MARIO'S BRAWL

THE MCA UNIVERSAL LAWSUIT

In Hollywood, Florida, a sixteen-year-old pinball wizard with the apple-pie name of Billy Mitchell was the best player in town. He had learned all the physics tricks: tipping the machine without tilting the solenoid, keeping multiple balls in play, trapping balls and flicking them directly into scoops or drop targets. This used to impress people. But not anymore: all the arcade loiterers were over watching a video game. Billy, who lettered in three sports in high school, considered video games beneath his abilities. "Video games were something new and different," he said in an *Oxford American* interview, "and I don't like new and different."

"But they started getting more popular," he said. "Everyone was standing around the *Donkey Kong* machine, and I wanted that attention." Mitchell, whose father owned a restaurant that featured arcade games, started devoting himself to long hours every day getting a feel for *Donkey Kong*: when Mario should run, when he should jump, when he should grab the hammer. Mitchell discovered a place to stand in one level free of dangers: perfect for bathroom breaks.

Mitchell also learned about the last board of *Donkey Kong*—in the 22nd level, the 117th total screen. The game was supposed to have infinite levels, which plateaued at the highest level of difficulty and simply cycled over and over. But the algorithm to determine how much time to give Mario per screen was written without knowledge that people like Billy Mitchell would treat *Donkey Kong* like a rental car on a racetrack, pushing it to its engineering limits. In this case, the limit was $100 \times (10 \times (22 + 4))$, which for any computer nowadays would run the same if that 22 was a 21 or a 23. But *Donkey Kong*'s Z-80 was an 8-bit chip, with a memory counter of only 256 places. Like an odometer hitting a million miles, it rolls back to 000001. For *Donkey Kong*, the rollover on board 117 causes a "kill screen"—Mario is simply not given enough time to complete the level before time runs out.

Billy moved onto *Centipede*, and *BurgerTime*, and *Pac-Man*. He was the best player anyone in South Florida had seen. When an arcade owner in Iowa, Walter Day of Twin Galaxies, started keeping track of reported top scores in games, Billy called up to question a reported *Donkey Kong* score of 1.6 million. He knew it was false because he hadn't cracked a million before hitting the kill screen, and if he couldn't, no one could. Billy was right: the seven-digit score was bogus. He's held the *Donkey Kong* top score more or less since then.

A 2007 documentary about arcade games, *The King of Kong*, shows a duel between Mitchell, whose ego and eloquence make him an easy villain in the film, and a challenger, sweet teacher Steve Wiebe, who lives in Mario's hometown of Redmond, Washington. Mitchell comes off somewhere between Harvey Keitel in *Bad Lieutenant* and wrestling's Mr. Perfect. He's clearly unwilling to give up his title, and hasn't played *Donkey Kong* for years. Yet the victory means so much to him he resorts to psychological warfare and character assassination against the guileless Wiebe. Since then, he and Wiebe have broken and rebroken each other's records: As of July 27, 2007, Mitchell still holds the live record, with 1,050,200 points. Hank Chien, a Harvard-trained plastic surgeon, videotaped a 1,068,000-point score in late 2010.

Billy wasn't the only one addicted to *Donkey Kong*. Those initial two thousand units were long gone from the Tukwila warehouse by the fall of 1981. Just about every unit that came off a boat from Japan was immediately put onto a truck to somewhere in Middle America. Why? Pop psychology would say that while most every other game offered a way to destroy, and *Pac-Man* offered a way to escape, *Donkey Kong* offered a way to rescue. That didn't affect the mimetics of the game play, but it certainly changed the motivation of the players: a girl's life was at stake here! Some desperate arcades had even started to buy a blatant clone, Falcon's *Crazy Kong*. Others bought expensive counterfeits.

Minowa Arakawa had Don James, his new head of operations (after having lured James away from Segale), hire some Washingtonians to manufacture the parts in Redmond. That way, the finished machines wouldn't have to ride the slow boat from next-to-China to get there. Plus, Seattle had tech-savvy workers and one of the world's great reserves of lumber for the cabinets. This reduced production cycle allowed Nintendo to manufacture more *DK*s while it was still popular with arcade-goers. Up to fifty units a day of the big ape were made in 1982, more than a thousand a month, more than *Radar Scope* ever sold in its lifetime.

Nintendo's distributors Ron Judy and Al Stone were two of the six people who piece by piece converted every one of the original *Radar Scope* games to *Donkey Kong*. They were being paid on straight commission, which had nearly bankrupted them in the early days. Now Judy and Stone were millionaires. Arakawa—whose wife, Yoko, had been another one of the six crawling inside machines with soldering irons—found himself responsible for a global property that brought in $180 million in its first year in the United States alone. That was more than any film released in 1982, save for *E.T.*

Amazingly, *DK* brought in $100 million in its second year, well beyond any other sophomore game other than *Pac-Man* and *Space Invaders*. "Video Games Are Blitzing the World," read a *Time* magazine cover in January 1982. Miyamoto's originality of concept contributed to *Donkey Kong*'s long-lasting success. There were tons of shooter games and maze games, but no other "ape-throwing-barrels" game. (Atari's *Kangaroo* that year was closest, with its evil monkeys and a high-jumping hero.) If Nintendo was just another flash-in-the-pan toy company, this was quite a long flash.

Arakawa had a new challenge: how to spend the money. The original plan of marketing the Japanese product overseas for an additional slice of profit was becoming inverted: America ate up the games like cheeseburgers. Nintendo needed an American hub, not just a rented warehouse. (Mr. Segale, presumably, was all squared away by this point.) Arakawa purchased twenty-seven acres of land in Redmond in July 1982. Nintendo could have paid in rolls of quarters.

Arakawa may have needed a proper headquarters just to hold back the people knocking on his door, cash in hand. Licensing companies left and right were eager to have Nintendo sign deals for the likeness of *Donkey Kong*'s hero and villain. Pajamas, breakfast cereal, Saturday morning cartoons, plush stuffed animals, Topps trading cards, Fleer candy. The B-side of the Buckner and Garcia novelty song "Pac-Man Fever" was "Do the Donkey Kong." Arakawa's worries now weren't that he'd go out of business, but that he'd leave money on the table.

Milton Bradley even adapted *Donkey Kong* as a board game: Kong himself was a toy that could throw small yellow barrels, as one to four Marios (drawn with a long chin and a bouffant mustache that would soon characterize Luigi) moved up the *Chutes-and-Ladders*–style board. The game was simple, but came with instructions longer than the prescribing information for most pharmaceuticals.

And, of course, *Donkey Kong* became a console video game. Taito offered a big chunk of its *Space Invaders* money to Nintendo for all rights to *Donkey Kong*. Nintendo knew to sell the milk, not the cow. American companies such as Coleco and Atari also vied for the rights. Yamauchi looked at who had the best technology, who had the most avenues for distribution, and who would fork over the most per unit sold. The decision from Kyoto: Coleco would get the exclusive rights. "It was the hungriest company," Yamauchi explained. It was also, notably, American. Atari was offering more money, but Coleco execs camped out in Arakawa's hotel room one night, imploring on Nintendo to honor Yamauchi's decision. Arakawa did, saying he was impressed with Coleco's passion.

Coleco received all tabletop and cartridge rights to *Donkey Kong*. In exchange, Nintendo received a lump-sum payment, plus a buck in royalties for every tabletop game, and $1.40 for each console game. Coleco packed *Donkey Kong* with every unit of its new ColecoVision game system: after six months of exclusivity there, Coleco would port it to rival consoles such as the Intellivision and the 2600s. The prestige of bundling such a popular game with its new console helped make the company half a billion dollars in sales, and $40 million in pure profit. Mario should have been called Midas.

In Kyoto, Shigeru Miyamoto was tasked with making a sequel. He had had huge plans for the original *Donkey Kong*, but had had to work with the sloppy seconds of *Radar Scope's* primordial ooze. Now, though, he had carte blanche—and a team to do the grunt work of designing it for him. Millions of quarters had given his initial vision validation. Gamers around the world wanted to go on another adventure with the heroic Mario.

Miyamoto wasn't feeling that, though. He wanted to rotate the love triangle, give the big ape some respect. Donkey Kong, being too big for 1982-era machines to make a playable character, would play the Pauline role, the helpless kidnapped one. A new character, Donkey Kong Jr., a smaller and more agile ape, would be the hero. He'd also get the game named after him, à la *Ms. Pac-Man*, gaming's most successful sequel.

That left one more character and one more role to fill. Miyamoto knew it was good drama to upend audience conventions, to make them all of a sudden have pity on a villain, and also to see the unexpected mean streak in the one they thought was a hero. So Mario would be the villain, the master who locks up his pet and won't let him go free. And tries to kill the son who attempts a jailbreak. It was a natural next step for the relationships, for the story.

Numerous licensers who paid big money to slap a grinning Mario and a snarling Donkey Kong onto their products must have been shocked. This was not how a brand was built! Miyamoto found himself accused of not knowing his characters, at a time when the characters barely were extant. But *Donkey Kong Jr.* was hardly a misstep, even if it too altered expectations. The single-jump button was still there, but Junior could climb up a series of chains and vines, as well as jump. There were items in the chains and vines, and by touching them Junior dropped them onto various enemies below. That replaced the hammer attack.

And the enemies! There were living bear traps, snapping madly and dragging unleashed chains behind them. There were yellow-and-purple birds that hopped around and glided through the air in deadly assaults on Junior. And there were sparks, living dollops of anthropo-morphic electricity that ever so slowly inched their way up the chains. Miyamoto had the "Snapjaws" move in two different ways, and colored them differently as a clue. It would become a Mario tradition: the recolored sprite attacking in a different manner. Mario himself showed up with an identical twin, to move a cage around: perhaps Luigi bor-rowed his brother's red overalls for the day.

Donkey Kong Jr. wasn't what anyone expected for a sequel, but no one expected *Donkey Kong* to come out of the guts of a space shooter. Nintendo was virtually printing cash by putting anything with Mario or Donkey Kong's face on it, so it crossed its corporate fingers and sent the game out into the world of 1982.

It was a hit. Notably, it was a different enough game from *Donkey Kong*—not a remake, not an improvement, but a new series of levels to conquer—that it seemed to have an almost negligible effect on the popularity of the original. Nintendo and Mario would learn this les-son well: a franchise character could appear in various different types of games and not glut the market—provided the games were all suit-ably different from each other. (Later franchises from *Army Men* to *Star Wars* failed to learn this, to their dismay.)

Coleco, which was still preparing its dominant ColecoVision, was contacted by MCA Universal, which wanted to invest in the company. As reported by Steven Kent in *The Ultimate History of Video Games*, the investment pitch in Los Angeles, including a walk-on visit by Univer-sal's wunderkind Steven Spielberg, was more assassination than assignation. Once the two companies' presidents were in the same room, Universal's president dropped the pretense of an investment and threatened to sue (read: destroy) Coleco if it shipped the Coleco-Vision with *Donkey Kong*. *Donkey Kong*, Universal felt, was an infringe-ment on its own King Kong character.

A telex (this was before e-mail) laid it on the line to Coleco: destroy all *Donkey Kong* property, stop any and all marketing, and give us every cent you've made off the ape. Universal sent the same telex to Nintendo of America. Coleco, desperate to have an unblocked path to release the ColecoVision, quickly agreed to fork over 3 percent of net profits to Universal. The profit-slice turned out to be worth almost $5 million. Coleco didn't inform Nintendo about this, which seems puzzling, since the lawsuit implies that Nintendo had licensed an illegal product.

Nintendo's initial response to the telex was similar to Coleco's: let's pay up to get rid of this quickly. They certainly had enough money lying around: $5 million of it might save a lawsuit. Anyone in gaming knew that success drew lawsuits: if not from Atari or Magnavox, then Universal. Wait, how about $7 million?

Then, Nintendo of America's lawyer Howard Lincoln had an epiphany. Lincoln, formerly Al Stone and Ron Judy's attorney, had the previous year arranged for trademark protection for *Donkey Kong*, paving the way for millions in lucrative licensing fees. Millions and millions, in fact. Nintendo had the money to fight this, if it wanted. It wasn't a six-person start-up anymore. Furthermore, Lincoln did some research and realized Nintendo had a tremendous case against Universal. *Donkey Kong* and *King Kong* were different animals. Arakawa was chagrined to not just pay some hush money, as Yamauchi wanted. But Lincoln convinced him it was the right thing to do.

A three-party meeting was held in Los Angeles, Universal's backyard, to attempt to straighten things out. Arakawa and Lincoln attended for Nintendo, along with reps for Universal and Coleco (who still hadn't told Nintendo it had capitulated). Nintendo said Universal was, to skip the legalese, full of it. There were lots of other unlicensed *King Kong* products on the market, and Universal hadn't gone after any of them. This was about Nintendo's money. Coleco sheepishly tried to get Nintendo to fold to Universal. But Nintendo wasn't budging.

Universal promised Nintendo it would send a chain of title for *King Kong*, documented proof that it owned the property. That would be the easy part of the legal battle, of course: the hard part was proving that *Donkey Kong* was a rip-off of *King Kong*. No one had ever asked a judge or jury to decide how close a video game had to be to impinge on a film. But no chain of title arrived in the mail at Redmond. When Nintendo asked again for it, Universal instead demanded a royalty payment. It was a foreshadowing of Universal's poor legal standing.

In a possibly perfidious piece of brinkmanship, Nintendo arranged a special meeting with Universal, to discuss matters. These sorts of meeting are only called when there's something to discuss, i.e., Nintendo caving in to Universal's demands. Universal's president personally attended, wanting to see the upstart Nintendo fall on its own sword and offer him royalties. But Lincoln and Arakawa merely reiterated their already-stated belief: we're not liable and won't be paying you anything. To quote Ice Cube, it was on like Donkey Kong.

"His reaction was shock," Lincoln recalled. Universal made movies, and its movements seemed reflective of this: big, bombastic, very entertaining, but as ephemeral as the fog around Skull Island. Nintendo, on the other hand, was a game company. Its lawyer just scored a major tactical victory, without the pieces on the board moving a whit.

As if the suit wasn't complicated enough, a new player entered: Tiger Electronics. Tiger had exclusively licensed *King Kong* from Universal for a handheld game. Universal realized that if Tiger kept that exclusive license, and *Donkey Kong* was shown to be the same as *King Kong*, then only Tiger would be able to sell *Donkey Kong* games. Furthermore, Tiger's *King Kong* game was a pretty blatant swipe from *Donkey*

Kong. (The layers of irony are like a lasagna.) Universal rejected the game. Tiger redesigned it to have bombs instead of barrels, and straight instead of crooked platforms. Also, the hero was given a fireman's hat.

Universal continued its aggressive actions, officially suing not only Nintendo but six other companies to whom Nintendo had licensed *Donkey Kong.* It collected royalties from all but two of them: Milton Bradley for the *Donkey Kong* board game (which refused to pay) and Ralston-Purina for *Donkey Kong* cereal (which offered a measly five grand, which Universal rejected). Combined with Coleco's payments, Universal was already making steady money off of a case that hadn't even started yet. This was the benefit of lawyering up: smaller companies backed down so fast, it was almost a legal form of theft.

Nintendo was seeing this through to the courtroom, though. Howard Lincoln had pulled in a hotshot trial lawyer named John Kirby to mount the Nintendo defense. *Universal City Studios Inc. v. Nintendo Co. Ltd.* lasted seven days. Kirby listened to Universal's legal team explain its case: the two have similar plots, they're both apes named Kong, so in conclusion give us the money. Kirby, in turn, highlighted every difference between the game and the film. He read deposed statements from Shigeru Miyamoto, explaining how the game was designed.

Then, Kirby sprung the trap. In 1975, Universal had sued RKO, the original makers of *King Kong.* Universal, in a case-winning argument, had proved that *King Kong* was in public domain, since the movie was from 1933. Universal didn't need to pay a dime to the "owners" of *King Kong,* because anyone could do whatever he wanted with King Kong. Kong was as unownable as Huck Finn. Then, Kirby asked for a summary dismissal of the suit. Granted.

The word "hubris" might not be strong enough for Universal at that time. It had, after all, knowingly collected millions of dollars, and started a half dozen lawsuits, all on a claim that it had proven, in the public record no less, to be bogus. How did it think it was going to succeed?

Judge Robert W. Sweet tore into Universal, in a blow-by-blow beating as thorough as it was brutal. First, Universal didn't own *King Kong*. Second, even if it did, *Donkey Kong* wasn't a copy of *King Kong*. Third, *even if it was*, it would be considered parody, which is legal.

Sweet was just getting started. Any company Universal had hit with cease-and-desist letters had the right to sue Universal to get back its "royalty" payments and more. There was one clear copyright violation that came to light, though. Judge Sweet felt Tiger's *King Kong* game, even with its superficial changes (a fireman's hat!) was a clear knockoff of *Donkey Kong*. Universal had to pay a license fee to Nintendo for Tiger's game. Universal's loss could only have been greater if the judge ordered back royalties to the planet Earth for its use in the film company's logo.

Universal countersued Nintendo, and the ensuing battle took a few more years to conclude. Universal lost every suit. In the end, it had to pay nearly $2 million to Nintendo to cover its rival's legal fees. This wasn't counting all the other lawsuits it had on its hands, or the millions in fees it spent trying to prove, in an "abuse of judicial process," that *Donkey Kong* and *King Kong* were one and the same.

Coleco got its money back (via Universal buying a chunk of its stock), but its lack of business fortitude was now public. It and Atari were both working on computers. Coleco was going to include *Donkey Kong* on a floppy disc as the pack-in game for its "Adam" computer. Adam premiered, playing *Donkey Kong*, at a Chicago trade show. Coleco was promptly contacted by lawyers from Atari. Nintendo had licensed the floppy-disc rights to Atari for its Atari 800 computer. Coleco had assumed it had them, as part of the console and tabletop rights. Yamauchi intervened, and bullied Coleco into shelving its unlicensed game. He almost certainly chose to play a game of chicken with Coleco because he remembered Coleco caving in to Universal. Coleco caved again. (The floppy-disc version for Atari's computer, the Atari 800, was never released.)

Nintendo's victory, in comparison, was unparalleled. Most other game companies either went out of business or were gobbled up by the big boys. But Nintendo faced down a muscular extortionist of a rival. Like a boy who realizes during a bully showdown that he has become a man, Nintendo learned how powerful it really was, after a mere two years. Howard Lincoln, for his part, rose from being Nintendo's lawyer to being its senior vice president and general counsel.

And trial attorney John Kirby was given a boat. The thirty-thousand-dollar sailboat was named, of course, *Donkey Kong*. Kirby was also given "exclusive worldwide rights to use the name for sailboats." Finally, as Mr. Segale before him, Mr. Kirby may have been rewarded with Nintendo's greatest honor. Starting in 1992, Nintendo released a popular series of games about a cute little pink fluffball. His name? Kirby.

4 – MARIO'S EARLY YEARS

THE VIDEO GAME CRASH OF 1983

Voice actor Peter Cullen may not have a recognizable name, but everyone's heard his pipes. For the last twenty years he's been everyone from the sad-sack Eeyore in *Winnie the Pooh*, to the villainous K.A.R.R. in *Knight Rider*, to the clicking flange-jawed Predator. He hit the trifecta of giant-morphing-robot cartoons in the early eighties, doing voices for *Go-Bots*, *Voltron*, and most memorably Optimus Prime in *Transformers*. (He still voices a CGI Optimus for the live-action remakes.)

But before Optimus Prime became his trademark role, Cullen was Mario. An animated anthology program called the *Saturday Supercade* on CBS in 1983 featured characters from various video games, all with brief cartoons in a half-hour show. *Q*Bert*, the hopping star of a maze game, became a fifties-style teenager on the run from bullies. *Frogger*, about a poor animal trying to cross a busy road, was now about an amphibious reporter. *Pitfall*, at least, was a more traditional action-adventure, since Pitfall Harry was a blatant Indiana Jones rip-off.

Mario was clearly the second banana (sorry) in the cartoon of *Donkey Kong*: Soupy Sales's titular gorilla was the lead. DK was a Bugs Bunny type, always one step ahead of his circus trainer, Mario, who was trying to recage him. Mario was reduced to the Elmer Fudd role. Pauline was recast as Mario's niece, who intervened on Donkey Kong's behalf when Mario grew too close to capture.

The slapstick portrayals didn't mesh with the game, where tension and death awaited every misstep. And the show gained an odiously revisionist second act when the *Donkey Kong Jr.* cartoon premiered the following year, featuring lonely Junior's quest to find his missing father. The show made DK seem to be a deadbeat dad, undeserving of his son's efforts at reunion. But perhaps the gentle good humor helped soften Mario and Donkey Kong's edges.

The two rivals, though, would be parting ways. Shigeru Miyamoto introduced a new human protagonist for 1983's *Donkey Kong 3*, Stanley the exterminator. Donkey Kong, residing in the upper center of the screen, and again in the heavy role, is hanging between two jungle vines. When he punches a hive, a staggering variety of bugs pile out, ready to attack Stanley with all-different attack patterns. The exterminator has to zap them all with his bug spray, then once they're gone grab some super bug spray and spritz Donkey Kong himself. (No little fun has been had with Stanley's only available target: the gorilla's rear end. The gorilla braces when he receives the bidet-style insecticide.)

Donkey Kong 3 was, behind the jungle canopy, a clever reworking of *Space Firebird*, Nintendo's old dogfighting game. Space games weren't selling that well, but the game play was almost identical. Besides, Miyamoto was working on two games at the same time (not counting the *DK3* adaptation *Green House* for the Game & Watch), and couldn't be expected to generate all-original content for both.

For that other game, Miyamoto was spinning off Mario into his own title. Mario was originally a carpenter, since he was at a construction site. But, a friend told Miyamoto, the overalls and hat and pudgy willingness to leap into nasty situations made him really more of a plumber. Hmm, Miyamoto thought. There could be a video game about plumbing. And Mario could be the star.

The idea he came up with bears as much relation to plumbing as *Pac-Man* does to fighting the paranormal. Mario, down in the cavernous sewers of New York, jumps around on platforms four stories high. Open sewer pipes emit a series of nasties—crabs, turtles, flies. Mario attacks not by hammer or bug spray, but by jumping on enemies. Furthermore, the platforms are mutable: head butting one from below buckles it like a plank-and-rope bridge, and flips enemies. If Mario collides with them while they're upside-down, he kicks them to the edge of the screen. Kick or bop them all offscreen, and the level is clear.

The enemies were all "palette-swapped," the same design with two paint jobs, which doubled the menagerie crawling out of the huge green drainage pipes. The Sidestepper crab started off red, but if not kicked offscreen after being flipped would turn a speedy blue. Good attacks and quick finishes rewarded Mario with points, as well as coins that went clattering around like a shanked football. The game's grand challenge wasn't just defeating the creatures, or winning before time ran out, or amassing valuable coins. It was finding an amalgam of all three. It was noticeably easier than *Donkey Kong* to finish a level, but—appropriate for a game located underground—much deeper.

The game was called *Mario Bros.*, which raises the question of who Mario's brother was. To create a sibling, Miyamoto palette-swapped

Mario himself. The plumber's red shirt was now black, and his blue overalls and red hat were now Day-Glo green. Better electronics let Miyamoto have a whopping six colors at his disposal. So Mario and his sibling received slightly different skin tones and hair colors. One pair of ugly-even-by-1983-standards indigo sneakers later, and taa-da!: Luigi was born.

Luigi's wardrobe has been updated slightly since then: his green hat now matches his green shirt, he wears blue overalls like Mario, and the indigo sneakers are exiled. His name supposedly came from an Italian bistro near Redmond, called Mario and Luigi's. Or maybe it's a pun: *ruiji* means "similar" in Japanese. Or, as some have pointed out, maybe someone at Nintendo was a cinephile, and remembered Yves Montand as Mario in 1953's *The Wages of Fear*, a stout mustached man with a hat, who had a tall lean friend named Luigi.

Luigi's controls were identical to Mario, which, of course, was even easier to program than a palette-swap. The game, though, was called *Mario Bros.* Wasn't Mario the *first* name? Thanks to what comic book fans call a ret-con (retroactive continuity), Mario's brief history was rewritten to have Mario be the family name. That made Luigi's name Luigi Mario. But then what was Mario's first name? Mario as well. Mario Mario. If he was a real person, he'd have had a rough childhood.

The two-player simultaneity was "inspired" by a 1982 Williams game called *Joust*, which in turn seemed to be inspired by *Donkey Kong*'s platform-jumping control scheme, combined with the sheer lunacy of crazy animals running around. In *Joust*, players mounted either an ostrich or a stork, which could fly by repeatedly hitting the "flap" button. They bounded around a board suspiciously similar in layout to *Mario Bros.*: a series of tiered platforms arranged like a split-level stairway minus the stairs. Due to a programming glitch that defined the ethos "it's not a bug, it's a feature," when the ostrich or stork crossed the far left side of the board, they popped through to the right side, like a secret passageway in *Clue*.

Joust was a glorified game of chicken. Players charged at flying monsters, and whoever had his lance higher when they collided won. The loser was, in a plot twist worthy of Gabriel García Márquez, transformed into an egg, and would hatch back into play if the winning jouster didn't come and stomp it within a few seconds. One final, crucial aspect of *Joust*? Players could—and did—attack each other, as well as the on-screen baddies.

Mario Bros. did not copy *Joust*'s singular attack style. Its rule was the same as in the previous game: if Mario (or Luigi) touched an opponent, he died instantly. It varied the types of attacks: jumping, flipping, kicking, or head butting the once-a-level POW block landmine, which wipes everyone out. The platforms were placed a bit closer, since Mario had to access them in a single jump. One final, crucial aspect of *Mario Bros.*? Mario and Luigi couldn't kill each other.

Cooperation in games wasn't a much-traveled avenue. Certainly, from *Pong* onward, people understood the joys of two-player rivalries. It was loved on the business side as well, since it gobbled up two quarters instead of one. Shooter games were more difficult to make two player. Put a second controllable sprite on an existing board, and whatever challenge there was gets ruined by double the laser fire. Beef up the number of enemies, and you ended up designing two games. And trying to throw more villains in the mix on the fly was pushing things in 1983. The solution, it seemed, was to turn whatever game you had into a duel, with the winner the one simply left alive. *Joust*, *Space Duel*, *Space Wars*, *Tank*, and numerous others found ways of turning any number of game genres into death matches.

But not *Mario Bros.* There was no easy way to hurt Luigi. The best players could do was to kick an enemy at him. The only honest way to beat Luigi was to outscore him, trying to trample the monsters and claim the coin reward before he could. This invested Mario in a taut, competitive friendship with his brother, one eye on the beasts and the other on the current high score. It was cooperative competition, rather than simply throat-slitting. And with no in-game story other than sewer stomping, the "story" became you versus your friend.

Mario Bros. made for the fourth *Donkey Kong* game in three years, not counting an Epyx game based on the *DK* game play called, in a probable homage, *Jumpman*. Plus, Nintendo finally acquired the *Popeye* rights Miyamoto had wondered about, and made a game for the spinach-eating sailor that clearly reflected its *Donkey Kong*–ish roots. But Nintendo was merely keeping pace. *Pac-Man* alone generated 1981's *Ms. Pac-Man*, 1982's *Super Pac-Man,* and 1983's *Pac & Pal* and *Pac-Man & Chomp-Chomp. Gradius, Space Invaders, Asteroids*, and *Galaxian* all churned out yearly arcade sequels.

These games didn't provide the only automated entertainment in the early eighties. The same quick-and-dirty aesthetic accounted for: disposable Freddy, Jason, and Michael Myers slasher movies; a barrage of TV spinoffs (*Knots Landing* from *Dallas*, and the *Facts of Life* from *Diff'rent Strokes*); and a cavalcade of synthesizer-y New Wave music (Depeche Mode, A-Ha, and the Pet Shop Boys). But people understood that when one fad in entertainment ended (bye, Howard Jones) another would take its place (hello, Huey Lewis and the News).

The same wasn't true of fledgling video games, barely a decade old as a business. Arcades had grown like overnight mushrooms in the quarter-rich atmosphere, and seen a generation of grass-smoking hippies and disco cats grow up and leave, turning into Walkman-wearing yuppies. The arcade culture had existed for a hundred years before video games, but video games made them ever-present places where you could bum a smoke off an older kid, watch *Yars' Revenge* masters ply their trade, listen to Kiss, and feel cool. But as with any game, the fun only lasted so long.

Distributors were now placing cabinets anywhere they could: supermarkets, restaurants, barber shops, drugstores, gas stations. They overloaded the market with too many games, games that weren't worth a quarter, games too hard for John Q-Bert Public. Distributors started going broke, since the machines they bought on credit weren't bringing in the cash to pay back the bank. The writing had been on the wall for a year already, when in 1982 Atari's projected earnings were reset to be less Daedalian. After that, it was a matter of time before game companies too close to the sun started to fall out of the sky.

Where the pinch was really being felt, though, was in the home console market, which was five years newer than even arcade video games. The market began with its own minibubble, when Atari released *Home Pong*. Literally more than a hundred competitors followed, all with their own *Pong*-style games. It was grossly expensive and impractical to require consumers to purchase an entire console to play one game.

Atari's 2600, released in 1977 as the VCS, had become the dominant gaming machine. But by 1983, its colorful graphics and varied gaming styles had become old hat. Too many companies—including Atari—were releasing too many games. Disgruntled Atari workers left to form their own companies, and sell their own 2600 games— Accolade, Activision, Acclaim (all named to come before Atari in the phone book). Simply buying "a" video game was now as inconceivable as buying "a" book or "a" sneaker: you had to know what type of experience you wanted, and which titles offered the best and most challenging game play and graphics.

Even knowing the game from the arcade didn't guarantee your port of the game would be the pick of the variorum of possible conversions. *Donkey Kong* was a prime example. ColecoVision players received three solid levels, while Atari 2600 players only got two so-so levels. Since the arcade version had four levels, both were abridgements. *Donkey Kong Jr.* was even more bisected: the Atari 2600 game was atrocious, but the Intellivision edition was like setting up the arcade in your living room. And the *Mario Bros.* Atari 2600 version was phenomenal. (The ad for it was not. It featured an actor dressed as Mario in a boiler room frantically fighting giant crabs coming out of green pipes. Then he operatically sings "Mario, where are you?" Apparently the ad makers never understood that the plumber in red *was* Mario.)

Conventional wisdom says the sheer number of these bad games was the primary cause for the video game crash of 1983. Certainly two bad games stand out. Atari's wretched *Pac-Man*, for instance, was manufactured to the quantity of 12 million cartridges. Atari had only sold 10 million 2600s, though, a decision as catastrophic as drying wet dynamite over a campfire. Add to that the other much-maligned 2600 game, the rushed *E.T.*, whose box-office ubiquity was tarnished by a hard, unfun game. These games' final fate is that rarest of things: an urban legend that's actually true. With millions of unsellable titles, Atari had to eat the loss and dispose of them. But it feared that if the games were merely thrown away they'd be stolen from the trash and resold, further cutting sales. So, in an act of overkill usually reserved for Rasputin, they pulverized the cartridges with steamrollers, dug a pit in an Alamagordo landfill, buried the games deep, and smothered everything with concrete.

But the way to avoid a bad game, as with a bad album or bad magazine, is simply not to buy it. Consumers might get burned from a shoddy product, but they'd learn not to touch that particular hot stove again. It's the most basic role of capitalism: weak products don't sell.

The real problem came from the retail side. Department stores, toy stores, and electronics stores needed to stock the latest games and consoles. Nowadays, and more or less ever since 1983, that has meant three or four home consoles, and maybe one or two portable consoles, plus a selection of games for each system.

Imagine what it was like in 1983. The Atari 2600 was still dominant. Its replacement, the Atari 5200, has recently hit stores. It was competing for shelf space with the ColecoVision and Coleco's new Gemini, Mattel's Intellivision and Intellivision II, the Bally Astrocade, the Fairchild Channel F System II, the Magnavox Odyssey^2, the Vectrex, the Emerson Arcadia 2001, and the VTech CreatiVision. Individual stores such as Sears and Radio Shack had proprietary systems as well—Tele-Games and the Tandyvision.

And these were just the consoles! Atari had branched out into computers with the Atari 400 and 800 personal computers. Add to that the Texas Instruments TI 99/4A, the Commodore VIC-20 and Commodore 64, the Timex Sinclair, the Apple II and Lisa, the Mattel Aquarius, and the Coleco Adam. Each one had its own software library. Each had a half dozen accessories. All were sold as game machines that could also run a spreadsheet or type a letter. None were compatible with the others. Just about every company had announced plans to ship a brand-new console or computer in 1984. And, in a bout of desperation, they had all begun to slash prices to draw in a customer base. When *Time* magazine had said the person of the year for 1982 was the computer, it didn't imagine the very next year there'd be an overpopulation problem.

The poor electronics retailer had seen this before, with VHS and Betamax, and before that tape versus videodisc. Eight-track versus cassette, record versus reel-to-reel, FM versus AM. Laserdisc, in 1983, was trying (and failing) to supplant videotape. But these format battles were usually two-party affairs. Retailers would stock both modestly, and allocate more and more shelf space to whoever was winning. But this rhododendron hell of a dozen different video game companies all trying to put the others out of business would bring everyone down—as well as any retailer foolish enough to try to stock a little bit of everything.

All through 1982 retailers had seen their groaning partitioned shelves grow dusty. Even for the Christmas season, consumers didn't want to commit to any one console, any one computer. Now, in 1983, store owners drew a line. They started pushing back unsold products. They demanded refunds, and refused to stock any new games or consoles. Time to get out of this cloud-cuckoo land, this nine-person game of *Joust*.

But the game manufacturers had no cash on hand to return to the stores, since neither their new games nor the existing inventory were being sold. One company, US Games, went bankrupt. Another, Games By Apollo, followed. Private companies that had entered gaming to rack up a quick IPO shuttered their doors. Public companies like Atari's Warner Brothers saw their stock prices plummet. System after system ended up being marked for clearance prices. What used to cost $300 was ratcheted down in $50 installments until it was being given away for less than it cost to manufacture. Forty-dollar games went for $10, then for $5—anything to get them out of the store. Like maggots on a corpse, a new crop of game manufacturers appeared, selling cheapo games already priced at $5.

The gaming retailers adopted the motto of the video-game-playing computer WOPR from 1983's *Wargames*: The only way to win . . . is not to play. They hesitated to stock any more video games. They absolutely refused to stock any more video game consoles. The glut of bad games had salted the earth of Sears and poisoned the well of Toys "R" Us. Kids would still be able to buy their GI Joes, Cabbage Patch Kids, and My Little Ponys. Toy stores, like arcades, would survive. But they'd never let another video game system pass through their receiving bays again.

PART 2

SUPER 8

5 - MARIO'S ISLAND

JAPAN AND THE FAMICON

Times were tough for U.S. game makers: Coleco collapsed. Milton Bradley, weakened from the Vectrex, was gobbled up by Hasbro, which didn't have any skin in video games. Mattel lost millions from its Intellivision flop, and stuck to selling Barbies and Hot Wheels. Warner sold the Atari business for parts, as documented in Scott Cohen's book *Zap*. The Commodore 64 and Apple II stayed strong, and became the home gaming systems of choice. Companies like EA, Epyx, and MicroProse vied to be to the computer what Atari was to the home console. Filling the void, VCR sales skyrocketed.

The American video game crash did not affect Japan at all. Or rather, it benefited Japan. Its retailers, shaking their heads from across the Pacific, had only stocked a negligible amount of most of the American video game systems. And those Colecos and Vectrexes that had made the trip were mere curiosities, no more a threat than wasabi peas are to Doritos in the States. The video game crash-and-burn gave

Nintendo an unparalleled opportunity: the chance to enter a billion-dollar market where the others had just forced themselves out in a Mexican standoff gone wrong.

President Hiroshi Yamauchi had had engineers working on a game-playing home computer for years, since before he asked Shigeru Miyamoto to refurbish *Radar Scope*. (He briefly considered buying and branding the ColecoVision, but they wanted Nintendo to pay whole-sale for it: *no-sankyu*.) He based it on Atari's wonderful 2600, which used a lesser version of Motorola's 6502 chip, the 6507, to generate its titles. Nintendo would upgrade to a specialized chip made by Ricoh. The Ricoh chip was specially engineered to produce sounds, accept inputs from a controller, and generate tricolored sprites. It outputted as much image and sound as an 8-bit processor could, which was good, because it was going to have to duplicate *Donkey Kong* using a fraction of the arcade game's horsepower.

Instead of a joystick, Nintendo's "family computer" (or Famicon) would use one of Gunpei Yokoi's innovations from the Game & Watch line: the raised directional pad. Joysticks broke with repeated use. Flat discs like the Intellivision's were better, but still didn't produce much tactile satisfaction. D-pads, little plus signs, were the future. There would be square action buttons as well, but only two. The sparse button selection was a "forcing device" to ensure developers made easy-to-play games. The controller was simple, elegant, and offered a diversity of options for designers.

Yamauchi believed in the Famicon so much he canceled Ninten-do's arcade division to focus funds and experience on it. Price was one of Yamauchi's no-compromise angles. The Famicon had to be cheap, cheaper than most everything else on the market. After all, Apple's Lisa and Xerox's Star were top-of-the-line machines, but flopped due to five-digit price tags. In fact, Yamauchi wanted a price point of under ten thousand yen, about seventy-five dollars—and wanted to make a profit off each console. This seemed a pipe dream, to double-dip from the two-part tariff business model. This model, most famously used by Gillette, sets a one-time price for the razor, and an ongoing price for the blades. Yamauchi insisted Nintendo profit from both the games and the consoles, no easy feat.

By 1983, Nintendo had released dozens of different Game & Watches. It had widened the screen, and then introduced dual-screen games that doubled the playing space. Most games were original, but franchise characters such as Snoopy, Mickey Mouse, and Donald Duck made appearances. Nintendo had smartly ported over one-level versions of its arcade hits: *Donkey Kong* and *Donkey Kong Jr.*

Mario had three different Game & Watch titles in 1983, doing three different jobs. He retained his contractor creds in *Mario's Cement Factory*, where he worked filling up cement mixers. For *Mario Bros.,* instead of adapting the sewer game, designers put Mario and Luigi to work in a bottle factory. (This version was ported to the Commodore 64 as *Mario Bros. II.*) And for *Mario's Bombs Away*, he becomes an ace commando, grabbing lit bombs from a battlefield and tossing them into the enemy camp.

This trilogy of games (none designed by Miyamoto) makes it clear what Nintendo was aiming to set up for Mario: a cartoonlike role as the eager employee, trying to cope in any number of stressful environments. No one who played *Mickey & Donald* thought "Hey, wasn't Mickey a sorcerer's apprentice instead of a firefighter? This guy's career is all over the place." Mickey was a symbol for Disney, and Mario would be that exact same symbol for Nintendo.

To accomplish this, Nintendo would ignore Mario's role as a villain in *Donkey Kong Jr.* Mario would jump with both feet into whatever challenge Nintendo put in front of him, be it war, monsters, or the perils of just-in-time supply chain management.

Mario's father, Miyamoto, moved on as well to new jobs. After *Mario Bros.* he worked to design a game called *Devil World*, the only game of his never released in North America. It was a maze game, with the clever conceit that the monsters in the maze would move the walls, instead of just chase the hero. That wasn't what kept it from U.S. shores, though. In the game's story line, a green dragon named Tamagon descends into Hell in order to fight Satan. The *Pac-Man*–style power pellets are replaced by crosses and Bibles. For an industry called devil worshipers by some extremists, a game featuring the devil (even as a villain) was a no-no.

There was a push to make a lot of games for Yamauchi's new game console. Nintendo was excellent at *nemawashi*, a Japanese gardening term for digging around the roots of a to-be-transplanted tree. *Nemawashi* referred to the business necessity of quietly laying the correct groundwork of success. For Nintendo, *nemawashi* demanded that a game console have many games ready for release, and many more in the pipeline. Otherwise, it'd be as deserved a failure as all the American consoles that rushed to market without any quality in their product. And they had to be a different breed of game, not necessarily engineered like arcade games to end quickly.

As soon as *Devil World* was finished, Miyamoto received a promotion. He had been working with his mentor, Gunpei Yokoi, who was on the Game & Watch development team and also pitched in overseeing the *Donkey Kong* franchise. But Yamauchi wanted to keep Yokoi working on Game & Watch: it was Yokoi's idea, and each new game added to Nintendo's coffers. Yamauchi decided his company's new golden boy, shaggy Shiggy Miyamoto, was management material.

Miyamoto supposed that Yamauchi saw in him a surrogate son—or grandson.

Miyamoto officially stepped back into a producer's role with his new position. He hadn't trained as a software designer: it wasn't where his skills lay. He knew enough to be able to explain what he wanted, how he wanted it, and how it could be done. Like Mario, just because he was good at a job didn't mean there wasn't a better fit for him somewhere else. Yokoi's management style was encouragement: he told future *Metroid* designer Yoshi Sakamoto, "If you can draw pixel art, you can make a game." Miyamoto continued the style of choosing carrots over sticks with his crew. (His leadership turned out to be better than his organizational skills: he needed an assistant just to keep track of things.) A new designer named Kazuaki Morita served as Miyamoto's protégé. Which put the thirty-something Miyamoto in the role of mentor.

Their first challenge was *Ice Climber*, which seemed like a polar-themed *Mario Bros.* Except that as Popo and Nana, the cute titular Eskimo kids, advanced to the top of the screen, it panned up with them. The "level" was about five screens high! Scrolling upward also allowed the cut-off lower screen to become a deadly obstacle if the climbers fell below it. Miyamoto also supervised a horizontally panning game called *Excitebike*, whose controls used one of motocross's elements, overheating, as the game's crutch. (Miyamoto bicycled to work instead of driving a car, so he had an interest in things two wheeled.) Both buttons sped up the bike: the A button was regular speed and the B button was a sizzling form of turbo power. Use it too much and the bike cooks. Use it too little, and get lapped.

The Famicon was released in Japan on July 13, 1983. Two controllers were hardwired into the white and maroon system, with vertical holding slots built into the console to store them when not in use.

Player one had a start and select button, with the power cord sticking out from the left. Player two, with the power cord to the right, had an internal microphone instead. The Famicon accepted sixty-pin game cartridges from a top-down slot, and could be expanded to accept certain discs and allow modem support. (Yes: modem support in 1983. America Online started in 1983 as well, as Gameline, a service offering modem support for the Atari 2600.)

The Famicon launched with three games, all ports of Nintendo's arcade hits: *Donkey Kong*, *Donkey Kong Jr.*, and *Popeye*. A dozen more games were in the works. This wasn't a mere arcade game, rigged to play just one game, or a rinky-dink piece of LCD electronics. This was a full-fledged computer! Yamauchi didn't get his wish of a price under ¥10,000, but the retail price of ¥14,800 was still on the low side for a console, and helped it gain market penetration.

Then the Famicons started to break. Computers were indeed difficult to make: one little mistake on one little chip could cause players' games to freeze or crash midsession. Reports trickled in of this happening with multiple consoles all over Japan. The batch of chips used in production, it turned out, was shoddy. Nintendo had put out a product with a bad component. When retailers found out, they would pull the Famicon off their shelves.

Nintendo had never made bad products, and it wasn't going to start now. In a move that echoed Tylenol's voluntary recall after a tampering scare, Yamauchi ordered a product recall of every single Famicon, even those without the bad component. Those who had bought one could send it in and have it repaired free of charge. Nintendo would rip out the entire motherboard, not just the bad chip, and replace the whole system. Yamauchi knew Nintendo had the money to essentially rebuild each Famicon manufactured or sold. The question was whether anyone would buy them, or let them back on shelves, once the recall was completed. Recalls done wrong tainted the brand forever. Done right, though, they could be a blessing in disguise.

Erring on the side of caution paid off. Japanese retailers liked that one high-tech company finally took responsibility for its errors and fixed them for free. (Nintendo continues to do so today, to the point of reapplying kids' stickers onto a new console if the old one has to be replaced instead of repaired.) Sales were great for the rest of 1983: Nintendo moved half a million consoles, and Sharp started production of a TV set with a built-in Famicon. And as those new games from Miyamoto came out, the Famicon became Japan's biggest-selling game console, selling three million consoles by 1984. Yamauchi even found a cheap way to drum up new arcade games: convert existing *Donkey Kong* and *Mario Bros.* cabinets to *Nintendo Vs.* machines, which played a series of beefed-up Famicon titles. Replacing it with new games would be as easy as restocking a vending machine. The same idea was reused for the *Play Choice* arcade games.

Miyamoto wasn't the only producer generating new games for the nascent Famicon. Yamauchi ran his R&D team with three divisions, run by three daimyos. (Daimyos were the medieval lords of Japan, all powerful save for the kingly shogun. Yamauchi, of course, was the shogun in this metaphor.) All could design games, hardware, accessories, whatever they wanted. Gunpei Yokoi was head of one of these three divisions now. Masayuki Uemura, who designed the Famicon, headed the second. Genyo Takeda, who would come up with the battery-save feature for the NES, headed up the third. All three of Nintendo's daimyos had expertise in hardware, not software.

In 1984, Miyamoto was given the honor of heading up a new fourth division. As a daimyo, his job was to rally his people to produce the most value, and the best advancement, to please the shogun— er, the president. Yamauchi-sama (no mere Yamauchi-san for him) was happy to play the role of judge; no game went forward without his express permission. He had a sixth sense for knowing what would sell well in which markets. Amazingly, he did this without ever playing a game, instead just watching a scant minute or two of game play. It's wildly out of character for both Yamauchi and his company, but the image of a drug lord refusing to sniff his own product does come to mind.

One of Miyamoto's "rival" R&D divisions decided to make a game called *Wrecking Crew*, and Miyamoto "lent" them Mario and Luigi to star in it. The brothers play demolition workers taking down a hundred levels of concrete and brick, which much be taken out in the correct order. To keep the cerebral nature of the game, Mario and Luigi can't jump. Mario received a makeover for the role: he gained a hard hat, switched to an all-red sleeveless ensemble instead of overalls, and trimmed his mustache to look like Tom Selleck's.

Mario also shows up as a bonus character in Nintendo's *Pinball*, in a bonus where he can save Pauline in a *Breakout*-style extra level. And there he is again as the line judge in *Tennis*, yet another game generated for the console's launch. And again in *Donkey Kong Hockey*: he and DK slap the puck back and forth, and whoever has the slower reflexes gets scored on. He also appears in *Mario Bros. Special* (only in Japan) in an awkward port of *Mario Bros.* made by Hudson Soft, and in *F-1 Race*, where he waves on the Formula One cars. Mario appears in *Punch Ball Mario Bros.*, another failed attempt by Hudson Soft to adapt *Mario Bros.* that involved, as you might expect, Mario punching a ball. And he's in the audience for the arcade game *Punch-Out!* It might be easier to list the Nintendo games of that time into which Mario was *not* shoehorned.

This was the Mickey Mouse philosophy, all right: could anyone remember Mickey as a cartoon character anymore? With a distinct personality? No, Mickey was just a mascot. Just a smile and a pair of ears. Donald Duck, now he had a personality. Goofy too. Mario was a brainwashing victim: what little there was about him—he could jump, he was a hero, he had a bushy mustache, he was a carpenter—had all been rewritten.

Nintendo's attempts to keep vague Mario plugging away at job after job were not promising for long-term success. One could go Sanrio's Hello Kitty route and have abstract form but no meaning. Or one could go the Bugs Bunny route and make a strong defined character. But to survive, Mario would need a consistent hook. Look at King Arthur, on whose story hangs various unrelated legends: the King Uther tale, Lancelot sleeping with his wife, the quest for the Grail. Yet everyone knows King Arthur's core; he was England's greatest king. Despite glaring contradictions (he can't pull Excalibur from a rock if he's already been given it by the Lady in the Lake), his core character remains the same.

If Mario was to be Nintendo's cynosure, he needed a constant narrative. Not just whatever ridiculous workplace needed a hapless light industrial employee: a world of his own.

6 — MARIO'S SUNSHINE

SUPER MARIO BROS. AND THE NINTENDO ENTERTAINMENT SYSTEM

hen the Famicon was released, in 1983, twenty-three-year-old Kōji Kondō heard about a job through his college in Osaka. He was considering graduate school to further his music studies. He wanted to play professionally, and had learned both the piano and the cello. He had even experimented with composing and arranging music using a computer, being one of the first digital audio converts of a still-analog world.

The position was with the people who had made *Donkey Kong*. Kondō loved *Donkey Kong*, and especially loved the brief little bursts of original music for each level. The job was nearby, in Kyoto. And it combined two of his favorite pastimes: video games and music. Kondō would apply, of course, but so would everyone else. He didn't have any demo tapes of his compositions. But Kōji had grown up with electronic music, playing the Yamaha Electone, a downmarket version of Hammond's drawbar electronic organ. He had developed the skills to imitate his English rock heroes—such as John Paul Jones of Led Zeppelin and Keith Emerson of Emerson, Lake & Palmer—in a cover band. He lived for this sort of music, and it must have shown in the interview.

Kōji Kondō got the job at Nintendo, and became a professional composer for video games. With all the games they put out they needed one: for *Mario Bros.* they stole a page from Looney Tunes and digitized Mozart's *Eine kleine Nachtmusik* for a score. Within a matter of months Kondō had scored two arcade games: *Golf* and a boxing game called *Punch-Out.* He learned about the challenges of writing music that would be listened to over and over without becoming annoying, bland, or too jingley.

He started working more closely with a man named Miyamoto, who was a few years older. Miyamoto had shaggy hair: Kondō was always scared of letting his grow out—for fear of not being employable. Miyamoto loved the groove bands Kondō did—and bluegrass too! The two of them worked together on a new endeavor, a secret electronics project that they said would change the world—although they said this about all their secret projects. And Kondō would get to score the transformation.

Mario needed a narrative in his new game, and Miyamoto was on it. He had designed side-scrolling racing games and vertical-scrolling "athletic" games for the Famicon, so why not a side-scrolling "athletic" game? With his protégé Morita, the pair might be able to get five or six decent levels out of it. By increasing the cartridge size by adding a chip, it could even be super. And it could answer the question of who Mario was.

Miyamoto was leaning strongly toward form. His game idea involved a fantasy land accessible by sewer pipes, where Mario would go on epic adventures in land, sea, and air. He would grow to a great size, and shrink back down. He would be able to control fire (which replaced an earlier idea of giving him a gun), and breathe underwater. He would battle living fungi, malevolent clouds, and demonic animals. In short, he would again be nothing like any previous iteration.

Here was the narrative: Mario the explorer. Miyamoto could retell the oldest tale in the world: the stranger coming to town. The Mushroom Kingdom, as it would be called, could afford an endless number of beasts, inventions, characters, tasks, environments, and challenges. Miyamoto didn't realize he was making a world as imaginative as *Star Wars*'s bestiary of planets, *Star Trek*'s galactic Federation, or the Marvel Universe's hero-clogged New York City.

Yes, Mario technically was still a plumber. An eldritch pipe would take him to the Mushroom Kingdom. There would be pipes everywhere, so much so that players would stop thinking it odd that open vertical sewage tunnels painted kelly green served as the only way to ever get from point A to point B. For consistency Mario still had his move set from *Mario Bros.*—the head butt, the jump-stomp, and the prone-enemy kick. Moves that never made it beyond the drawing board included a rocket pack and a second kick attack.

Figuring out the controls was itself a matter of control. Miyamoto wanted up on the directional pad to be the jump control, freeing A and B for actions. No, no, others said, jumping is too important to not be given its own button. His coworkers wore him down, and Miyamoto eventually agreed to make A the constant jump button, with B for fireballs when tapped, and running when held. By "losing" the argument, Miyamoto showed he would let the better idea win, even if it lost the daimyo a bit of face. Ironically, this commitment to quality gained him unparalleled face.

One of the biggest changes was the background: every previous Mario game had had a black background, the better to make the colors more vibrant. Most all games followed this rule. But *Super Mario Bros.* (the game was given a superlative adjective) took place on a beautiful bright day, with a Montana-worthy horizon of periwinkle sky. A few scattered clouds and distant mountains (the clouds and the bushes were, in fact, the same fluffy image colored white or green) made for a feeling of scope, that this two-dimensional land truly existed. It was, in a word, happy.

Happy was a guiding light for the project. Difficulty was a double-edged sword for any game: too easy and there's no replay challenge, too hard and you repel players. How to keep people playing regardless of what was happening? Keep 'em smiling. Therefore, the villains were cute mushroom "Goombas" toddling around on stubby legs, Venus's flytrap "Pirhana plants" with luscious rep lips, and white squid "Bloopers" that resembled curious bells.

The music, most of all, was happy. The score for level 1 (or, to use the game's nomenclature, World 1-1) is an infectiously happy synthesizer salsa. When Mario has an underground level, a bass-heavy score fraught with tension kicks in. When he's underwater, the music is soothing and muted, almost submerged. And when Mario grabs a power-up star, the beat turns as fast and frantic as anything this side of Beethoven's Ninth played at 33-1/3 speed.

This was all the work of Kōji Kondō, the new hire. Kondō had a limited palette of sounds to work with. Forget writing for piano: he had two monophonic channels, a synthesized triangle wave, and a white-noise generator. Try to write good music with a hearing tone, a wooden block, and two chanting monks as your "band." It was possible, of course, but it would first require writing a synthesizer program that could turn sine waves into piano licks.

Sneaking into the Famicon's source code led Kondō to discover an extra sound channel: a pulse-code modulation channel designated for sound effects. And those two monophonic channels could be used together to create harmonies. He set up the white-noise generator as percussion, with the triangle wave working as a bass. Drums, bass, chords: the band was starting to come together, all inside a computer chip. He passed on what he had discovered to others, penning the section in the computer-language cartridge *Famicon BASIC* on sound programming.

Some things couldn't be taught, though: they needed trial and error. Kondō didn't write just one theme to *Super Mario Bros.*, he wrote lots. Each one he played over footage of gaming sessions, and kept in a loop in his head. Was the score fast enough? Was it too fast? Did it contrast with the sound effects he had for the actions: the *sproing* of a jump, the smack of an enemy's hit? Did a section go on for too long before repeating, or not long enough? He grew satisfied with the underground music, the battle music for bosses, and the underwater music. But not the main theme.

Eventually, Kondō perfected his little score. The secret was to write multiple minisongs, each a few seconds long, and string them together. They were a series of pop hooks destined to worm their way into the world's auditory canals. When played in a row, they somehow never sounded like one song on repeat. They even sped up in tempo as Mario's time ran out. The song's lyrics and title, "Go Go Mario," are awkward and probably best forgotten. The first two bars: "Today, full of energy, Mario is still running, running / Go save Princess Peach! Go!" But the melody is unimprovable.

If this hadn't been a Nintendo game, it might have ended with World 1-4, or World 2-4. Both times Mario defeats a large adversary, a "boss." A princess comes out at the end of each fight, and says "Thank you, Mario" . . . followed by "But our princess is in another castle!" (Complete with royal thumbs-ups that might be mistaken for middle fingers.) The use of the word "Our" instead of "the" or "Your" includes the player alongside Mario as questers for the princess's freedom. And to have the same bad joke delivered level after level turns Mario into some sort of Odysseus, forced to storm castle after castle, never to reunite with his Penelope. (Or Toadstool, as the princess was execrably called in the American edition.)

Further mixing the character's and the player's adventures were the Warp Zones. Scattered here and there were secret chambers, with "Welcome to Warp Zone!" displayed over three identical pipes. They all led to different levels of the game. It was a built-in cheat, letting Mario bypass vast swatches of the game if he wanted. Another bit of humor, addressing just how Brobdignagian the game had become: what book lets you know you can skip ahead to page 320 if you want?

It must have been frustrating for Yamauchi, not a patient man, to watch the development. His A-team of designers produced a great game, gave it a perfect end point, and then added a dumb joke to explain why they had to design another four levels to play. And then the *same* dumb joke again. And again! Shades of *The Agony and the Ecstasy*, with the pope continually asking Michelangelo when the Sistine Chapel's ceiling will be completed, and the painter responding, "When I'm finished!"

In the end, *Super Mario Bros.* had thirty-two levels, and eight boss battles. Mario could gain a hit point by eating a mushroom, and grow much larger in size. He could gain temporary invincibility from sparkly stars. He could throw bouncing fireballs if he touched a flower. He climbed beanpoles to the sky, fought off a reptile king, and battled a series of turtles wielding hammers, wings, and spines. He saved any number of women who were not our princess. He jumped on floating platforms, avoided flaming windmills, and ducked living bullets fired at him. He would gain another life if he found a "1-up" mushroom, or collected a hundred coins.

While the game took forever to make, it also took many hours to play through completely. This was *Donkey Kong* if each level was ten times regular size, and if the levels never repeated. Each board had so many hidden coins and power-ups, so many enemies and dangers, so many secrets! This wasn't a simulation; it was a world to get lost in, as replayable as a favorite book or movie or album. It was supposed to ship in the summer, but Miyamoto askd for a few more weeks to fix bugs. It shipped on Friday, September 13, not the most auspicious of dates. When it arrived in Japanese arcades, players kept plopping quarters in long after they defeated King Koopa, just to find all the Easter eggs. Everyone played it as Billy Mitchell did, trying to wring the computer chip of every last secret.

Now if only someone would sell it. Yamauchi had hit wall after wall trying to get the Famicon, an established hit on its way to selling more than 19 million copies in Japan, on American shelves. Japan had about 120 million people at that time, so almost one in six owned a Famicon. Yet video game consoles remained radioactive to U.S. retailers. It was their loss, of course, but also Nintendo's.

Before Famicon's success, Yamauchi sat down with Atari and offered them a sweetheart deal. Nintendo would make Famicons, and Atari would sell them as an Atari product, with Nintendo taking a hefty slice of the revenue. Nintendo would lose its darling distribution network, but it trusted it would be in safe hands with Atari. The deal fell apart, mostly because Atari itself fell apart during the '83 crash. Nintendo was left without an American partner. Atari was left to kick itself over letting a golden goose fly away.

After the Famicon had proved itself in Japan, Yamauchi sent it (and Arakawa) to electronics trade shows. The console received a new Americanized name, the Advanced Video System: Famicon was too Japanese. It worked with a typing keyboard, played songs with a music keyboard, and featured dozens of great games. Attendees thought it was a quality product, but doomed. Who'd try to sell a new video game system now, in 1985? This wasn't selling coal to Newcastle, it was selling smog to Los Angeles.

How to break in? If Mario really was Odysseus, questing away forever, maybe Homer had the answer to Yamauchi's problem as well. The Greeks gave their rivals the Trojans a big wooden horse as a surrender gift. The Trojans took it inside their fortress—and out poured the Greeks. All Nintendo had to do to sell their video game system . . . was to hide it.

Gunpei Yokoi was tasked with designing a twentieth-century Trojan horse. It was a foot-tall robot that could move its head and arms, pivot, and pick up certain objects. It was the Robotic Operating Buddy, or R.O.B. R.O.B. wasn't that functional: only two lackluster games were designed that used him, *Gyromite* and *Stack-Up*. But R.O.B. made the video game console a robot that happened to come with an accessory that worked as a video game system. Toy stores sold robots no problem. And, Nintendo ported over its recent arcade hits like *Duck Hunt* and *Hogan's Alley* complete with the Zapper, a light-gun peripheral.

American audiences must have been familiar with Homer. Toy stores once again rejected the console (again rechristened: it was now the Nintendo Entertainment System, or NES, with a sleek gray makeover), even with the robot and the gun. It was a pretty lousy ruse: toy manufacturers weren't dolts, and knew a game console when they saw one.

Arakawa thought this was Nintendo of America's end, and wanted to pull out. One company could only be so lucky: refurnishing *Radar Scope*, winning the Universal lawsuit, and making a ton of money in a scant three years was enough. Arakawa had opened up a successful Chuck E. Cheese in Vancouver, and then two other restaurants. Maybe resurrecting the home video game market wasn't worth it. He was at heart a contented person, satisfied with his victories so far.

Yamauchi was not, at heart, happy. He always wanted more and bigger success, a curse peculiar to captains of industry. If American chains weren't buying, Nintendo would start trotting the damn things door to door. The machine sold in Japan, after all, and it would sell in the United States if someone had the guts to realize one bad year did not make all video game systems Kryptonite. Games were huge in Japan, huge in Europe—hell, huge in Canada still. Even in the United States, arcades were still doing okay. Kids still played (and bought) games for the Commodore 64. The market was ready, the product was ready: he just needed to convince the idiot retailers.

Yamauchi had a hundred thousand NES units shipped to a warehouse in Hackensack, New Jersey, and had most of his American staff move out there as well. That fall of 1985, they'd hand sell as many systems to as many toy stores, electronics shops, and department stores in the New York City area as they could. The Manhattan-based toy manufacturers would notice all the local toy shops were stocking the NES. They'd see that it sold. They'd get the message, and start buying it on a national level. That was the plan.

Arakawa raised Yamauchi's bet: any unsold Nintendo Entertainment System, he promised retailers, could be returned for full value. No retailer could lose a dime by stocking the NES, just floor space. Yamauchi had refused to offer such a guarantee—why don't you just cut the price in half, or stuff the machine with twenty-dollar bills?—but Arakawa went behind his father-in-law's back and made the promise. A desperate measure, for a desperate time. His small team worked nonstop every waking hour to set up holiday displays in toy stores. If this didn't work, to quote Bill Paxton from that year's *Aliens*, "Game over, man." For their effort, they were rewarded by having their Seattle flight back home for Christmas cancelled due to fog.

As with *Radar Scope*, the NES sold some but nowhere near all of its units for the Christmas rush. Fifty thousand units out the door wasn't great, but it was a start. Enough to convince the next test market, Los Angeles, to try in early 1986. (Toy stores were more willing to try new products in the non-Christmas months.) Then Chicago. Then San Francisco.

Just in time for the fall '86 toy season, with the seeds sown in four big markets, Nintendo began a national launch. The big N signed up with toymaker Worlds of Wonder, who was selling a pair of hot products, Teddy Ruxpin and Laser Tag. They'd sell the NES as well, for a trifecta of must-have products. Mattel handled distribution in Canada.

Yamauchi had one more trick up his sleeve for the country-wide rollout. That game Miyamoto had taken forever to make was finally done, and a recent hit in arcades. He had cannily started selling Famicons packaged with it, just like Colecovision did with *Donkey Kong*. Japanese sales were high. He'd do the same overseas in the United States. Every NES, sold for a mere $130, would come with the console, two controllers . . . and a copy of *Super Mario Bros.* For an extra twenty dollars customers got a Zapper and a second game, *Duck Hunt*.

Thirty-four million U.S.-sold NES systems later, Yamauchi seems to have made the right call. The ultimate legacy of the game, though, can be seen throughout the many worlds of geekdom it cultivated, a vast nerderie of games, book, movies, music, and shows that have moved from niche to limelight. (A preferred word for geek, *otaku*, comes from the Japanese.) Mario was dense, and called for deep explo-ration instead of facile button mashing. It rewarded the extra energy to explore it. A generation of fans with the first fix of gaming depth started rewarding other deep games with huge sales. No exaggeration: the RPG series *Dragon Warrior* is by Japanese law not allowed to be released on a weekday, since too many people take off school or work to start leveling up.

Mario's shadow has fallen outside of games, since fans of depth didn't only want it in 8-bit form. Think *Harry Potter*, *Twilight*, *Star Wars*, *The Matrix*, *Lord of the Rings*, *Lost*, even comedies such as *Arrested Development* and *30 Rock*. These very different books, movies, and TV shows weren't inspired by Mario, of course, but their *fans* have been. Instead of passively ingesting their entertainment they study it in miniature, read up on each new installment, create and maintain wiki sites to document all its facets. A big film can't arrive anymore without a tie-in comic prequel, an alternate-reality game in the weeks prior to release, extra scenes shot for the special-edition home release, and what *Spaceballs'* Brooklynite Yoda called "moichindizin'." The cross-platform blockbusters that fuels the modern entertainment economy are fanned by, well, fans. And all those enthusiasts, like torches lit by one eternal flame, were indoctrinated into existence by a single fire flower.

7 – MARIO'S BOMB

THE LOST LEVELS

mitation is the sincerest form of flattery. Just ask the Great Giana Sisters.

In 1987, Rainbow Arts made a game called *The Great Giana Sisters* for various computers. It was an almost perfect replica of *Super Mario Bros.*, except with spiky-haired girls as the leads. Nintendo found out about it, made some threats, and Rainbow Arts pulled the game off shelves.

Or ask *All Night Nippon Mario Bros. All Night Nippon* was a popular Japanese late-night radio show, which asked Nintendo to change up the game's sprites for a promotional giveaway. Some of the levels had their sky colors changed from blue to black (it is night, after all), and various bad guys had their sprites replaced with eighties singers and disc jockeys.

Or ask *Super Bald Bros.*, a hacked version of the game where Mario and Luigi have no hair. Or replaced Mario's face with that of glam rocker Alice Cooper. Or made Mario Russian, or a pimp, or simply hat-less. Or replaced Mario with characters from a grab bag of other games—*River City Ransom*, the *Teenage Mutant Ninja Turtles*, or *Bomberman*. (Worst of all would be the *Super KKK Bros.* hack, about which nothing more will be said.)

The samizdat hacks were merely the logical reaction to Miyamoto's philosophy. He had designed *Super Mario Bros.* to be not just played but studied. Certain valuable boxes were invisible, findable by heuristic trial and error. Players spent hours leaping into the air at every point of every level, looking for them. They discovered Mario could get an extra life if he jumped high enough on the level-ending flagpole. They found the "minus levels," including one water board that simply extended forever until time ran out. They found the invisible walls, where Miyamoto had cached extra loot. They even watched the odd anime movie *Super Mario Bros.: Great Mission to Rescue Princess Peach*, which features Peach escaping from her own video game, Mario searching for magical items to restore a prince who had been transformed into a dog, and King Koopa demoted to working at a grocery store.

After investing so much time in a mere game, not everyone wanted to let it go. The NES was a computer, after all, and computers could be hacked. A cottage industry of NES hackers was emerging. They learned about the technical changes made when the Famicon became the NES. While the Famicon was top-loading, for instance, the NES was side-loading. Its controllers were uniform, and had round instead of square buttons. (Despite passing a "million-punch test," the square buttons were jamming.) The mike and modem support were gone. And, oddly, the game cartridges were bigger, 72-pin instead of 60-pin.

That was to accommodate the 10NES chip, Yamauchi's newest brainstorm. Atari and other console makers couldn't stop outside parties from making games: anyone could whip together a game, and shove it into a 2600 cartridge. The 10NES was a lockout chip: before the NES did anything else with a cartridge, it checked to see if the inserted game cartridge had a 10NES chip. If it did, game on. If not, no dice.

This additional chip added cost to every unit, but it allowed Nintendo to once again control distribution. If you wanted to make a game for the NES, Nintendo had to approve it. Yamauchi signed up as many Japanese publishers as he could: Komani, Capcom, Bandai, Taito, Hudson Soft, Namco. The more the merrier: third-party content (i.e., games not made by Nintendo, or by companies Nintendo hired) was how the Apple II grew successful. Yamauchi limited them to five games a year; any more, and the market might get glutted. Some companies went so far as to create shell corporations to put out additional games while keeping to the letter of Yamauchi's law. Few American game publishers wanted in: they stuck with computer games.

That first launch year, 1986, America bought three million NES consoles. The following year, six million more. Worlds of Wonder was cleaning up with the NES, but the company faced bankruptcy since it had a veritable sleuth of unsold Teddy Ruxpins on its hands. Nintendo ended up hiring the WOW sales force from the floundering company. Yearly, Nintendo was bringing in millions from the console, more millions from its own games, and more millions still from third-party developers' games. Arakawa even got a licensor, MGA Entertainment (of future Bratz doll fame) to import the Game & Watch titles from Kyoto to the United States. Add on arcade games and licensing, and Nintendo was living out Naomi Klein's description of a modern company's "race toward weightlessness: whoever owns the least, has the fewest employees on the payroll and produces the most powerful images." To this day, as journalist Osame Inoue points out, it continues to have an employee-cost ratio in seven figures—that is, divide the profits by the staff and each employee ends up bringing in over a million dollars a year.

Now if only they could get a sequel for that most powerful of images. *Super Mario Bros.* would end up selling an astounding forty million copies. As in Japan, one in six Americans bought a copy. That number would stand as the world's bestselling game for over two decades, thanks to every NES buyer getting one. It wasn't just dumb kids playing. When Booker Prize–winner Salman Rushdie was asked what he did while in hiding after Ayatollah Khomeini issued a *fatwa* calling for his death, he said he mastered *Super Mario Bros.* (He's since based a book on the game's themes.) To celebrate the game's twentieth anniversary, Japan released a set of eighty-yen Super Mario stamps. This was some game.

In lieu of a proper sequel, Mario and Donkey Kong were going to star in an educational game, *Donkey Kong's Fun With Music*. Players would be able to jam alongside Donkey Kong on the upright bass, Mario on the keyboard, Pauline on vocals, and Junior on the drums. While jamming, players would learn about rhythm, and how to sight-read music. Miyamoto and Kondō both loved music, and this was a perfect way to make learning a true joy.

But the music project was canceled. The first U.S.-released game in the series, *Donkey Kong Jr. Math*, was a dud. Junior had to answer math problems by maneuvering through vines and chains littered with numbers, picking the right integers and actions to get the correct number. It was fun, and reinforced math fundamentals, but it was challenging. There was another game, one that taught basic English reading, called *Popeye's English Game*, or *Popeye no Eigo Asobi*. Obviously, it was for Japanese audiences, and not released in the U.S. After swinging 0 for 2, Nintendo gave up on the NES being a learning machine.

Another never-finished game was *Return of Donkey Kong*. It was a remix of the first three *Donkey Kong* games, with the clever conceit that Mario (with his jumping) and Junior (with his swinging ability) would have to navigate the same board in two different ways to get from point A to point B. The game would have redesigned levels from all three games, adding challenges for both sets of characters. It was two different new games in one, masquerading as three warmed-over games.

All these games that never made it out of development hell must have been frustrating. Great ideas, great execution, and they get killed because people wouldn't understand them. People just wanted more of Mario in the Mushroom Kingdom. More of the same, just, you know, a little different.

Miyamoto, possibly with a raised eyebrow, decided to deliver on exactly that. His new protégé, Takashi Tezuka (memorably credited as "Ten Ten"), would do most of the work for a *Super Mario Bros.* sequel that would look and play like the original. Gamers would be immediately comfortable: this was what they wanted. Question mark blocks! Smashable bricks! Mushrooms! Digital comfort food!

Then, they'd go grab that mushroom, which in the previous game made Mario super. And they'd see what a little difference could do. (Insert maniacal laughter here.) In this game, the first mushroom would kill Mario. Boom, dead. Miyamoto could never pull a stunt like that with an arcade game: folks would demand their quarters back. But home console players would have touched the hot stove, and learned: okay, the mushrooms are all deadly.

Except only certain mushrooms were deadly, not all of them. That was only the beginning. The swimming "Blooper" squid here could swim on land and air. One endpoint could only be reached by climbing a vine, which in the previous game was just for bonus levels. A new element was rain, which could stir up from nowhere to push Mario back. All jumps now had to be weighed against the possibility that a freak shower would blow Mario off course.

Developers have a code of conduct about how to make a proper game. No blind jumps, for instance: Mario had to see both ledges. Miyamoto wouldn't break those commandments. But he'd certainly tweak them. If the first game had Mario schlep his way up a pyramid to get a 1-Up, this one would create a similar obstacle course that led to a worthless poison mushroom. Mario's warp zones took him forward in the first game? The warp zones in the sequel might take him back to the beginning of the game. Level after level, Miyamoto was pranking the player.

This was exactly, precisely, what video gamers had said they wanted. They wanted a game just like *Super Mario Bros.*, but with new challenges. But did they really? Or did they want the illusion of difficulty? The thrill of accomplishment, without a constant ramp-up in difficulty? Just because all NES owners had a copy of *Super Mario Bros.* didn't mean they all mastered it. This was a true continuation of the series, in that it started out at a difficulty level higher than the last level of the first game.

The finished game was released in Japan in 1986, and met with mixed reaction. Japan had become a testing ground for new Nintendo products. And if the more accepting Japanese crowd thought it was too hard, imagine the American audience's reaction. The Big N couldn't release it: skittish retailers already were saying the NES was a one-year fad, and this game might prove them right. Mario's lone appearance for that year would be as a guest referee in *Mike Tyson's Punch-Out*. (Arakawa scored a coup signing up the then-heavyweight champ for his likeness to be added to the boxing game.)

Miyamoto didn't have time to go back to the drawing board: his team was already working on another game. He had tried vertical and horizontal side-scrolling, so this one would be a top-down tile-based game. Each board would be a grid populated with traversable ground, obstacles, enemies, and hazards. The square hero would run from board to board, free to explore a vast map of territory. He could even find hidden caves, just like from Miyamoto's childhood, to further his fantasy quest.

And since Nintendo's two biggest franchises were named after the hero and villain of a love triangle, why not name this one after the captured heroine? There was an American name he had come across, reading about F. Scott Fitzgerald: Zelda. Sounded like a princess. And keeping with the triangle theme, he'd make the MacGuffin device a mystical triangle called the Triforce.

While Miyamoto and company were limning *The Legend of Zelda* (in the credit he was "S Miyahon"), other designers were hard at work at transforming a standalone video game into a Mario game. *Dream Factory: Heart-Pounding Panic* (*Yume Kōjō: Doki Doki Panic*) was an Arabian-themed NES game, based on a Fuji Television cartoon. Players could choose one of four family members to play as, each with a different skill. They used genie lamps to hop into a backwards midnight world, rode flying carpets, and fought giant rodents, masked opponents called Shyguys, and living desert cacti. One opponent was a bow-wearing cross-dressing dinosaur who shot eggs from his (her?) mouth. Most notable was the family's attack: they pulled vegetables out of the ground to hurl at opponents.

What Nintendo would do, to make a new Mario game, was the same thing hackers were doing to make an Alice Cooper game. They'd swap out the sprites of the four main characters, and replace them with Mario folk. Imajin, the son, was changed to Mario. Papa, who was strong, became Toad. Mama, who had a springy jump, was Luigi. And

Lina, who could float if her jump button was held, was Princess Toad-stool. The lizardlike villain became Bowser once again.

Yume Kōjō's plot of someone attacking dreams was replaced by Bowser attacking the kingdom for a second time. A few other changes were made, to generally make the game easier than the original. (No point going through all this just to release an equally hard game!) But even when it was finished, it didn't feel in the same spirit as the other Mario games. There were hit points. Mario didn't get bigger or smaller. There was no score—and hence no way to compare friends' best games. No Goombahs or turtles. If Mario jumped on an enemy, nothing happened: the bad guy would just keep trundling along, like a rhino with a bird on its back. And suffice to say no one in the *Donkey Kong* games ever picked and threw rutabagas.

But Yamauchi's gut, once again, was proven right. 1987's *Super Mario Bros. 2* went on to sell more than seven million copies. It was a step down from 40 million, to be sure, but about 6.75 million more than *Dream Factory* would have gotten sans Mario. Indie comics hero Scott Pilgrim was a fan: he named his fictional band Sex Bob-omb after a *SMB2* villain. The game prompted a video game giveaway for drinking Pepsi's soda brand Slice, which gave Nintendo millions in free publicity. It's one of the more successful Mario games, even if everyone agrees that it doesn't play like a Mario game. It's been rere-leased for multiple Nintendo consoles as well, where its reputation has been rebolstered. So, though, has Miyamoto's original take on a *Super Mario Bros.* sequel. Now known as the *Lost Levels*, it's considered by some to be his *Finnegans Wake*, his dissertation on form.

8 – MARIO'S SMASH

SUPER MARIO BROS. 3

"C aptain" Lou Albano had a lot of gimmicks in his decades of professional wrestling. He'd been both heel (a bad guy) and face (a good guy). He was billed as a captain—Albano served in the army, but had never gotten three stars on his lapel. He played up his Italian heritage as part of the tag-team group the Sicilians. He wore often-unbuttoned Hawaiian-print shirts. Even when he wasn't wrestling but merely "managing"—which allowed him to throw a punch or two but mostly keep out of harm's way—he was one of the most popular stars of the squared circle.

Albano's biggest trademark, though, might be his beard. It was a wily goatee, grown down and out over years, and it looked like a tiny patch of Gandalf mixed in with an extra large hank of tiki bar bouncer. He weaved rubber bands into the graying beard, and hooked more rubber bands to his earrings. Another rubber band was pierced into his cheek. He resembled an uncle who had rummaged through a junk drawer trying to be funny.

As wrestling got more mainstream in the eighties, Lou Albano seemed the personification of its fun. If Hulk Hogan and André the Giant were the strong men, Albano was the joker who stole the show. He showed up in a Cyndi Lauper video. And a Brian DePalma movie. And an episode of *Miami Vice*. He was game for anything, loved getting a reaction from a crowd, and was able to sell it to the back row. Like many wrestlers, his biggest fans were children.

Maybe this was because he was a dead ringer for Super Mario. He had a beefy thickness run to fat by years of good living. His hair and mustache were full and bushy. He certainly looked like a plumber from Brooklyn—he was from Westchester, close enough to get the Noo Yawk accent right. And at five feet ten, he'd allow a tall actor as Luigi to play Laurel to his Hardy.

The only thing wrong, in fact, was the beard. (Well, that and the rubber bands.) Mario didn't have a beard. Ever canny in ways of promotion, Albano shaved it off on live television, in front of Regis Philbin and Kathie Lee Gifford. Soon he was outfitted in custom red overalls, a blue work shirt, and a big red cap. Veteran actor Danny Wells played Luigi. Together, they hosted the *Super Mario Bros. Super Show*!

The syndicated show mixed live-action and cartoons. Albano and Wells, in a basement set, had mild adventures that acted as bookends for each show. Guests would show up—one time it was Ghostbuster Ernie Hudson—with a problem for Mario and Luigi to solve. Sometimes they'd do double-duty as mustached women—Mariana and Luigiana. The show's theme song doubled as dance instructions: "Do the Mario! Swing your arms from side to side. Come on it's time to go. Do the Mario! Take one step and then again." Between the bookends were *Super Mario* cartoons, which Albano and Wells voiced as well. The cartoon was light adventure with a lot of pop-culture parody. On Fridays, Mario and Luigi hosted a *Legend of Zelda* action cartoon. This setup allowed the show to run five days a week and yet only be half-animated.

Also airing in the fall of 1989 was NBC's *Captain N: The Game Master*. He wasn't a real captain either, incidentally, but a teenage Nintendo fan who got sucked into a video game world. He met up with various Japanese-based third-party characters—Simon Belmont from Konami's *Castlevania*, Capcom's *Mega Man*, and Nintendo's own *Kid Icarus*. Notably absent was, of course, Mario, which was like visiting Egypt and not seeing the pyramids.

Captain Lou's bookended segments were dropped after a year, in favor of a bunch of "radical" teens called Club Mario. The cartoons in the middle remained. Eventually they all aired in one big loop in syndication. The following year, a new Mario cartoon with no live-action component was introduced, called *The Adventures of Super Mario Bros. 3*. Working actor Walker Boone took over the Mario role. The year after that, the show was renamed *Super Mario World*. If a quality Mario cartoon could not be made, then the audience would have to settle for quantity.

This came to a head with a live-action production so abysmal it merits comparison to the underground cult classic *Star Wars Holiday Special*: the *Super Mario Ice Capades*. Teen hosts Jason Bateman and Alyssa Milano are backstage, wearing sweaters that can be carbon-dated to December 1989 (his is Cosbyrific, hers has no shoulders and is Day-Glo yellow) talking about how good Bateman is at *Super Mario Bros.* When he calls himself a "video prince," the screen starts to flash. Bateman says it's a computer virus that will magically infect all the computers in the world if it's not stopped. Then Mr. Belvedere appears.

Christopher Hewett, the British actor who starred in *Mr. Belvedere*, floats on the ice as King Koopa, to take responsibility for the virus. He's not skating but being pushed around on a chair designed to look like Bowser's brick castle, against a Mushroom Kingdom backdrop that's actually quite good. Hewett's wearing a green velvet jacket, red plaid pants, a jester's hat, and about nine seconds' worth of green makeup.

A surprisingly authentic-looking Princess Toadstool skates out, complete with a head bigger than a prize-winning pumpkin. She calls on the Mario Bros. to help her, and they float down from the sky. They too have heads the size of dishwashers. Peach calls out to a bunch of children to help them, Luigi uses a fireworks gun to shoot all the Goombas dead, and Mario and kids twirl around Koopa until he explodes, replaced (via trick photography) with a white phosphorus blast. The princess pins the Purple Plunger of Bravery on Mario and Luigi for their efforts. The audience at home received no such prize for the effort of watching it.

Shigeru Miyamoto couldn't control how Mario was marketed or licensed. The various comics and cartoon shows about his adventures were, as continuity quibblers say, noncanonical. But Mario himself wasn't a creature of "canon." He was a pop culture superstar, even making it on the cover of *Mad* magazine. There were more important things to worry about.

Nintendo used to be an arcade company. Now it made arcade games, Game & Watch titles, NES games, plus two new consoles in the works, and all that licensing revenue. As producer, Miyamoto was overseeing the baker's dozen of staff members who were actually designing and coding each game. It took him a while to feel comfortable stepping back, but the *Dream Factory* fiasco helped him distance himself.

Miyamoto was management now, and developing his own Sphinxlike style. Instead of saying "let's make a maze game," he'd ask his staff to consider a game built around a chase, or around moving walls. This helped engender the creativity in others, and also led many to mythologize Miyamoto as a Delphic oracle who spoke exclusively in puzzles, about making puzzles. Mario was a purposeful blank, and Shigeru was a purposeful cipher. In truth, though, he was often just tongue-tied trying to say what he felt, and when he tried to explain it sounded like a fortune cookie.

He stayed hands-off for the sequel to his beloved *Legend of Zelda* game, letting Kazuaki Morita program it. He also guided another role-playing adventure, called *Mother*, which was too unusual to be released in the United States. Ironically, one of the elements that made it odd was that instead of a medieval fantasy, it took place in the United States and starred an American boy named Ness (ha-ha) with a baseball bat. At one point a boy asks Ness if he's played *Super Mario Bros. 7*. Ha-ha again.

But Miyamoto couldn't stay away from Mario: there would indeed be seven *Super Marios* one day. The sour taste in his mouth from *Super Mario Bros. 2* was a powerful propellant. It took many games for him to feel the dreaded "sophomore slump," but here it was. Here was the dumped superstar, back to redeem himself. Whatever *Super Mario Bros. 3* would be, it would also serve as a quest of honor.

All the verbosity of being an artist and experiencing change and taking risks boils down to doing something different. Sometimes it's dramatic: Jackson Pollock deciding to drizzle paint instead of spreading it. Sometimes it's flexing a new muscle: Woody Allen trying dramas instead of comedies. Sometimes it's mercenary: Madonna's new look for each song. But it's always necessary. Artists can't simply redo the exact same thing over and over. Artistry, perhaps, is at its core being able to control change in interesting ways.

Miyamoto was not someone accustomed to change: his parents told him to not "change vessels," meaning to stay who you are regardless of circumstances. That was why he still biked to work, still kept the same rescued-castaway haircut, and not incidentally still worked at Nintendo rather than go start his own firm. "I don't really chase after the American dream—that idea of continually changing with success," he said. But unless he wanted to make *Lost Levels II*, he would have to change.

Miyamoto had gotten into game design in the tail end of the arcade era, and was now comfortable in the home console world. Not many of his cabinet colleagues made the jump: not *Space Invaders*'s Tomohiro Nishikado, Atari's Nolan Bushnell, or even one of Miyamoto's idols, *Pac-Man* creator Tōru Iwatani. They were all masters of their era's technology, but they lost that mastery with the advent of new innovations. Without a master narrative guiding them beyond engineering prowess, they were back at square one.

So what was Miyamoto's master narrative for Mario? Was it the athletic exploration that he poured into *Super Mario Bros.*, whose magic he wasn't able to bottle a second time when he went back to the well? Or was it something even more basic than that? Something that would not only allow for a regular series of great Mario games, but of a roster of other great franchises? Miyamoto's decisions for *SMB3* would set the stage for the rest of his life.

Miyamoto decided that gameplay was king. How Mario interacted with the world was the core of the game. This was a slight change from *Lost Levels*, where the game play was mostly identical to the original, except much more difficult. Now, though, he wanted new ideas, new opponents, new powers for Mario. That was why people said *Lost Levels* wasn't Mario, not because it varied from some ethereal formula but because it did *not*.

So Mario got a series of "suits" he could wear. The frog suit made him swim faster. The bizarre Tanooki suit turned Mario into unmovable stone, let him fly, and gave him a tail to hit enemies. (Mythological Japanese tanuki attack with a less family friendly weapon: their heavy testicles, wielded like morning stars.)

That creative game play, built around running and jumping, was what was missing from *Lost Levels*. Certainly it was missing from many of the side-scrolling imitators that had sprung up, where the sole challenge was in navigating incredibly difficult boards and fighting incredibly easy foes. Miyamoto added more and more power-ups and extra lives in the earlier stages, and held them back as the game progressed. That helped new gamers keep playing, without making experienced ones feel like they were playing a baby game.

Miyamoto also decided to end the one-man-show operations. *SMB3* was a collaborative effort, which meant every contributor would have a section, a character, an obstacle they could point at and say "that was mine." His job was to produce games, which meant giving others the tools so they could shine.

Perhaps the most innovative element of *SMB3* was the game board. In the previous games Mario was exclusively seen from the side profile. But Nintendo had had success using two views in the *Zelda II* game: tile-based when traversing a large map, and side-scrolling for the fights and town/dungeon exploration. It let Link's journey feel more epic.

In Mario, though, it would create another abstraction level, a thinning of the barrier between our world and Mario's. Level 1 begins with a small map, with a squarish Mario facing a fork in the road. The right fork is locked, forcing him to go to the left, to the square labeled 1. After that is 2. After that he can choose from another fork, to move ahead to 3, skip it via a side path to 4, or bypass both 3 and 4 and go straight to the Picture Game, a slot machine game where players can win extra lives and coins if they hit the right buttons.

This built upon the warp zone concept, where Mario could jump ahead multiple boards. Here it's not a secret hidden door but right in front of you, clear as day. If you want to go fight the bad guy at the castle, you can do it in a mere seven boards. But if you want to fully explore the world, you have 12 boards' worth of adventure ahead of you. This game, more than any other before it, was built to reward the completionist. Simply winning wasn't the goal anymore. The new goal was to visit every location the game offered, do every activity, soak in each experience. This wasn't a race, it was an amusement park.

SMB3 cribbed many other stylistic tricks from theme parks. Each level had its own theme—ice, grasslands, an inventive Giant Land where all the enemies and obstacles are four times normal size. Each level had its own theme music. Each had its own new enemies, and new powers for Mario to acquire. Each had a distinct layout: Pipe Land was a big confusing maze, Ocean Land was an archipelago of semiconnected islands, and Koopa's castle was hidden in the dark. Level 3 leads Mario to a Japan-shaped island chain, with a castle smack-dab in Kyoto. Players received multiple audiovisual clues as to location identity, and each level was as separate as Tomorrowland is from Main Street, USA.

Miyamoto's success showed why the Mario cartoons never caught on. Mario isn't about jumping on mushrooms and fighting turtles any more than the heritage of Italian-Americans. It's about play, what Croatian-born psychologist Mihaly Csikszentmihalyi called "flow." The fun of "flow" is its feeling of accomplishment and fulfillment while engaged in an activity. Anyone who's ever lost happy hours tinkering with a car engine, shopping for clothes, talking with friends, or playing music has experienced flow. The sweet spot when a game's not too easy or too hard, the just-right porridge, is flow. Showing a tennis fan a documentary about the polymers in her racket would interest her as much as Mario's players would be interested in a cartoon.

Nintendo itself learned that it would be richly rewarded for increasing the "flow" of gamers. Arakawa put a toll-free phone number in the thick instruction booklet of Miyamoto's original *Zelda*, in case anyone was confused. Four people manned the lines. They were soon swamped, many times over. And not just for *Zelda*: for *Super Mario Bros.* and *Punch-Out* and every other Nintendo game.

Arakawa increased the number of operators exponentially: eventually two hundred people staffed the lines. (The staff increased up to five hundred for the holiday rush.) He removed the toll-free number, and they still called. It's among the best jobs in the Seattle area for hard-core gamers: a small cube outfitted with the newest game systems, manuals of past tips and tricks, and a hot line that never stops ringing. And it further cemented Nintendo's reputation as caring for its customers.

Nintendo also expanded on its fan club newsletter, secretly working on what would be *Nintendo Power* magazine. (*Super Mario Bros. 2* graced the cover of the first issue, July/August 1988.) Everyone in the fan club got a free subscription. The idea came from Japan, where millions of copies of *Dragon Warrior* games had been sold because of a write-up in a manga magazine. The same plan worked stateside, with Nintendo as its own publisher. Soon the Nintendo Club was like the National Geographic Society, with millions of members. The magazine offered screen-capture walkthroughs of popular games, previews of upcoming titles, game-related comic strips, and tips for masterful performance. The first issue featured a list of *Super Mario* high scores: among them was thirteen-year-old Cliff Bleszinski, who'd grow up to make *Gears of War*. It was the Nintendo hot line between two glossy covers.

But simply putting Mario on the cover for *Super Mario Bros. 3* wasn't enough. Nintendo knew it had a tremendous game here, a deep, deep experience that it could use to show off its versatility. It also knew that this was Mario's final outing for the NES: folks in the home office were working on an improved gaming console. Arakawa was working a deal with McDonald's Happy Meals to distribute toy likenesses from the game. But *Super Mario Bros. 3* needed a big publicity stunt to open it. Something a big Hollywood movie would do.

That thinking eventually truncated down to "make a Hollywood movie." It so happened that work on a feature version of Universal's *The Jetsons*, scheduled for a holiday 1989 release, was six months behind. Would Nintendo be interested in making a movie about the allure of its games? When someone else offers to pay for an hour-and-a-half commercial for your new product, you say yes. The fact that Universal, which not five years previous was suing Nintendo up and down for stealing *King Kong*, was now offering to foot the bill for a feature-length Nintendo ad speaks to Nintendo's clout. It could not only get a movie green-lighted, it could have Voldemort fund it.

The result, *The Wizard*, was a monumentally awkward fusing of video game culture and family melodrama. A preteen Fred Savage and a teenage Christian Slater go on a road trip with their possibly autistic younger brother, Jimmy, who is the eponymous wizard at video games. Only Nintendo games, of course: much of the film's dialogue is about particular Nintendo titles. When a rival game-player is introduced, for instance, he uses Nintendo's Power Glove peripheral.

The three brothers (plus a girl they pick up, Jenny Lewis) travel to California for a video-game tournament. Jimmy's gaming prowess is portrayed as akin to Dustin Hoffman's mathematical ability in *Rain Man*. He's even an expert at games he's never played before. The tournament-winning game, by the way, which all the characters gush over, and which Jimmy wins to incredible roars from the crowd, is *Super Mario Bros. 3*.

SMB3 was released in Japan in 1988, but not on U.S. shores until 1990. In the meantime, *The Wizard*, despite opening in fifth place at the box office, stoked the fire for its release. The movie was clunky, but it definitely whetted the appetite for its target audience. (And its cast and crew escaped relatively unscathed: Fred Savage made *The Wonder Years*, Christian Slater became a leading man, director Todd Holland went onto helm *The Larry Sanders Show* and *Malcolm in the Middle*, and Jenny Lewis sings with the band Rilo Kiley.)

Super Mario Bros. 3 moved millions of copies its first day of release, February 12, 1990, two months after *The Wizard* hit theaters. The game would go on to sell 18 million copies, setting a Guinness record for the most popular game not bundled with a system. It's since been beaten, but only by other Nintendo games. The continual bettering of the Big N's profits started a thousand Nintendo-is-buying-us rumors from toy companies such as Mattel and Hasbro.

Miyamoto was vindicated. He once again had topped himself, and in a way people loved. *Super Mario Bros. 3* is still considered one of the finest video games ever made, for any system. And with his last great success, Miyamoto was finally able to feel comfortable in the producer role. Like the athlete who can't retire until he has that world championship, Miyamoto was ready now to let others share in the fun of trying to fold, spindle, and mutilate gaming's leading man.

But only on Nintendo systems. Around this time Nintendo was approached by a small Texas game developer, who had come up with a side-scrolling game program. After adapting (and sprite-swapping) some boards of *Super Mario Bros. 3*, which they dubbed *Dangerous*

Dave in Copyright Infringement, the Texans converted all of the game's first level to the PC. If Nintendo gave the thumbs-up, it would have a perfect DOS-based port.

The corporate thumb, though, pointed down. If gamers could play Nintendo's games outside of the NES, they might stop buying the NES. As a computer game maker, no matter how profitable, Nintendo would be following, not leading. So it turned down what would have been some nice short-term money to ensure its long-term stability. Discouraged but not beaten, the indie developers moved to Dallas and developed an original PC side-scroller, *Commander Keen*. Then the game engine's inventor, John Carmack, devised a way to simulate 3-D first-person graphics on a computer. He, and id Software cofounder John Romero, went on to create the classics: *Wolfenstein 3D, Doom, Quake,* and the entire shooter genre. They all might have been Nintendo exclusives, if Nintendo had been willing to share Mario with the computer.

9 — MARIO'S BROTHERS

THE NES AND THE GAME BOY

higeru Miyamoto's reputation as a Steven Spielberg or George Lucas of video games was being built with every new title. But games are a young franchise compared to film. Spielberg, Lucas, and their seventies ilk were building on close to a hundred years of filmmaking grammar, from cutaway close-ups to ending with a big explosion.

Video games were barely twenty years old: their storytelling grammar was still being developed. Miyamoto would more properly be compared to Charlie Chaplin or Buster Keaton, a gifted prodigy whose breezy onscreen antics belie how incredibly difficult it was to pull off. Miyamoto's mentor Gunpei Yokoi, then would be in the D. W. Griffith or Cecil B. DeMille role, the patriarch whose work was the foundation upon which all others build upon. Anyone who uses a directional pad, after all, is playing a Yokoi game.

Yokoi certainly racked up internal accolades for his work, serving as one of Yamauchi's top R&D daimyos. But he was an inventor first, and seemed to have a side business of inventing new profit centers for Nintendo, and finding new leaders to run them. First came the Ultra Hand and various other devices. Then the Game & Watch series, which continued throughout the eighties. Then his handholding for Miyamoto on the *Donkey Kong* series. When Miyamoto was given his own R&D division, Yokoi worked with new talent to create games like *Clu Clu Land* (a maze game) and *Balloon Fight* (which copied everything from *Joust* that *Mario Bros.* didn't). Yokoi's team was fast, learned quick, and got better with every game.

After mastering the basic programming skills, Yokoi let his crew run wild with *Kid Icarus*, which merged the *Ice Climber* verticality with more action. Then came *Metroid*, an outstanding achievement that merged multiple play styles, horizontal and vertical action, and a tense, gripping, science-fiction atmosphere. Plus, it has a stunner of an ending: Samus Arau takes off his spacesuit to reveal that "he" is really a she, gaming's first great heroine.

But by 1989, the Game & Watch franchise was dying down. Why buy a whole system (albeit a sliver of one) to play just one game? Yokoi began brainstorming a handheld gaming system with removable cartridges. They'd been tried before, but the results were poor, hard to decipher, and worst of all expensive. Yokoi understood price, hardware, playability, and consumer interest. He could do it.

Price, as with the Famicon, was king. It had to be cheap, but not cheaply made. Yokoi insisted on using existing technology instead of cutting-edge hardware, which was both expensive and untested by time. It was his philosophy: *Kareta Gijutsu no Suihei Shikou*, which awkwardly translates to Lateral Thinking of Seasoned Technology, or applying new ideas using off-the-shelf parts. (*Kareta* can also be translated as the elegant "mature" or the condescending "withered.")

Technology, memory, transistor speed: everything grew smaller and cheaper. So why pay for top-dollar top-shelf parts, and have to pass that cost onto the customer? It was Island Economics 101: import materials, add value, sell at a profit.

There would be no backlight, for instance. Backlights were expensive, they ate up battery, they were heavy. Sure, people would complain the "Game Boy" (as it was being called) couldn't be played in the dark. But their unspoken desire for a light, cheap, long-lasting product outweighed the backlight's pros. There would also be, alarmingly, no color—another battery drain. Yokoi instead proposed a grisaille color palette: all gray, or rather a Soviet olive-green. He almost gave himself an ulcer worrying about Sharp's investment in the screens, especially when an early version was too hard to see head-on, and reflected a glare from an angle. But he and Sharp worked it out at the eleventh hour: the four different shades of green-gray pixels displayed fine. "Creamed spinach color," as a rival's advertisement snidely put it.

Yokoi was indulgent in other areas. Each Game Boy would come with ear bud headphones. This allowed a more private gaming experience, let the games exist in stereo instead of the mono speaker, and saved more precious batteries. A battery pack accessory would let gamers play 24-7. Two-player games would be possible with a link cable and a connector port. Many other small touches, like an on-off switch that locked in the cartridge, made the device durable and smart.

Yokoi's team was at work on a suite of launch games, which read like a minihistory of gaming. First was *Tennis*, an update of *Pong*. Then *Alleyway*, a tribute to *Breakout* and other paddle-ball games. Then *Baseball*, a shared love of the United States and Japan. Of course, a Mario game was in development as well. The Game Boy would play identical to the NES, so developers already knew how to program for it.

Minoru Arakawa decided the Game Boy would have *Tetris* as a pack-in game, not Mario. Nintendo had been a part in a years-long battle over who owned rights to Alexis Pajitnov's falling-block game. (The whole story is excellently told in David Sheff's *Game Over*.) Like the Brooklyn Bridge, most of the people who said they owned it—this included a reformed Atari, who found a way around the lockout chip and were going to sell a NES *Tetris* without Nintendo's approval—were sold bogus licenses. Turns out the Soviets never sold it in the first place—and all the millions of *Tetris* fans were all playing ultimately stolen games.

Arakawa went after the rights hard, following his own gut feeling that America would love the game in handheld form. He flew to Moscow to personally meet with the Soviets, and offered some of Nintendo's cubic mile of cash. He walked away with console rights, handheld rights, and the eternal ire of Atari. Mikhail Gorbachev even weighed in, personally promising a rival company's execs that Nintendo wouldn't get the rights. It did no good, and Nintendo kept its rights. (Welcome to capitalism, *tovarich*.)

Tetris was a masterpiece. Puzzle games turned out to be the Game Boy's bread and butter: no fancy graphics needed, and its portable nature let it be the new crossword puzzle or Rubik's Cube. Plus, it meant that people wanting a Mario game still had to plunk down another thirty dollars to buy it. Just to be safe, Mario received cameos in *Tetris* (he and Luigi appear in two-person games), *Tennis* (he's the player) and *Alleyway* (the blocks form his face at one point). Only *Baseball* escaped him.

Miyamoto was grinding away producing other Mario and Zelda games, so Yokoi and his new protégé Satoru Okada would try to shrink down the Mario experience without losing the grand scope. It would get a new name—*Super Mario Land*—because the conceit was this wasn't the Mushroom Kingdom but a whole new land to explore, Sarasaland.

Many minor details were different. Mario still attacked by jumping, still grabbed coins and mushrooms, still shot fireballs and gained invincibility with stars. But instead of Princess Toadstool, Mario was saving a dark-haired princess named Daisy. He rode a submarine in one level, and an airplane in another. He could bypass boss fights by running past them out of the room. The final boss wasn't King Koopa but an alien named Tatanga. And Okada gave Mario a reason to be universally attacked: Tatanga has hypnotized all the inhabitants. There were twelve levels, not as big as previous Mario adventures, but still a lot for a cartridge the size of a Ghirardelli chocolate. It wasn't necessarily worse, just . . . off. Whatever the Platonic ideal Mario game was, this was not it.

No matter. The Game Boy sold out in Japan upon its launch in April 1989, and sold out in America four months later. (Toys "R" Us offered to be the exclusive home of the Game Boy: Arakawa was smart enough to say no.) Millions upon millions of each of the four launch games were sold. President Bush was photographed using one. It was huge in Europe, much bigger than the NES. A Russian cosmonaut took one into space—to play *Tetris*, of course. *Super Mario Land* alone sold 18.4 million copies over its lifetime. It more than made up for no NES Mario game released in 1989. The Game Boy would go on to sell a flabbergasting 118 million units. There are more Game Boys in the world than people in Mexico. You could tile half the states in New England with Game Boys. Nintendo, it seemed, could do no wrong. The prestigious *Japan Economic Journal* that year named Nintendo the best company in Japan, besting Toyota.

Nintendo was so confident, it even closed the book on one of its first cash cows, the Game & Watch. The final game, *Mario the Juggler*, was Nintendo in a nutshell. Its simple premise was that Mario had to keep juggling. It was, in fact, a redesigned version of the original Game & Watch game *Ball*, from ten years earlier. Simple, inexpensive to make, proven popularity, a certain Italian mascot: all of the Big N's grace notes. Long-running TV shows have aired final episodes that weren't as contemplative, respectful, or tributary. One wonders if Gunpei Yokoi wanted to include Mario bowing a tearful farewell as an LCD curtain fell.

The Game Boy had loads of room for improvement. Any system with a color screen was a better game-playing machine. Atari's Lynx and Sega's Game Gear both claimed that: both used backlights, too. Their games were graphically superior to regular NES games, let alone Game Boy's four flavors of creamed spinach. But—as Yokoi knew they must—these handhelds gobbled up batteries at a shocking rate, six every four hours. A fraction of the Game Boy shelf space was allotted to whatever high-price, high-quality, high-weight competitor was out there. They never caught on, despite years of marketing and many solid games.

Gamers already had a Game Boy by then. They already equated portable consoles with puzzles, low-impact gameplay, and inexpensiveness. Sega, Atari, and TurboGrafix had color screens, but did they have a Yokoi? Did they have a Miyamoto? If not, too bad. Every new all-green Game Boy title made competitors green—with envy.

10 - MARIO'S DRIFT

SEGA, THE GENESIS, AND A VERY FAST HEDGEHOG

Every issue of *Nintendo Power* contained a Howard and Nester comic strip. Howard was the clueless do-gooder, and Nester the wild child. They'd jump into game worlds (whatever was on the cover the previous month) and pass on a game tip. Nester looked like a skate punk waiting for puberty. Howard was a tall gangly redhead in a bowtie—the red hair tying into the Richie Cunningham/Jimmy Olson/Archie Andrews trifecta of unthreatening all-American rubes.

Nester was fictional, hence his name, the NES-ster. Howard, though, was based on Howard Phillips, one of the American branch's first employees. (And yes, there was a Howdy Doody quality to him.) Phillips had been the first person to think that *Donkey Kong* was a better game than *Radar Scope*. He was one of the original six who had converted the two thousand units shipped over from Jersey. During the Universal lawsuit, he flew to New York to demonstrate *Donkey Kong* in court. A few years later, he moved to the New York area and spent months setting up World of Nintendo displays. He helped choose which games from the hundreds of Famicon titles would be NES launch releases. His current job was to evaluate games up for review, passing on notes for changes. Most designers admitted his suggestions were right on the money. After the NES launch he had been given the official job description, on business cards and everything, of Game Master.

As a *Nintendo Power* editor, Phillips helped come up with the modern strategy guide. Images of each board of *Super Mario Bros.* were stitched together to display every obstacle and villain Mario would face, and printed small enough so a good dozen screen were included per row. The result looked like Cinerama film strips from a virtual world. The board stretched on for miles, branching off into multiple avenues, sometimes betraying when an underground jaunt didn't correspond in length with its aboveground stretch.

This was done to help sell the games, but it had a value beyond mere marketing. The guides helped gamers through tough sequences, which not only kept them playing but showed them facets of the game that only experts would otherwise find. Strategy guides for video games now bring in over a hundred million dollars a year. In addition, every game (no matter how small) has a dozen or more fan-made walkthroughs, contributed and collected at sites like gameFAQs.com. The Mario game walkthroughs are the length of Victorian novels.

"Howard" disappeared from the strip two years into its run, replaced by just Nester. This was because Howard Phillips himself left Nintendo, poached away by LucasArts to be their games guru. Nintendo was in continual expansion, so having someone leave was almost unprecedented, especially from the job of "spokesgamer." (It still is: Nintendo employees stay on for decades.) The coolest job at the coolest company had its downside, though: long hours; low wages—despite

Nintendo literally making billions each year, it paid its employees con-
servatively; and poor job security. Howard Phillips had clear competition as company mascot, competition who sold millions of games every
year. Nintendo's focus was shifting from gamers (like Phillips) to games.
And there just wasn't anyone in creation who could be a worthy rival to
Mario.

Since the late 1970s, Sega wasn't so much the Pepsi to Nintendo's
Coke as it was the RC Cola. It had been Rosencrantzing and Guilden-
sterning its way around the gaming world for decades, always buffeted
by the wake of others, rarely the one making waves.

Sega began life in 1940 as Standard Games, running penny arcades
on military bases in the territory of Hawaii. A decade later, under the
name of Service Games, it merged with American expatriate David
Rosen's company, which was putting photo booths around Tokyo. The
combined venture was called Sega Enterprises—SeGa for Service
Games.

Sega was bought in 1969 by Gulf + Western, an American *zaibatsu*-
style conglomerate parodied in the Mel Brooks film *Silent Movie* as
Engulf + Devour. Rosen stayed on as Sega moved from electromechanical hits like *Periscope* to video games such as *Zaxxon* and *005*, a James
Bond knockoff. The arcade titles (including *Congo Bongo*, a suspiciously
familiar game about an angry ape throwing things) brought in $200
million worth of quarters over the years. But Sega also tried its hand
at some home consoles—1981's SG-1000 and a cheapo sequel a few
years later. Gulf + Western dropped Sega like a hot potato in 1983,
thinking that gaming was a bubble that had just burst.

Sega's third console was the Mark III, which it quickly renamed
the Master System. Its merits were dubious: it was backward compatible with two previous game systems no one knew about; it could
accept cards or cartridge-based games; its mascot was an egg-shaped

spaceship name Opa-Opa. When Opa-Opa flopped as a character, Sega replaced the spaceship with Alex Kidd, a monkey boy whose dull, difficult, different adventures (in subsequent games he fights ninjas, then playing cards, then fights a boss called Mari-Oh [!], then is a BMX rider) gave him little identity. Alex was a winded rival's sad attempt to "make" a Mario by plopping the same character in radically divergent games.

Then, like the dawning of a new day, came the Genesis. Called the Mega Drive in Japan when it was released in 1988, it was a 16-bit system, allowing for exponentially better graphics, sound, and—most crucially—speed. More than sixty possible colors, eighty movable sprites on screen at a time, and a resolution rate that was actually slowed so that the processor could have more juice for faster animation.

Any 1988 console would (and should) be leaps and bounds better than the NES, which was five years old. The paradox of launching a game system was how to attract third-party support when they would only make games for a system with a big install base . . . which of course would only happen with third-party support. Sega was having little luck attracting vendors to design for their great machine. Nintendo had inserted exclusivity clauses for all of its third-party designers, to starve any possible competitor. If they released a Genesis game, they'd be breaching their contract.

Furthermore, Nintendo wouldn't let companies make their own products: everything was made by Nintendo, to further its control of distribution. This micromanagement came to a head during a chip shortage in Japan, where Nintendo both slashed orders down to a fraction of their size and forbade companies from finding their own U.S. or European chips. Those who complained could see their chip allotment cut further, and fewer mentions in *Nintendo Power*. Making your business partners codependently kiss your ring in exchange for such paltry treatment was a recipe for misery, and game makers no doubt hoped Sega would offer an escape hatch from the draconian Nintendo.

The Genesis sold for $189, nearly double the NES price. It was backwards compatible with the Master System, not much of a feature since few in America had one. In Japan, it wasn't doing particularly well: it was third, behind the NES and then NEC's Turbo-Grafx 16. The TG-16 was very popular in Japan—it had a 16-bit graphics chip before the Genesis did—but it cheated with an 8-bit microprocessor and wasn't as robust a machine. Still, Nintendo's and NEC's market advantage of being there first and building a customer base shut Sega out. (The Genesis and the TG-16 launched in the United States around the same time: the Genesis's superior games would essentially end NEC's chance of American success. It ranked a distant fourth in the U.S. market.)

Sega made bold moves to win over American audiences, which in toto would achieve so much success that any claims of Nintendo's coercive monopoly would crumble. It allied with Tonka to distribute its systems. It called out Nintendo by name in its ads, running side-by-side pictures that Sega's Japanese exec thought were in bad taste. It made its own series of sports games, paying out millions to the biggest names in the field—Joe Montana, Tommy Lasorda, Arnold Palmer, Pat Riley, and (in a possible bid for industrial sabotage) hockey's Super Mario Lemieux—for their names and likenesses. (Nintendo had stayed far away from athlete licensing ever since Mike Tyson was accused of spousal abuse.) It lured computer game giant Electronic Arts, which Nintendo had never hired, to make Genesis games. Sega even hired the King of Pop, Michael Jackson, for a beat-em-up called *Moonwalker*. It happily sold its games to Blockbuster.

And, in 1991, it unleashed its Sonic boom. *Sonic the Hedgehog* was a new genre of game, a mix of racing game and platformer. Sonic's goal was ostensibly the same as Mario's: trek from one end of the world to the other, while picking up all the goodies. But while Mario's focus was on replaying each level until all the treasures were found, Sonic's was on lightning-quick reflexes and the adrenaline rush of caroming up hills, through loop-de-loops, around lateral twists, and then banging into pinball bumpers to do it all again backward. Sonic used only one button, jump. This was done to simplify game play—Mario and his wardrobe of costumes seemed baroque by comparison. Even Sonic's jump was literally sharp. He spun into a quill-lined ball to bowl over others. Each impact with an opponent presumably left them covered in barbs.

Sonic's creator, his Miyamoto, was Yuji Naka. Naka was young: he had been in high school during the crash of '83. He was from Osaka, and had grown up a generation removed from the war. He spoke fluent English, but loved Japanese synth-pop. He was handsome. Figuring he'd learn more with on-the-job training, he never went to college, and talked his way into Sega as a programmer. He had cut his teeth on the *Phantasy Star* line of role-playing games, which were easily among the Master System's best. He had a hard time managing staff, preferring to do everything himself. For fun, and to show off, he built an NES emulator for the Master System.

Sonic was different: he was the poster child for the ADHD generation, an anime speedster with spiky hair, a constant smirk, and what in retrospect would be the defining hallmark of the nascent 1990s: "attitude." He looked like Mickey Mouse channeling Sid Vicious, or Felix the Cat as a base jumper. Sonic's finger waggled at you from the title screen, like he was on *The Jerry Springer Show* (which also premiered in 1991). If you left the controller idle while playing, he impatiently tapped his feet. As a character, he was expressly built to showcase Nintendo's weaknesses. Mario was jolly: Sonic was rude.

Mario was happily unrushed: Sonic's express purpose was to rush. Mario changed into lots of clever outfits. Sonic didn't have to change: he was as ruthlessly perfect as a shark.

This was new for Nintendo. Plenty of people had made inferior side-scrolling platform adventures. They were fan fiction at best, people who didn't understand what made Mario tick trying to duplicate his efforts. Naka's *Sonic* was a four-fingered glove across Nintendo's cheek. He cast all of Nintendo's positives as negatives. Affordability and creativity became inferiority and impotence. Nintendo was popular? Well, as the middle-school logic goes, it's not cool anymore if everyone likes it. If Nintendo was the jovial uncle Mario happy to play with the kids, then the Genesis was the rebellious teen cousin Sonic who drove too fast and snuck cigarettes.

This argument between corporate mascots is, of course, risible. Sega and Nintendo were in the same business, operating under the same rules. Corporate philosophy may drive a board of directors' meeting, but for the designers trying to digitally paint a background or map out some extra processing power, it was academic. Yet this was a serious issue for the young consumer. Mario was lame and Sonic was cool, went the new social paradigm. You could still play a Mario game, just like you could go pick flowers for your mom if you wanted. At school you pretended you were allowed to stay up late to watch the overtime, you said you loved all the hit new music, and you praised Sonic for being def and rad and bitchin'.

Worst of all for Nintendo was, appropriately, Sonic's speed. From its launch day on June 23, *Sonic* was the Genesis' new pack-in game. Anyone who recently bought a Genesis with *Altered Beast* packed in could receive a free *Sonic*. Sega even retrofitted a version to play on the Master System. *Sonic* soon appeared in a hit series of cartoons, comic books, and all the merchandise that went in between. Sega dropped the Genesis's price to $150, and set up a domestic gaming division to makes games for American audiences. After fifty years in the gaming business, Sega was an enfant terrible.

Nintendo hadn't had an easy climb to the top, but once it was there it continued to act like a team down by fourteen, instead of up by twenty-one. (Psych journals have reported on this "overdog" effect, showing that teams work harder when they have more face to lose.) It made toy stores, who usually had a "December 12" policy of not having to pay for any shipments until well into the Christmas season, pay up-front for everything. It continued to manufacture all cartridges, putting third-party vendors at Nintendo's mercy during parts short-ages. It set up its own divisions in the United Kingdom and Canada. It went after rental companies like Blockbuster. It attacked Taiwainese software pirates. For all the billions it was bringing in, it took almost no risks. Such was the benefit of controlling the distribution.

Sega found a way to challenge Nintendo despite not having avail-able third-party support, or an established fan base, or known brands. *Sonic* wasn't a perfect game—it was very short, and too easy. But pointing that out in public would be treating them as equals, which played into *Sonic*'s and Sega's game. For Pete's sake, Paul McCartney was just in Japan, and he passed up a visit to Mount Fuji to meet Shigeru Miyamoto. Any Beatles stopping by Sega headquarters? "Sega is nothing," Yamauchi said to a reporter, a quote that ended up pasted onto many Sega employees' doors.

Minoru Arakawa's strategy to fight Sonic, then, was to do little other than cross his fingers that Sega went bankrupt. Mario licensing was big: the first of a dozen *Nintendo Adventure* books had just hit bookstores, featuring choose-your-own-adventure style adventures for Mario. Nintendo already had its new 16-bit console in develop-ment. It would be foolish to rush it to market too early, or to launch in the United States and Japan simultaneously: Japan was the acid test for gaming. (One that Sega failed, incidentally.)

But maybe they could gin up a new Mario game, a sort of hail Mario pass. Gunpei Yokoi's team had designed an excellent Game Boy puzzle title, which built on the success of *Tetris*. The screen starts out full of blocks in one of three hues, and the player has to drop two-block units down to clear the rows. It played like starting a half-lost game of *Tetris*. And, it was a Mario game. The game field was a bottle, the blocks were viruses, and Mario had to drop "pills" to clear the board. It was closer to waste management than medicine, but *Garbage Man Mario* didn't have a good ring to it. *Dr. Mario* did, though. And since its graphic needs were so basic, quality versions could be made for the NES, Game Boy, and the arcade. (Where one of the big hits of the year was Sega's own puzzle game, *Columns*.)

Dr. Mario did quite well, selling more than five million copies, further establishing the puzzle genre as a viable field. *Tetris* had given gamers a jones for puzzle games. And while great ones were hard to make, imperfect ones practically grew on trees. For the Game Boy especially, it seemed half of all the new games released were puzzle games: *Boxxle*, *Pipe Dream*, *Qix*. But only a few had the simplicity of game play and design to be intuitive: *Dr. Mario*, *Tetris*, and *Columns*. (In fact, Nintendo released a combo cartridge called *Tetris & Dr. Mario*.)

Another *Dr. Mario* accomplishment was to upgrade Mario to the star of a game that had nothing to do with Mario's wheelhouse of jumping, costumes, turtles, saving princesses from King Koopa, etc. It was a puzzle game, pure and simple. Having Mario be in it was fine—discovering him in a Nintendo game was like finding the Alfred Hitchcock cameo, or searching out the word Nina in an Al Hirschfeld drawing. But to *name* the game after him? Who would see the word "Mario" and think "puzzle game"?

Dr. Mario wasn't phoned in, and Nintendo felt its quality earned the right to have Mario on the cover. Mario was a celebrity endorser, Michael Jordan in overalls. While Sega was building its mascot Sonic with mercenary aplomb, Nintendo turned Mario into the Good House-keeping Seal of Approval.

Sonic's rebellious attitude apparently wasn't a whole-cloth invention from Yuji Naka. He cut ties with Sega's Japanese headquarters—he wasn't being paid what he deserved, he said—and went to work for one of Sega's new U.S. divisions. He brought a slew of Japanese designers with him; the development team was a little bit of Tokyo in the heart of Los Angeles. It was as if Naka couldn't stay, but didn't really want to leave, either. There is a philosophical term invented by Schopenhauer for being equally hurt by staying too close or staying too far away. It is called the hedgehog's dilemma—think prickly animals needing to huddle together for body heat.

Naka continued working on more *Sonic* games, eventually weaving in a supporting cast—Tails the fox, Knuckles the Echidna, another hedgehog named Amy Rose—that reinforced Sonic's bad-boy image. Amy Rose pined for Sonic—but he was too busy to ever notice. Tails looked up to Sonic like a younger sibling. Knuckles was Sonic's bitter rival. All existed to smartly shine Sonic's rising star, and make him the centerpiece of the game.

Mario, on the other hand, didn't need a crew of characters who all said how awesome he was. He was kept purposefully mute, a mere avatar for the audience, his specificity of look and demeanor making him that much more universal. Nintendo would not change its actions just because a competitor had finally made some grounds in terms of market share.

Besides, the next Mario game in the pipeline would crush Sega.

PART 3

SWEET 16

11 - MARIO'S CLASH

THE SONIC-MARIO SHOWDOWN

The man behind the Nintendo Entertainment System was Masa-yuki Uemura. Uemura had grown up in Japan's poor postwar years without much money. He taught himself engineering, and successfully built a remote-controlled airplane from bits of scrap he found in a junkyard. This skill led him to study electrical engineering in college, and then to work for Sharp with the new technology of solar cells. He specialized in optical semiconductors, which were the infrastructure of the power source.

Part of Uemura's job was explaining this new technology to potential clients. One day around 1971, Sharp sent him, with his thatch of thick hair parted evenly over a growing forehead, to a potential client in Kyoto. It was a toy and card manufacturer named Nintendo. Uemura and one of Nintendo's engineers, Gunpei Yokoi, hit it off, as only two grown men still interested in designing toys can. Yokoi's knack for finding the fun in everything, combined with Uemura's knowledge of the solar cells, could bear fruit.

Or it could bear arms. This solar-cell technology could be used for a light gun game. Shooting a light gun at a sheet of such cells would light up only the one that was hit. It'd be as direct as pushing a button on a calculator. But it would require a whole screen of photodiodes, which was impractical.

It would take an engineering genius to think of a practical solution; luckily, two of them were working on the project. The trick was to reverse the iconic thinking of the gun as the transmitter and the screen as the receiver. If the gun were the *receiver*, all you would need was one small photodiode in the cannon. For the screen to be the *transmitter*, whatever image it currently showed would have to be replaced (when the trigger was pulled) for a single frame with blackness, then another frame of blackness save for the white target. If the photodiode ever saw white, then it was aimed at the target at the time of firing. Thus was born Nintendo's Beam Gun, one of its first hit electronic games. Out of this technology grew a slew of Nintendo products: the *Wild Gunman* electromechanical arcade game, the *Laser Clay Pigeon Shooting System* (which set up in bowling alleys), and the NES Zapper.

Uemura stayed on at Nintendo, and became not only its technical guru but also one of President Yamauchi's wisest advisors. When he saw the Magnavox Odyssey, he told Yamauchi that Nintendo could get into the same business, if it partnered with someone with experience making mass-market electronics products. That led to a partnership with Mitsubishi, and the Color TV Game 6 and 15.

Once the Game & Watch line was a hit in 1980, Uemura started work on a new home console, this one cartridge-based. Just a few years had made for a tremendous increase in technology speed, and for much less yen. Arcade-quality graphics, stereo sound, and screens brimming with sprites were now possible. He could even make a 16-bit system, more powerful than most personal computers at the time.

Uemura remembered, however, that this was Nintendo. Yamauchi would have a fit if he saw how much 16-bit processors cost. Uemura scaled down his ambitions to 8 bits. Yamauchi helped lower the costs in his own way: brutal negotiations. He promised Ricoh a sale of three million semiconductors, only if they were sold at the bargain price of two thousand yen each. Nintendo's computers would cost less to make and could be sold for less, while still being an order of magnitude better than the Atari 2600 and its ilk.

The Famicon took a few years to develop, and as it moved to the United States and became the NES it lost many of its computer features. But it still had flaws. While the Famicon was top-loading, the NES was set up like a VCR, with cartridges inserted sideways. Too much pressure, or too much use, could make the connector pins bend. And the wide alley collected dust. Notoriously, people tried to fix their dusty systems by blowing into the NES, and onto their cartridges' exposed pins. Moist air, though, was to computer parts as garlic was to vampires. Uemura knew that the "zero-insertion-force" drive on the NES was a mistake, even if it hadn't affected American sales. He'd not make the same mistake again on his new video game system.

The mere fact that Yamauchi allowed a successor to the NES took years of argument. The Atari 2600, the Apple II, the Vic-20: all became dead as the Sargasso sea once their successors were announced. Consumers didn't want to buy a system with a death date, developers didn't want to program for it, and retailers didn't want to stock it. And for every successful successor—the Commodore 64 for the Vic-20— there was an Edsel-ish Atari 5200. Yamauchi didn't want to pull the brakes on the gravy train just yet.

He had already experienced one hardware failure—the Famicon Disk System. It was an add-on peripheral that accepted proprietary three-inch floppy disks, which contained more storage than a regular Famicon cartridge. That is, until developers started putting extra chips in the cartridges, making games that started out life as disk games, like *Super Mario Bros.*, playable on the NES. The disks' other feature was their erasability: when you're done with one game, wipe it clean at the game store and load on another. But the idea of paying for a license was new: what if you wanted to replay the old game? Yamauchi didn't help by inflicting onerous licenses on any store who wanted a Disk System hub. Despite selling in the millions, the Disk System never made it out of Japan.

And Nintendo's "Family Computer Communications Network System"—using the Japanese Famicon's modem capability—wasn't the huge success Yamauchi had envisioned either. People needed a computer, a screen, and a modem to download recipes, trade stocks (the NintenDow?), and read sports scores. But it also took a societal evolution, and society was still getting used to video games and computers. It would be another decade before "the series of tubes" (as a joke t-shirt put it, depicting Super Mario navigating some pipes) would snake their way into the world's homes. Not even the game sellers showed much interest in joining "Club Super Mario," a supposed pipeline for new product information.

The Turbo-Grafx-16 and the Genesis were gaining market share. Their graphics were undeniably more detailed: they were better engines for gaming. People hadn't stopped buying Nintendo games, but "Nintendo" was no longer synonymous for "video game." Arakawa's laissez-faire strategy wasn't working. Nintendo had to act—but when? Like a squad leader waiting for the right second to order his archers to fire, Yamauchi waited, and waited, and waited. One day in

1988, he saw the whites of their eyes, and gave the order: Develop a 16-bit game system.

The new system would be called the Super Famicon, the Super Nintendo Entertainment System in America. The entire console was given the adjective of its most popular game series, Super Mario. (That Mario's face wasn't emblazoned on the D-pads was a sign of restraint.) Backward compatibility would have cost an extra seventy-five dollars per unit, so Yamauchi and Awakawa decided to forego it. It was a tough call, but being inexpensive was worth the ire of NES owners.

Uemura decided that, as with the NES, the SNES would be designed to showcase the audio and visual aspects of the game. Its microprocessor, the 65816 (this was still the era when chips were numbered instead of named) dated from 1984, so by 1990 it was well understood, and widely available at a low cost. Two additional chips were used in tandem to make the graphics. The SNES, essentially, could show a digital photo slideshow if it wanted.

The sound was beefed up, too: eight-channel, 16-bit sound (including a digital signal processor good enough to be in a synthesizer) that was almost completely removed architecturally from the graphics. You want a digital voice? A clip of a song? A barrage of sounds effects for a character's actions? Can do.

The controller was changed from a brick to a more ergonomic dog's bone shape. There were now four rainbow-colored action buttons, not just two or three. In addition, there were two shoulder buttons. This broke away from Nintendo's original simplicity. But if a designer needed six distinct buttons for six different actions (think *Street Fighter II*), the SNES could do that. The Genesis couldn't.

What the SNES couldn't do, though, was lift. The Genesis has a beefier processor, which let Sega games run as fast as its spiny mascot. The SNES would never be able to do that, and it wisely didn't try. What made Nintendo so successful wasn't its hardware but its games. And, of course, its acumen; locking up third-party developers, doling out needed chips only to the companies that pleased Nintendo the most, testing out concepts in regional markets, selling the razors cheaply and making a fortune on the blades.

Shigeru Miyamoto's team was given a mere fifteen months to get to know the SNES, learn to program it, and spit out the first three games. His producer job became a writ-large version of a Game & Watch classic; running to the *Pilotwings* development team, then going to check in on the *F-Zero* group, then racing over to Team Mario. Miyamoto didn't drink, so for stress relief he smoked and hit the pachinko parlors. But he had grown into the producer role with aplomb. At last, Miyamoto was living the artist's dream; to imagine an idea, have others do the work, and receive all the credit!

The Mario atelier was designing *Super Mario World* with two different goals in mind. One was to create a worthy follow-up to *Super Mario Bros. 3*. A new item, a feather, let Mario fly. A spin jump lets Mario crouch down to career up extra high. Mario's fire flower not only killed bad guys, but also made them turn into valuable coins. And to make Mario's powers less of a crapshoot, players could gain and stockpile power-ups, deploying them when needed.

The other guiding principle was to show off what the SNES could do. Certain yellow bricks spun when hit, an animation the NES would have been hard-pressed to do convincingly. The bricks themselves were given softer edges, like well-worn toy blocks, which made Mario seem more like a toy himself. Mario now had a white circle on his hat, with a red M on it. His overalls were a lighter blue, more suggestive of denim. He could duck, be cartoonishly scorched, and shriek in comic horror at his fate.

Sometimes showing off and making a good game went hand in hand. Miyamoto, for years, had wanted Mario to do one specific thing he could never attain with the NES architecture: ride a freakin' dinosaur. Now Mario could. In keeping with the series' nomenclature confusion, the dinosaur he rode was called Yoshi (big Y)—but the species of dinosaur was also called a yoshi (little Y). Taxonomy was never Miyamoto's strongest suit. While Mario stayed the same size, Yoshi started out small, and needed to be made bigger by his signature attack: gulping down enemies.

Many game changes were to strike the right balance for the best flow. Halfway through every level was a checkpoint: if Mario died, he would come back to life at the checkpoint, instead of the beginning. After playing through a level once, Mario could quit mid-level, just by hitting start. These functions, along with plentiful warp doors, worked as a virtual fast-forward button, letting gamers replay their favorite parts.

These changes seemed minor, but there were more substantial alterations. The world maps looked more like maps than grids. Moving the far mountains slowly as Mario walked, called parallax scrolling, augmented the illusion of depth. Redrawing all the sprites to look more 3-D helped too. Finishing an area called the Special Zone caused a sprite swap, turning piranha plants into pumpkins, giving turtles Mario masks to wear, and switching many other map and creature colors around.

But the drop-dead date of November 21, 1990 (its Japanese release), was unavoidable. Miyamoto had been late with all three *Super Mario* games, and didn't like the feeling that ready or not, out this one would go in time for Christmas. One of his quotes has become regularly used in game design: "A late game is only late until it ships. A bad game is bad until the end of time." The finished game has a hefty seventy-two levels, and rewarded players who found its dozens and dozens of secrets. It could have had even more, Miyamoto rued. But he still considers it his favorite of all the Mario titles.

Super Mario World was the pack-in game for the SNES, so it was the default guide to the new game system. The SNES sold for twenty-five thousand yen, a little over two hundred dollars, more than the TG-16 or the Genesis. It sold out in mere hours. New shipments were sent to stores at night, to avoid falling off the truck into the underground economy. *Super Mario World* would move three and a half million copies in Japan, and the SNES a whopping 17 million units.

Three days after the U.S. launch on August 13, 1991, American stores were out of consoles too. Some retailers started bundling the system with additional games, tacking on another C-note worth of goods onto a two-hundred-dollar purchase. Almost 13 million people paid for *SMW* bundle units domestically, close to four times the number in Japan. More than 23 million SNESes were sold stateside overall. The system even earned America's ultimate compliment—it made it on *The Simpsons*, where fan favorite Ralph Wiggum called his principal's boss "Super Nintendo" instead of "superintendent." Every game system since has launched with various retail "bundles," adding mandatory extra controllers or games to beef up the store's sales.

Promoting the SNES on Pepsi and Kool-Aid packages helped young people know about the product launch. Oh, and Kraft's Super Mario Macaroni & Cheese, and Sunshine's Super Mario cookies. And the four-pack of Shasta sodas—Mario Punch, Luigi Berry, Yoshi Apple, and Princess Toadstool Cherry. Mario's face was as sure a sign of unhealthy food as high-fructose corn syrup. (A golden opportunity was missed to rebrand Nes-Quik to SNES-Quik.)

But as Gore Vidal said, it's not enough to succeed: others must fail. The SNES and *Super Mario World* were both smashes, but gamers didn't abandon Sega just because Nintendo had a 16-bit system. There was finally a balance in the video game world. Nintendo's years of writing its own rules for retailers and customers were coming to an end. It could no longer, say, try to muscle Blockbuster out of renting its games for three dollars for three days. If you wanted to rent a SNES game, Nintendo preferred you did so from a hotel room, for seven dollars an hour. But the big N wasn't the only game in town anymore.

Perhaps that's why a third style of NES was designed, and released in 1993 for a mere fifty dollars. It played the same NES *Mario* games, but removed the zero-insertion-force port for a top-loading toaster-style slot, and a dog-bone controller. It also lost the expensive 10NES chip, so it could play unlicensed games. Sega still put out Master System games despite the Genesis's popularity. Nintendo—without acknowledging it—was taking a page from Sega's book, and keeping the fan base for the previous system happy.

For this redesigned NES, Miyamoto tried his hand at designing a puzzle game, with the seemingly simple *Yoshi*. (Around this time he also began fantasizing about a toy game as devilishly simple as Enzo Rubik's Cube, which is still just a daydream twenty years later.) The *Yoshi* screen was only four columns wide, and pieces (they looked like Mario villains) fell two at a time. Mario had to shuffle the pieces so like fell on like. It was fun for what it was, but nowhere near *Tetris*, or even *Dr. Mario*.

Nintendo also rejiggered a Japanese golf game, *Mario Golf*, as *NES Open Tournament Golf*. The American release had fewer courses, easier holes, and more replayability, thanks to adding prize money for good performance. It was a microcosm of the difference between what Japan wanted—hard simulation games to be studied and then discarded—and the United States—fun arcade-style endeavors that could be replayed over and over.

Assuming, of course, that America wanted Nintendo at all, instead of Sega.

12 – MARIO'S GALAXY

SPINOFFS GALORE

ustin Hoffman—two-time best actor Oscar winner, six-time nominee—wanted to play Super Mario. That there would be a movie made about Mario was eventual: it couldn't be worse than action movies about paintball (*Gotcha!*), gymnastics (*Gymkata*), or skateboarding (*Gleaming the Cube*). For pity's sake, the Garbage Pail Kids and Howard the Duck had movies.

And one of the greatest actors in the world wanted to play him. It was too bad. Nintendo wanted Danny DeVito: you couldn't get a better physical match. And DeVito was in more family friendly movies: kids knew the Penguin from *Batman Returns* more than Carl Bernstein or Ratso Rizzo.

But Danny DeVito wasn't interested: he was directing, producing, and acting in *Hoffa*, with Jack Nicholson as the union leader. Nintendo's producers signed another comic actor, who like DeVito was trying to move beyond just comedy. They landed him for five million dollars: he was taller and thinner than Mario, and he wasn't Italian, but he did have dark hair and a family film pedigree. Tom Hanks it was.

Nintendo, in perhaps not the best use of its seasoned technology mindset, didn't want to pay five million for its lead. It wanted Bob Hoskins, a versatile British actor the approximate size and shape of Mario, who was asking for less. Kids knew him from *Who Framed Roger Rabbit?* and *Hook*. So Nintendo went with Hoskins, and in the first of many dire signs, fired Tom Hanks for not being a bankable movie star. (This could have made his career: would Hanks have won Oscars for *Philadelphia* and *Forrest Gump*—would he have even been cast—if he was fresh in people's minds as Mr. Super Mario?)

For Luigi, producers picked a rising star named John Leguizamo, also great with impressions, who passed over a starring sitcom deal for the role. The film used Princess Daisy (of the Game Boy's *Super Mario Land*) instead of Princess Toadstool as the heroine, probably because Daisy wasn't called Toadstool. Daisy was written as Luigi's love interest, as played by Samantha Mathis. (She and Leguizamo dated during filming.)

King Koopa went to Dennis Hopper, an old hand at playing villains. (And a step up from Mr. Belvedere.) But this King Koopa wasn't a big evil turtle but, strangely, a human who had evolved from a *Tyrannosaurus rex*. The whole movie had a devolution theme, with the parallel world Mario and Luigi go into being attacked by biological forces of decay. It's way more David Cronenberg or David Lynch than Walt Disney.

The directors, Rocky Morton and Annabel Jankel, seemed like a fine choice on paper. The British partners had cut their teeth directing New Wave videos for Elvis Costello and the Talking Heads. They also created Max Headroom, that definitive eighties character, an emblem for the bizarre world we thought computers would make. After capably directing a standard thriller (*DOA*), they were ready to handle a big budget (forty-eight million dollars, a lot in those days), a large cast, and a lot of action and special effects.

The set for the alternate universe "Dinohattan" was the interior of an old cement warehouse outside of Wilmington, North Carolina. It was big and crowded, with lots of extras dressed up for a rave. Various NES and SNES equipment was used in the movie: the devolution gun, for instance, was a clearly repainted Super Scope. Bits like that made the *Blade Runner*–inspired production design the most interesting part of the film.

The directors had a shoot-length argument with the studio over whether they were making a movie for adults (they filmed a scene with strippers, which was cut) or for children (they refused to have Mario and Luigi in costume, thinking them silly, but eventually relented). Production ran very long: Leguizamo and Hoskins started doing shots of scotch just to make it through the day. Hoskins hadn't known he was making a video game movie until his son told him who Mario was. Rewrites to the script were done on a daily basis. Rocky Morton reportedly poured a cup of hot coffee over an extra, because he wanted his costume dirtier. Leguizamo drove a van drunk during one shot, and braked too hard. It caused the sliding door to slam on Hoskins' finger: he wore a pink cast for most subsequent shots. The crew started to wear T-shirts with rude phrases the directors had said, as a form of protest.

The result, a film that seemed embarrassed and apologetic about its very existence, was not fun for kids or adults. It opened in fourth place over Memorial Day weekend of 1993, and within a month had dropped from the top twenty. The dinosaurs of *Jurassic Park* chased it out of theaters. Morton and Jankel retreated into directing commercials. Hoskins told the *Guardian* it's "the worst thing I ever did."

Leguizamo at least got a relationship out of it—until Mathis dumped him for new costar River Phoenix. But, as with true film flops, it disappeared from theaters so quickly that most people weren't even aware of it. It didn't even get nominated for a Razzie—for that, Mario should thank his lucky star sprites he came out the same year as three Sylvester Stallone films.

GAME DESIGNERS IN KYOTO WERE EXCITED FOR A REASON that had nothing to do with Hollywood. Uemura had designed eight "modes" for the SNES, called Mode 0 through Mode 7. This gave designers eight different game machines to program. Mode 7 was the most dramatic: It allowed the camera to scale and rotate a 2-D surface, creating what appeared to be a 3-D world. It was a narcissist's dream come true: the world literally revolved around the character. And if that surface was, say, a racetrack, you could continually move the point of reference to simulate velocity.

Mode 7 was the place to be. Certainly it wasn't something that the Genesis or the weak TG-16 could do. Shigeru Miyamoto based two of his three launch games around Mode 7 architecture: the third was, of course, *Super Mario World*. *Pilotwings* started life as *Dragonfly*, a game about gun-ladened insects involved in dogfights. By the time the game was finished, the insect combat theme had morphed into a more simple concept: flight simulator. The ground got very blurry up close, but players only saw the ground right before a crash—or a safe landing.

F-Zero went in another direction—and went there at about three hundred miles per hour. The year was 2560, humanity had used alien technology to perfect society's ills, and bored billionaires had started a hovercraft league as a sort of twenty-sixth-century polo; the new sport of kings. Miyamoto gave his developers a lot of freedom to follow their bliss with the games: the insect combat game could lose both the insect and the combat angles. The racing game could develop very strong anime influences. So long as they played well, and looked good, their content was secondary. Not unimportant, mind you. But 3-D was new, and people would take a year or so to get used to it before they wanted to do more than just zoom around in (forced) three dimensions.

Topping the wish list was a two-player racing game. But simply doubling the Mode 7 via a split screen would make the racers move comically slow: no way this would ever pass as *F-Zero 2*. But slower would work fine for a go-kart race, where no one's expecting speed. That idea freed up the team to give the characters big cartoony heads, in the spirit of fun. One of Miyamoto's designers drew up a character to sit in the kart—a man wearing overalls. This was probably a homage to Miyamoto's Mario. To further the tribute, another designer added Mario's head to the guy in overalls. It looked pretty good. All of a sudden, the team realized they had been building a Super Mario game all along: *Super Mario Kart*.

Well, if it was a Mario game then some changes had to be made. The oil can weapon used for *Spy Hunter*-style spinouts would become a banana peel. The weapons that would shoot forward from the karts could be turtle shells, which ricocheted around in Mario's world. A power star, as in every other game, made whoever grabbed it temporarily invulnerable. A mushroom would parley a burst of speed. A feather would hop you up in the air. Best of all was the lightning: it shrunk everyone save for you. The tracks became Mario-centric as well: one was inside Bowser's castle, and another aped the Donut Plains from *Super Mario Land*.

As for the racers? Mario himself was a given, naturally. But the original idea was that each racer would have different abilities, like in *Super Mario Bros. 2*. That roster—Mario, Luigi, Toad, and the Princess—would be four racers right there. Yoshi, the breakout character from the last Mario game, was a fifth. Bowser the villain would be sixth. A welcome throwback was *Donkey Kong Jr.* And lacking a better eighth, a Koopa Troopa was given the last spot. (In future installments he was replaced by Mario's evil twin Wario.)

The characters were all drawn from multiple angles, since otherwise they'd always be facing the camera (as in games like *Doom*) and thus would always look like they were racing you backwards. This was a revolutionary idea for 1992, if you'll pardon the pun, despite also giving them a distinctly underrendered look. Single-player gamers were given an aerial view of the whole map, with all eight characters ratcheting for pole position. Kōji Kondō even wrote music that sped up in the final lap.

Between the one-person computer races, the cup races, and the two-person options, players had a nearly endless combination of races to try. Miyamoto and company were cognizant enough to realize the real challenge lay not from the weapons, but the buddy sitting next to you. He (or very often she—*Super Mario Kart* is famously popular with women) is out to get you in ways you'll never guess. The Guinness World Records lists *Super Mario Kart* as the most influential title in gaming history, beating *Tetris* and *Grand Theft Auto*. (There are five other Mario games on the list, and another seven Miyamoto-associated titles.) Over fifty kart-racing titles have come out since then, for everything from *Nicktoons* to *South Park*.

Super Mario Kart, combined with *Dr. Mario*, showed that Mario was able to exist as a character beyond Jumpman. The clever idea of having the Mario crew be racing rivals served to further deflate Bowser: who could be scared of this guy squatting in a little putt-putt ride? It helped free later Mario games from having any real semblance of danger. You never want to lose, but aren't scared that Mario will get hurt. By who, his impotent go-kart buddy over there?

Nintendo at this point was in the odd position of being America's most favorite *and* least favorite company. Most everyone loved their products, and it was clear that the NES and Game Boy games had some extra advantage to them that Sega and NEC lacked. Nintendo had made gaming a lifestyle, a community, not just something the friendless did. This was parodied in Gary Larson's *Far Side* comic: proud parents watching their son play the NES dream of a newspaper want-ad section (from the future of September 2, 2005). "Looking for good Mario Brothers players. $100,000 plus your own car." "Can you save the princess? We need skilled men and women. $75,000 + retirement." "So you laugh in the face of killer goombas? Call us."

On the other hand were more problems than even a Power Glove could hold. First of all, Nintendo was a Japanese company, when Japan was seen as an economic superpower trying to conquer us, as in the novels *Rising Sun* by Michael Crichton and *Debt of Honor* by Tom Clancy. (Those authors, incidentally, would later license video game adaptations of their books.) Both sides of the Pacific agreed: the Japanese *were* different.

Second, Nintendo advertised to children, who controlled many family purse strings but didn't have the BS detectors of adults. Adults played too, and Nintendo was working to place its products in electronics stores as well as toy shops. But its fan base was eight- to thirteen-year-old boys.

Third, Nintendo was enormous, controlling about 85 percent of the video game marketplace. It raked in billions every year. And it used its heft to insert onerous clauses into business contracts no one with any choice would agree to. For instance, Nintendo invariably was paid in full from just about everyone they did business with. It had no accounts receivable, despite being hugely liquid, and easily able to offer credit to its vendors.

Fourth, Nintendo's fear of "pulling an Atari" and letting the market be flooded with shoddy cartridges turned into a miserly refusal to let anyone else manufacture Nintendo cartridges. This left Nintendo with fewer profits that it might have had. But an unexpected windfall of sales would make the stock price fluctuate—up with the good news, then down when the spree was over. The risk was the dip might be greater than the extra sales, leaving Nintendo with the absurd choice of either doing nothing and making a profit or decreasing shareholder value due to better-than-expected sales. Nintendo chose slow and steady. Nabisco had done the same thing with Oreo cookies recently, underselling the market and leaving hundreds of millions of potential cookie sales on the table, to avoid a jittery Wall Street.

The best thing for Nintendo, really, was Sega. Sega grabbed hundreds in millions of dollars in sales, set up Nintendo's first console rival with the Genesis, and helped retailers have more of a say in their video game business. Nintendo had been an unstoppable power, yes, but now it had competition. And with it came a reason other than artistic satisfaction to release quality games. That would result in better sales, better deals for third-party vendors, and more discounts for retailers. Nintendo *was* the game industry for a while, but the Genesis's arrival made it a two-person race. Seeing the writing on the wall, Nintendo allowed its vendors to make Genesis games. It was nice to level the playing field, but this move also reduced the number of "exclusive" titles for the Genesis.

Proof of Nintendo's new ingenuity could be found at a 1994 gaming trade show. Arakawa wanted to impress people more so than usual, and contacted a company that could develop real-time computer graphics. At the trade show, the virtual Mario was going to talk. All they needed was a convincing Mario—someone other than Bob Hoskins.

Vocal actors learn to be broad, so the personality comes across more. "Italian plumber from Brooklyn," for most voice actors, would signify a "fuhgeddaboutit" type of voice. Having their cherished icon sound like Joe Pesci in *Goodfellas* would have been terrible, disastrous. But one auditioner, not knowing who Mario was, went for more of a Chico Marx.

His chipper falsetto started pouring forth, in a genial ramble about how nice it was to be there, how much he liked everyone, and how they'd all go make a pizza. "It's-a me, Mario! Wee-heee!" Mickey Mouse via Milan. The actor, Charles Martinet, got the job working the Mario-in-Real-Time (MIRT) device, thanks to the spicy meat-a-ball accent. Small sensors were glued onto his face, and he hid behind an Oz-ian curtain for the trade show. On the MIRT monitor, an on-the-fly animated Mario conversed with everyone who walked by, talking video games, Italian food, plumbing, family, whatever.

Martinet has gone on to voice countless Mario cartoons and video games, buttoning down just about every appearance since. (He's also the voice of the Cat in the Hat, and records in fluent French and Spanish.) Even though Mario rarely says more than "whoa!" and "whoo!," the same person has been recording it anew for each new game for two decades. Martinet is also Luigi, Wario, Waluigi, Baby Mario, and a handful of smaller characters. After the big-screen debacle, Nintendo finally found the right actor to play Mario.

13 - MARIO THE JUGGLER

MARIO PAINT

eople mixed up the two prominent men named Howard at Nintendo of America. Howard Phillips was the Games Master and star of the *Nintendo Power* cartoon. Once Philips left, though, VP and general counsel Howard Lincoln wasn't mistaken for anyone else.

Many people say they had a Norman Rockwell childhood, but Lincoln has the evidence. He and his Boy Scout troop posed for Rockwell's painting *The Scoutmaster*: Howard is the boy just to the right of the campfire. He grew up to be an Eagle Scout, got his law degree, and then took on two clients who ran a modest import business.

Those two clients were Ron Judy and Al Stone, and when NOA brought them into the fold, and then needed a lawyer, they brought him in. He had been a Nintendo exec ever since the *King Kong* fiasco, and he and Arakawa had complementary skills. Lincoln brought the press-savvy glad-handing, while Arakawa was more of a CEO, keeping

the operation running smoothly. Despite their titles, Lincoln sometimes seemed more like a corporate president, especially since he
talked with reporters more often than Awakawa.

Lincoln was also white: he had an aquiline nose and Johnny Car-
son's knowing grin. Most of the NOA higher-ups were Japanese: for a
division with "America" in its name, its management didn't look
much like America. In fact, there had been criticisms that NOA had so
few black employees. By 1992 Nintendo had upgraded to a more
diverse workforce, but the complaints about the company were just
beginning.

Despite turning iD Software away, Nintendo decided that maybe
one or two educational computer games might not be too harmful to
its hegemony. So they allowed Interplay to release the self-explanatory
Mario Teaches Typing for DOS and then Mac. When the world did not
collapse in on itself, Nintendo followed this up with a pair of DOS-
based digital coloring books, with line drawings of Mario and Luigi in
action that kids could print out at home.

Keeping with the educational theme, Nintendo released a trio of
educational SNES games, the *Mario's Early Years* series. It was a
McDonalds-worthy attempt to turn Mario into every child's friend,
someone Mom and Dad would find friendly and inoffensive. (Years
later there would be whole colleges devoted to ludology, the study of
games.) But no matter how good Mario's edutainment games were, he
could not break out of his fun-buddy box to become a teacher. The
reverse is true as well: imagine 1992's Barney the Dinosaur, the lowest
of low-hanging pop culture targets, trying to sell an action-adventure
show to teens.

Nintendo's goodwill efforts, such as a hands-free controller so
paralyzed kids could game, were backfiring in ways it couldn't imagine. Senator Slade Gorton (R-Wash) had asked Nintendo (with its

Scrooge McDuck money vault of cash) to save the Seattle Mariners baseball franchise, which would otherwise be moving down to Florida. He had helped lure baseball back to Seattle, after the Seattle Pilots left after its first year, 1969, to become the Milwaukee Brewers. Gorton had already been turned down by Bill Gates of Microsoft. Arakawa called up Yamauchi, and was shocked to hear his father-in-law agree, offering seventy-five million dollars of his own money. Gorton structured the deal so others controlled the team: Yamauchi wanted little say. It was the sort of lousy deal—expensive, little chance of long-term profits, and absolutely no short-term gains—that prompted conspiracy theories that the Japanese were trying to buy the world.

This was maybe the first time Nintendo's contacts with U.S. senators was positive. Every year another politician would make a speech or hold an inquiry about video games: were they too violent? Should they be regulated? Did they harm the nation's children? Were they letting American companies compete? One of these was symbolically held on December 7, Pearl Harbor Day. Nintendo felt it had done many things right: it refused to show blood in any game, for instance, which severely cut into its profits for a gruesome title like *Mortal Kombat*. What could be wrong about helping Seattle keep its team?

When word got out Nintendo was trying to save the Mariners, it was branded not as a helping hand but as Japan trying to buy our national pastime. Even some Japanese thought it was in poor taste. A commission of baseball owners was formed to decide if the move would be allowed. Commissioner Fay Vincent's initial comments against the purchase came off as more anti-Japanese than pro-American. Things looked bleak.

The deal's savior may well have been the managing general partner of the Texas Rangers, who helped convince the other owners that the Nintendo purchase was best for the game, and for America.

That owner had a notable name, George W. Bush. His father was the president, who counted Japan as a key trading ally. Bush Junior convinced the other owners to approve the purchase. He would go on to use his powers of persuasion as a politician himself, getting elected as a two-term governor of Texas, then president.

Miyamoto wasn't involved in the Mario educational games; they were done by outside firms. But he thought the flow potential of coloring a Mario image on screen was strong. It was part of his team's job to draw everything in the game, after all, and his team loved its jobs. So what about a drawing program? This would be Mario's oddest departure from the platformer genre yet, since unlike puzzle or sports games a painting simulation wasn't even a game. No time limit, no points, no dangers, no characters, no bonuses. But to Miyamoto, Mario was about play, not just gameplay.

The biggest immediate hurdle was the interface: the SNES controller wasn't calibrated to move as fast or as accurately as a mouse. Even if it was, asking players to gain that supple movement just in their thumb was a too-tall order. Mouse users moved their whole hand, and the device scaled down that movement. It just wasn't replicable in a directional pad without a fatally fast cursor. Miyamoto had recently quit gambling in honor of his fortieth birthday. As a follow-up, he quit smoking and started exercising. If he could accccomplish all that, he could get over this hurdle.

They needed a mouse. This gibed with Yamauchi's long-term vision of Nintendo as a communications company. Its NES, after all, started off life as a Famicon, with a keyboard and a modem and an AOL-like network. Sega forced his hand to release a 16-bit system, and to close the book on having the world funnel every aspect of life—work, play, cooking, sports, finance—through the NES. Arakawa had his doubts about the idea, and preferred to keep the company focused on games, instead of trying to compete with Silicon Valley. But getting a computer device into homes was a great second chance for Yamauchi's strategy of Nintendo as a communications company.

For starters, *Mario Paint* (which would come bundled with a mouse and mouse pad for sixty dollars) offered a decent painting simulator, complete with a gray mouse with two purple buttons. Line drawings of various Mario characters were included, for coloring fun. A tool let players place individual pixels, just like the designers at Nintendo did, to recreate favorite characters. (It was more difficult than it appeared.) Players could design their own stamps, move them around, and make an animated short. (More than a decade later, the first of Web comic *Homestar Runner*'s animated episodes was made this way, with a presumably hacked ROM of *Mario Paint*.) The practically mandatory *Mario Paint* strategy guide included pixel-by-pixel images of about every Mario character under the sun, and then some.

As an addition to the animation feature, *Mario Paint* featured a Music Composer, so the stories could have music to them. (There was another, more complex way of adding music, but it involved many AV cables and at least two VCRs.) Previously, Nintendo had been pushing the Miracle keyboard for the NES, touting its educational nature. Not many were sold. Now it had stealthily given players a music simulator program, hidden in an arts and crafts activity. A good portion of today's game developers probably got their start designing and animating with *Mario Paint*.

As a salve, two minigames that used the mouse were included in *Mario Paint*. Gamers could also click on each letter of MARIO PAINT on the title screen for more Easter eggs. But what Miyamoto had designed made few pretenses of being a game. Most saw it as a toy, a digital Crayola set, l'il PhotoShop. And it was.

Now that the mouse was in place, a bevy of other games were made with mouse controls. Finally PC-based games with complicated on-screen menus—including *Populous* and *Civilization*—could get ported to a console. But mouse devices require a flat surface like a desk, not a couch or a coffee table littered with controllers. And wouldn't people who wanted to play video games using a mouse play on their computer?

A few years later, Nintendo tried the online endeavor again, with the Satellaview modem. It hooked into Japanese Super Famicons, and for a subscription fee allowed them to upload new games on a special blank cartridge. Many were older titles—the addictive block-matching game *Undake 30 Same Game* (pronounced saw-me gaw-me) and *Excitebike* were two—repopulated with the Mario crew. What new content the Satellaview had was the sort of stuff that wouldn't sell well in stores—a sequel to the forgotten *Wrecking Crew*. Its success was limited by the Internet, which began offering much more gaming content, such as SNES and NES emulators, for an unbeatable price—nothing.

As if it were being paid by the Dickensian word, Nintendo spent 1992 and 1993 cranking out Mario game after Mario game. There were so many that they could afford to take a risk with a *Mario Paint*: anything branded Mario was good. So along came *Yoshi's Cookie* (the rare multiplatform game for Game Boy, NES, and SNES), another Yoshi-and-Mario puzzle game that added a Rubik's-Cube flavor to block-clearing. *Super Mario Land 2: 6 Golden Coins* for Game Boy continued the Sarasaland adventure. The educational PC game *Mario Is Missing* (later for the NES and SNES) tried—without much success—to merge Mario-style game play with *Carmen SanDiego*'s geography fu, teaching about the world based on retrieving what Bowser stole. The very similar *Mario's Time Machine* had Bowser once again stealing artifacts.

It was an arms race with Sega, who was only too willing to put up record numbers for Sonic games. In the same two-year time period, Sonic went from starring in one game to ten, including two games that make it into the bizarre name hall of fame, *Waku Waku Sonic Patrol Car* and *Dr. Robotnik's Mean Bean Machine*. Arcades, Master System, Genesis, Game Gear; action, racing, puzzle: Sonic was there. Sega capped off 1993 by introducing the Sonic the Hedgehog balloon into the Macy's Thanksgiving Day parade, the first such balloon based on a video game character. (True to form, Sonic went too fast, and crashed into a Columbus Circle lamppost.) Some were natural fits—a pinball game is perfect for a character who rolls into a ball and bounces around. Some were not—Sonic as a traffic cop arresting speeders smacks of hypocrisy.

Sonic's comfort in Generation X culture—alternative rock, grim and gritty superheroes, ironic detachment—was not something that Mario could compete with. Mario was politesse and friendly—his years of tormenting an exotic pet were way behind him. Still, they were both role models compared to the other games out there. A *Time* magazine cover featured Mario, Sonic, and fearsome predators from three game series: *Jurassic Park*, *Mortal Kombat*, and *Star Trek*. Mario and Sonic, at least, didn't seem eager to kill you.

An early attempt to try to edge Mario up—the first-person shooter *Yoshi's Safari*—was an embarrassment. Players sat on Yoshi as he wandered around a Mode 7-animated track, and blasted away at anything that moved. Players could use the Super Scope light gun to blow the Goombas and Koopas away. The gameplay's cutesy graphics clashed with the kill-'em-all mentality. Certainly Mario's actions didn't match up with anyone sporting a save-the-whales pin on their backpack. (A later *Pokémon* game reused the shooter idea, but had players take pictures of animals, a family friendly compromise.)

A much better response to the times was spinning off the villain of *Super Mario Land 2*, Mario's evil twin, Wario, into his own game. Wario as a name worked on a variety of levels—in English it suggested war and wariness, the literal flipside of Mario. In Japanese, *wariu* means bad. He was given a gin blossomy nose, a mustache like Charlie Brown's sweater zigzag, and a big, mean build that piled on the muscle and fat. He wore yellow and purple—although, of course, for the Game Boy that was green on green.

If Mario started off life as a carpenter, Wario was a deconstruction worker. He was the titular star of *Wario Land: Super Mario Land 3*. The game may well have been designed by the Zucker Brothers, or at least Jacques Derrida: Wario is a sneering greedy bully, knocking over anyone who stands in his way. The positive goal of trying to get a high score is recast as pure avarice. With enough gold coins, Wario can buy a castle. And with a castle, he can rub it in Mario's face. (Wario's eyes are green, after all.) He moves like an angry ape, and is immune to most damage since he knocks over whoever he touches. But Wario never has easy access to the enemies he wants to clobber, so he has to puzzle out how to reach them.

The antihero nature of Wario must have had its attractors, especially since it didn't seem to change the mechanics of the gameplay so much as the framing of it. He's since been the Manicean star of over a dozen subsequent games, including a rare crossover into another franchise, *Wario Blast: Featuring Bomberman!* Many of these use his concupiscent invincibility as its key platforming mimetic. He shows up in the Mario racing or sports games as well. (A villainous Luigi, named Waluigi and with a purple-and-yellow color scheme, followed a few years later.)

As with politicians stopping by *Saturday Night Live* for an awkward chat with the comedian dressed up as them, Mario and Wario worked best apart from each other. The only platform game that featured both of them was 1993's *Mario & Wario*, which was never released in the United States. Wario had, in a lackluster evil plan, put a bucket on Mario's head. Players used the SNES mouse to help a flying fairy named Wanda make Mario avoid obstacles as he marched blindly forward.

But perhaps it was Mario and Wario's pairing that kept it from U.S. shores. You couldn't pretend Mario *was* Wario if they shared a screen and were facing off against each other. Wario was the Mr. Hyde, the Angelus, the Darth Vader. Just as Miyamoto's *Lost Levels* challenged the concept of game play by critically ignoring the rules, the Wario *weltanschauung* showed the inherent falsity of any game—including Mario's games—where the purpose was measured in personal gain. But as long as Wario existed, with his cackle and his Walter Huston gold fever, Mario got to stay as pure in motives as a saint. San Mario del Regno Fungo.

THE U.S. SHORES ENDED UP BEING A TENSE PLACE TO BE IN 1993. Yamauchi was tired of seeing declining profits from the American division, which had let Sega build up momentum. He never played video games, but was invincible in Go, the game where one move changes everything. He made one of those moves when he created a chairman position for Nintendo of America—and gave it not to Arakawa but to Howard Lincoln. An American, in charge of the American division. As if this wasn't a clear statement, he publicly shamed Arakawa, saying the son-in-law would be let go if the lethargic performance continued.

Yamauchi may have been trying to force a crack in the friendship between the two men: believing that great men could only be great alone. It didn't work. Arakawa and Lincoln continued to work well together, according to reports of the time, taking more initiative stateside for game design, and going after Sega in new ads. They also cranked out *Super Mario All-Stars*, a SNES game collecting the first three Super Mario NES titles. Those were all tactical decisions, though. To really take on Sega, they would have to make some bold strategic moves. Little did they know one of these moves would create Nintendo's all-time greatest rival—and give that rival the very technology to bring Nintendo to its knees.

14 — MARIO'S ADVANCE

NINTENDO'S DISCS

I f the human mind is divided into the ego, superego, and id, then Mario is the id: working off of instinct, never having much of a plan, always able to leap into the middle of things. We all become younger as we play Mario, because when we're Mario we simply play.

Miyamoto has given us more Freudian pop psych than that, though: his elfin warrior Link is an excellent ego. "I am not Link," Miyamoto joked, "but I know him!" While Mario has just the clothes on his back, Link has a cache of rubies, bombs, arrows, a series of swords, various other items, and a broad swatch of Hyrule to explore. Different games for different parts of the psyche. Both Mario and Link try to save princesses, true. But few imagine Mario as more than asexual, wanting to save the princess because Bowser is bad and needs a time out. Link, on the other hand, is a teenager after the girl of his dreams.

Link's SNES debut *The Legend of Zelda: A Link to the Past* has been voted by *Entertainment Weekly* as the best video game of all time. It took the tile-based action adventure of the first Zelda and added many elements from role-playing games (RPGs) for the sequel, combining them for a game that plays just as well today, despite blocky visuals. The biggest change was the Dark World, a nighttime level which repopulated the world with new villains, and doubled the size of the game. Further replayability came from trying to boost Link's statistics by finding, say, every last Heart Container piece. Miyamoto found a new flow balance: give players the choice of scouring or charging forward.

Miyamoto also oversaw the Zelda Game Boy outing, *Link's Awakening*. The setting was moved out of Hyrule—perhaps in tribute to *Super Mario Land*, which also left its homeland for a new (all-green) world. That may also explain Mario and Princess Toadstool's cameos (as pictures on the wall): was Link secretly in the Mushroom Kingdom?

Link would not appear in a Nintendo game for another five years. It was an eternity in the video-game world: five Christmases where millions of boys could have paid hundreds of millions of dollars to swing virtual swords and clobber Octorocks. Certainly Nintendo didn't let Mario take a year off between games: his mug was on something or other every other month. But the reason why Link didn't appear officially for five years might have had something to do with an embarrassing unofficial appearance, still joked about in the same terms as *Ishtar* and *Battlefield Earth*. As bad as Link and Zelda look in these awful games, someone else in the story—Nintendo—ends up looking worse.

IN 1994, NOT MANY PEOPLE HAD HEARD OF MOORE'S LAW— Intel cofounder Gordon Moore's prediction from way back in 1965 that transistor usage could double every two years. But everyone was living through the implications: what was top of the line in 1990 wouldn't be so in 1992, much less 1994. Special effects went from Patrick Swayze walking through a wall to a liquid-metal robot to computer-generated dinosaurs to Forrest Gump shaking hands with John F. Kennedy.

Within a year or so of the SNES's release, fans started spreading rumors about what would come after it. The words "multimedia" and "interactive entertainment" were thrown around like they referred to specific software applications, instead of generalities. It seemed clear, though, that previously separate aspects of life would blend together, just as previously separate forms of media would merge. One word: cyberspace.

It all boiled down to the concrete technology of compact discs. These thin twelve-centimeter circles of plastic had a central layer of aluminum indented much the way a vinyl record or wax cylinder was. A laser bouncing back and forth read so many thousands of infinitesimal "pits" a second it boggles the mind. Massive amounts of data could be stored on one disc cheaper than a cassette. Entire double-disc music albums, saved with undegradable sound quality free of pops or skips. Entire encyclopedias. Entire museums' worth of art.

Everyone involved in technology wanted to be part of it. Nintendo and Sega were in a dilemma: developing a new console would shut the door on their successful SNES and Genesis platforms. But new competitors like NEC and 3DO were already prepping CD-ROM-based video game consoles. Appropriately enough for the makers of Mario and Sonic, the task for Nintendo and Sega was knowing exactly when to take the running jump.

Nintendo went first, announcing a deal with Sony back in 1988 to codevelop a CD-ROM game system, which would also have a cartridge slot for SNES games. Sega countered in 1991, saying a CD-ROM system would be ready *that year* attachable to any Genesis. But it only expanded the size of the game, not the quality of graphics. Sega CD was a dud. Nintendo's CD would have been similar—offering more game, but not better game—and it died after years of quiet delays.

But Nintendo, like a paranoiac whose brash actions truly do get others conspiring against them, created a self-fulfilling prophecy in its urge to quash the competition. Its deal with Sony allowed the Japanese electronics giant the licensing rights to the special game-playing format it used, Super Disc. Big mistake. Nintendo's fortune had come in large part from owning licensing rights for NES and SNES games. It would never have that with the Sony console: Sony would get sole licensing fees for each CD-based game. As Sony execs got ready to enter the multibillion-dollar gaming industry, Yamauchi sensed they would steamroll over friend and foe alike.

It helps to imagine what happens next being the actions of *Degrassi* kids, not Consumer Electronics Show attendees. See, Lincoln and Arakawa had been two-timing Sony with Philips, Sony's Netherlands-based rival. And Nintendo threatened to break up with Sony if Sony wasn't cool with this. Sony swallowed its pride and announced its "exclusive" deal with Nintendo at CES, and double-dealing Nintendo the *very next day* talked about how it's now exclusive with Philips, that hussy, for a CD-based console.

Philips was little more than a rebound partnership, never destined for more than a few brief awkward weeks. It was working on the CD-i, which it wanted to make into the standard format for game-playing consoles, the same way it had successfully come up with a standard format for CDs with Sony back in 1982. A deal with Nintendo would kill two birds with one stone, it felt, and help create a CD-ROM standard for games. Every game would play on every player.

And once the standard was set, the golden age of information was imminent.

Nintendo had massively profited from proprietary media formats in the past, and planned on doing so well into the future. Any system that was based on CD-ROMs was copyable. The big N had made a mint on lockout-chipped cartridges, which was very tough to copy. Any ten-year-old with a PC could plunk a CD-ROM into a burner (which were getting affordable) and make a perfect copy of a game for the cost of a blank CD. Without the lockout chip, Nintendo felt it was signing its death warrant with a CD-ROM system surer than dealing with Sony.

But it was a long time dying. Sony came back to Nintendo despite the Panasonic deal, and the three agreed to give Nintendo the game royalties it wanted and let the games be playable on Panasonic's CD-i as well as the Sony/Nintendo console. Now the only problem was all the CD-based games were flops, and expensive ones to boot. Nintendo decided to sever ties with both parties at once, and convert its CD-based games in development into regular SNES titles. It just, like, needed some space, man.

Before being dumped, Panasonic had gained rights to produce its own *Legend of Zelda* and *Mario* games for the nascent CD-i. And like e-mailing embarrassing love letters postbreakup, it released them to the world in 1994. Well, it released them to whoever was watching TV at 3:30 A.M.: with no better avenue of getting the CD-i into stores, Philips shilled them via infomercial. Philips saw it as a bargain: a game system, stereo, karaoke machine, and video player all in one. The few insomniac viewers, though, just saw a seven-hundred-dollar game machine, and passed.

Much has been made about how terrible Philips's sole released *Mario* game, *Hotel Mario*, is. Bowser has taken over the Mushroom Kingdom, and kidnapped the princess. So far, so standard. He's turned the whole place into a series of themed hotels, which is admittedly odd. But every Mario game introduces new elements: riding a dinosaur and turning into a statue seem odder than Bowser's Donald Trump ambitions. The sole feature of *Hotel Mario*, though, is a series of single-screen boards filled with open hotel-room doors. Mario has to shut them all, while avoiding obstacles and enemies and finding ways to go from floor to floor. Miyamoto clearly had no role in producing this. It was, as one Internet wag put it, the NES game *Elevator Action* without the action. Or, a puzzle game without anything too puzzling: you simply walked to a door to close it.

Even odder was that *Hotel Mario*, whose mechanics would easily be playable on an Atari 2600, was used to launch a new seven-hundred-dollar console that was touting enhanced graphics and unparalleled game play. To make it seem more complex, animated full-motion video segments were added between levels. Previous games had a pixelated Mario with a line of word-ballooned dialogue over his head between levels. Now there was broadcast-quality animation cut scenes of Mario and Luigi traipsing through a tree hotel, an underground hotel, and a cloud hotel, between what seemed like levels of a lesser Game Boy puzzle game.

As with a lot of flops, *Hotel Mario* is nowhere near as bad as critics say. Still, it's a fair shake to call it one of Mario's worst games, if not the worst. If Philips hadn't pulled the plug on its game system, it would have seen some much better Mario games. *Mario's Wacky Worlds* was a traditional side-scroller featuring Mario in ancient Greece, an Aztec temple, an all-neon world, an all-plaid world, and so on. *Mario Takes America* was going to merge real video footage of American cities and landmarks and allow a computer-generated Mario to fly around them like Superman.

This was nothing compared to what happened to poor Link. He

was stuck in three bad games: *Link: the Faces of Evil*, *Zelda: The Wand of Gamelon*, and *Zelda's Adventure*. The first two games, developed in concord, used the side-scrolling format from *Zelda II: Link's Adventure*. Where exactly to begin? The subpar animation? Casting nonactors for live-action sequences? Game play that supposed took two entire years merely to play-test for bugs? Choppy, disappointing level design? The games' plots at least showed promise: *Faces of Evil* starts off with a bored Link practically begging for some adventure; he gets it when a villain kidnaps Zelda. The other two finally make Zelda the star of the show, instead of Link.

But *Zelda* was never about plot. Indeed, one's head could explode if all the games were considered one story, since Link is always meeting Zelda and villainous Gannon for the first time. Imagine trying to explain why James Bond has stayed forty years old for forty years, while changing faces and hair color. Better to accept the story as a constant retelling, and don't dwell on continuity matters. Mario has made a cottage industry of jokes about how Bowser had only one playbook—kidnap the princess—and *this* time it'll work! He's utterly incapable of coming up with any other plan. Aside from that one time he obtained a degree in hotel management.

Nintendo deserved the mess of *Hotel Mario* after its poor behavior in the CD-ROM debacle. It was the sort of behavior only the cool kids would try to get away with. Certainly Sony was left holding the bag of a half-developed CD-ROM/SNES console. It could swallow the loss, or try to finish the console and compete with one of the most dominant, and litigious, companies in existence. Sony execs wanted vengeance, though, and decided to keep developing. Even without SNES support, it could find some CD-ROM PC games to bring over.

In determined defiance to the any CD-based graphics and derring-do, Nintendo and Shigeru Miyamoto chose this as the time to release their new Mario game . . . a *Donkey Kong* port for the Game Boy. Huh? The first four levels of this version were faithful to the four levels of the arcade hit. Then, right when Mario gets Pauline back, Donkey Kong charges back on screen, and grabs Pauline once again. Mario has four different levels to traverse before another fight with the big guy. Then another four, and another four. A total of a hundred levels, ninety-six of them brand-new.

It was a clear passion project, Miyamoto returning to his first game. And he definitely deserved to follow his muse wherever it went; Hiroshi Yamauchi was becoming a billionaire thanks to it. But it was the exact opposite of hip, cool, or edgy. It was a tribute to a fifteen-year-old game much of Nintendo's audience was already too young to remember. Other people were promising graphics as good as a movie— and Nintendo was still trying to sell *Donkey Kong*? Didn't they know the future was CD-based?

Sony's half-baked console, before the drama happened, was going to be called Nintendo Play Station. Now, it would just be Play Station. Nintendo sued, saying that it owned the name. After a brief run of a few hundred SNES-capable Play Stations, Sony went back to the drawing board, and designed a machine without any SNES port. One deleted space later, the spelled-solid PlayStation was released, featuring 3-D polygon graphics, massive environments, full-motion videos, and graphics better than the arcade. Leagues better than anything the SNES could produce, Mode 7 or not.

Philips and Sony, pinky-swearing that no one would get between their friendship again, patched things up. They collaborated once again on a new format for a CD-based technology, the DVD, in the hopes it would become a global standard. It of course did. And, as Nintendo feared, the copyable nature of Sony's CD-based PlayStation's games led to gamers burning vast libraries of unbought games, playable via a soldered-on modchip. In one last twist, this ironically led to a massively increased install base for the PlayStation—because, like Napster did for music, it let you play games for "free." The piracy Nintendo so feared was Sony's bread and butter.

15 – MARIO'S KART(RIDGE)

VIRTUAL BOY AND OTHER THREE-DIMENSIONAL FUN

t this point in the early nineties, *The Simpsons* was the go-to joke for overcommercialized characters. Bart's often-pirated face looked out from T-shirts, mugs, hats, and dolls. Creator Matt Groening has a collection of such items, favoring the cheap plagiarized knockoffs. Cartoon characters are the hill-kings of branding, unfettered by the base-level dignity of celebrity actors, musicians, and sports stars. The Teenage Mutant Ninja Turtles, like Ado Annie in *Oklahoma!,* just cain't say no.

But Springfield's finest have nothing on Mario and company. Yamauchi wanted Mario's face to appear as often as possible, anywhere it could. To encourage this, he took the counterintuitive step of prohibiting any Zelda or Link merchandising. If someone wanted a Nintendo character for a doll or mug, it was Mario or nothing. Everything you'd expect to see Mario's face on has had his face on them: board games, Valentine's day cards, jigsaw puzzles, bedding, water guns, pens, toys.

Want some battery-powered tech? How about a Mario bike alarm, singalong AM radio, walkie-talkie, calculator, clock, or musical toothbrush?

The real creativity came after the easy-to-brand items had been plastered. Who, for instance, thought of using the Mario-plumbing connection to manufacture a licensed handheld shower? It features a plastic Mario and Luigi on each other's shoulders as a handle aiming a hose of water. "SCALD PROTECTION," notes the all-caps packaging. Perfect for washing off the Mario shampoo with the Mario bath sponge and playing with the Mario bath toys! (All real, by the way.)

Once out of the scald-resistant shower, dry off with a Mario towel, and put on Mario-branded sunglasses, belt buckles, ties, suspenders, slippers, Nike sneakers, T-shirts, jackets, sweatshirts, sweatpants, underwear, Halloween costumes. Hungry? Chow down on some fruit snacks, lemonade, energy drinks, candy bars, cereal, candy, lollipops, ice cream bars, or ice cream sandwiches. Carry around your stuff with Mario-quality folders, fanny packs, suitcases, backpacks, or glasses cases. What stuff? Why, cups, egg cups, cup dispensers, pens, Pez dispensers, cookie jars, cookie cutters, place mats, scratch-off cards, wallpaper, stickers, stamps, 110 film cameras, light fixtures, pins, golf balls, curtains, computer mouses, mouse pads, trophies, phones, remote-controlled car phones, music boxes, sleeping bags, temporary tattoos, wallets, phone cards, umbrellas, trash cans, Viewmasters, finger puppets, balls, flash drives, banks, greeting cards, coloring books, storybooks, holograms, and calendars.

For Mario fans not old enough to drive, how about remote-controlled cars and helicopters? Or Mario fuzzy dice, windshield screen, floor mats, car deodorizers, antenna toppers, and car seat covers? There are almost a hundred different types of Mario-branded key chains alone.

Who decided to green-light a Mario ceiling fan? To go with the Mario ceiling fan pull? A Mario Rubix Cube? Speakers? Tissue box? Bandages? Computer cover? Debit card? Dry erase board? Was there a decision to have every single purchasable item have a Mario version of it? Or even make up new items, like a piece of jewelry called a "bow biter" that lets Mario and Luigi hang from your shoelaces? Or a Super Mario cross-stitch? Or a $6,999 (insured for eleven thousand dollars-plus) solid-gold Mario pendant, with diamonds in red, blue, white, and black? (The same people make a Bart Simpson pendant, thanks to yellow diamonds.) At least there was history with, say, a Mario-brand set of hanafuda cards.

As new collectible trends arose—Beanie Babies, pogs, lunch boxes, figurines, plush chairs, trading cards, Christmas ornaments, stress relievers, K'Nex, Dots (a Japanese fad that mixed Lite Brites with Lego blocks), or Byggis (a Swedish Lego knockoff), Mario was there. Things that aren't even designed as collectibles have a market among this Mario mania. The neon signs saying "Nintendo AUTHORIZED REPAIR CENTER" showing Mario gamely holding a flathead screwdriver, for instance, fetch four hundred dollars. Arcade games sell for reasonable rates, considering they're twenty-five-year-old computers that weigh as much as a safe.

Nintendo must have, at some point, said no to a Mario marketing opportunity it deemed contrary to the character's youth appeal. There are Mario lighters. There are Mario slot machines, albeit ones that use play money. Moving onto the unlicensed (and illegal), Finnish police have confiscated tabs of acid with Mario's face on them. In the nearby University of Copenhagen they sometimes serve Mario-themed shots: the Super Mario is equal amounts of grenadine, Blue Bols, and tequila silver, and a 1-Up (whipped cream, green frosting, milk, vodka, and Melon Bols) looks disturbingly like the green-and-white mushroom.

Long years of lucrative evidence have proven to Nintendo that licensing is a double-plus-good endeavor—people pay the company to advertise Mario! For a character that doesn't exist outside of commercials, the more exposure the better. This was why Nintendo traded up its advertising firms in 1990, going from McCann-Erickson and Foot, Cone & Belding to the giant Leo Burnett. One of Burnett's first ads, for *Super Mario Bros. 3*, didn't feature anything as pedestrian as game play, but instead millions of cheering Mario fans, ending with a satellite view of Earth, and all the fans making Mario's smiling face. Mario wasn't a fun character, the star of a nifty game. He was an idol, to be worshipped and adored. Graven images helped that process.

HASBRO WORKED FOR YEARS ON A DEVICE NICKNAMED Sliced Bread, a virtual-reality machine that would enter it into the video-game world. Hasbro killed Sliced Bread in 1995, after forty-five million dollars' of investment. Nintendo was hoping for better luck than that. The Kyoto office was developing an in-your-face console as well. If this worked, it would break new ground. It wouldn't be as impressive as the Nintendo network perpetually in the skunk works, true. But that was Yamauchi's vision for Nintendo, not Arakawa's or really anyone else's. As a result, the father-in-law would every few months talk about how we'd all soon be playing online games and trading stocks from our SNES, and then nothing would happen. (There was at least one decent-size network test, to let people play the Minnesota State Lottery via the SNES. It was scrubbed because ten-year-olds would likely end up gambling—and with their parents' money.)

Pushing games into virtual reality would be a game-changer for the game-makers. Suddenly the Genesis, the PlayStation, the 3DO, all the other consoles with high polygon counts and fluid character movement would look as jerky as claymation. "In videogames," Yokoi wrote in his memoir, "there is always an easy way out if you don't have any good ideas . . . CPU competition." Nintendo was going to press for full 3-D, just like a monster movie from the fifties. Already it was cutting prices on the SNES, so that the Genesis would have to follow suit. If the 3-D gamble worked, everyone else would go broke playing catch-up.

One way it had already succeeded was in avoiding violent games, the sort that sold well among older (read: Sega) audiences but drew the ire of parents and Congress. Sega tried to play it safe by making its own game ratings system in 1993 it hoped Nintendo would adopt. Nintendo didn't bother making its own: instead it adopted the Entertainment Software Ratings Board's letter-grade system instead (with M reserved for what would get an R in the movies). Sega (and 3DO, who had its own system as well) tried to claim the high ground for gaming morality, but the level playing field of a unified system put an end to that pipe dream.

In the meantime, M-rated or not, Nintendo needed some new games. It had to live up to the recent New Yorker cartoon of Santa booking a lunch meeting with Mario and Luigi. Nintendo needed 3-D, by hook or by crook. They had a 1993 hit thanks to two English designers, whose special "Mario chip" was digital steroids, flooding an SNES cartridge with extra oomph. Miyamoto worked the pair to tighten up their flight game's playability, drafting a story about talking animal pilots onto the superb technical display. They even included actual spoken dialogue, to simulate intercom chatter among the furry space aces. *Star Fox* was born, a new Nintendo franchise.

The Mario chip, which was marketed as the "Super FX chip," indirectly led to *Donkey Kong Country*, the first *DK* title not made by Miyamoto. Instead it was made by a second-party company, Rare, which had a long history porting arcade hits to the NES and designing surrealist classics like *Battletoads*. *DKC* was a fun side-scrolling action platformer: much closer to *Super Mario Bros.* than to *Donkey Kong*. To clear the air, it begins by introducing the angry Donkey Kong from the original series, now aged and called Cranky Kong. Cranky's son, Junior, is now all grown up, and the current Donkey Kong. Very confusing, made even worse by subsequent games that negated this already-revised history: Cranky Kong was canonically the grandfather, Junior the father, and the new DK the grandson. From the people who brought you Mario Mario and five reincarnations of Zelda.

But the big boast, like *Star Fox*, was 3-D graphics. And with no expensive Super FX chip, either, to cut away from profits. How, when Pixar hadn't even released *Toy Story*, could there be fully 3-D characters in a mere SNES game?

The magic formula came from *Aladdin*, a recent Genesis platformer with outstandingly good graphics. It looked just like the cartoon! In fact, it was: Disney animators had drawn all the sprites. There were enough pixels in sprites to allow for a variety of drawing styles, not just the Lego-style pixel-by-pixel building that game developers were used to. In fact, if a company acquired high-end rendering hardware from Silicon Graphics, as Rare did, it could make its own computer-generated images, save them frame by frame, and add them to a game as the sprites.

That was the secret behind *Donkey Kong Country*: prerendered graphics. And it looked a whole lot better than most of the clunky, jittery 3-D of some 32-bit competitors with their lackluster launch games. Why buy Atari's Jaguar console (a sad attempt to be first to market, and with a monstrosity of a controller that looked like a cable box) or the seven-hundred-dollar 3DO when the mere SNES still was cranking out such great 3-D games? It sparked a shortage, and became the hot Christmas toy of 1994, beating *Sonic and Knuckles*.

But there was a downside of trumpeting such 3-D graphics: they became expected. The console of Mario was now the console of 3-D, thanks to *Star Fox* and now *DKC*. Whatever Nintendo did next had to be 3-D, to keep the new brand up. For *Killer Instinct*, an arcade fighting game, that was a no-brainer. Rare was making it, using the same pre-rendered graphics but for an intense fighting game that merged *Street Fighter II*'s depth of fighting with the gory *Mortal Kombat* death moves. A lot of its bells and whistles were lost in the port to SNES, and most all of them lost for the Game Boy port, but the gameplay held up. The same couldn't be said for *Stunt Race FX* and *Vortex*, whose slow frame rates killed the attempted realism.

Miyamoto wouldn't let that happen to Mario. Ever since *Star Fox* he had been working on *Mario FX*, a 3-D game for the SNES, but the graphics and gameplay just weren't there yet. They might never be: that was okay, it was all a part of *nemawashi*. What was important was that Mario not look like one of the "Money for Nothing" furniture movers. The Mushroom Kingdom worlds had to be the friendly places kids grew up visiting, not a harshly geometric backdrop. Every Mario project Miyamoto had made was a new style of game (first-person for *Yoshi's Safari*, racing for *Super Mario Kart*, art for *Mario Paint*). Just because 3-D was popular now didn't mean that *Mario FX* wasn't still a game too imperfect for release.

Mario was Miyamoto's baby, in other words: the developer protected his character. That was his job. In fact, protecting Baby Mario would become the basis of the next title, *Super Mario World 2: Yoshi's Island*. The story, which gleefully did away with past games' continuity, had a stork carrying Baby Mario and Baby Luigi attacked by a minion of Baby Bowser. Baby Mario falls on Yoshi's island, and Yoshi has to carry the helpless hero (wearing a red hat he hasn't grown into yet) on his back. This allowed Miyamoto to play with new game-play forms:

Yoshi collects various eggs, which bounce along behind him until he uses them. He can briefly transform into various vehicles, but can't take Baby Mario with him during the change. And Baby Mario can become Super Baby Mario, capable of flight, and with a cute red cape. Miyamoto used the Super FX chip to augment the game's graphics, but in subtle ways: some villains were 3-D, and the chip helped the graphics have finer resolution.

But the Nintendo marketing team rejected Miyamoto's game. This was akin to correcting the pope on scripture. The game play was fine, but the graphics weren't good enough. Maybe something more like *Donkey Kong Country*. Could it be more like that?

No one puts Baby Mario in the corner. Miyamoto, who had been uncharacteristically critical of *Donkey Kong Country* for its "mediocre game play," now had to change his game to look like the flavor of the month? He wasn't going to have it. They wanted distinct graphics? Fine, he'd give them distinct graphics. But his way.

That was how *Yoshi's Island* became the first video game that looked as if it had been drawn not only by hand, but by crayon. Baby Mario looks like a political cartoon who dropped a sash identifying him as Tariff Agreements. Yoshi looks like a middle-schooler's doodle. The backgrounds were made to look like rough sketches of mountains and trees, not pixel-built, and certainly not waxy CG creations. It was a living comic book.

Yoshi's Island, with its new look and characteristically fantastic gameplay, sold more than four million copies. It wasn't as flashy as *Donkey Kong Country*, which had sold twice as many units, but it held its own. Rare, meanwhile, got its revenge on "Dr. Miyamoto" (as many in the industry called him) in its *Donkey Kong Land* Game Boy game, which obviously would have none of the fancy graphics of *Donkey Kong Country*.

The game opened metafictionally, with Cranky Kong congratulating DK on the success of his SNES game. "Course, put a few fancy graphics and some modern music in a game, and kids'll buy anything nowadays . . . Back in our days, understand, we had an extremely limited color palette to work with, and we still made great games . . . No way you could duplicate that feat today, Donkey my boy! No siree!" Donkey Kong goes on to to prove his aged, out-of-touch, fourth wall-breaking ancestor wrong, by having the same sort of side-scrolling adventure as in his SNES version, sans CGI. (Rare later made it up to Doc Miyamoto by, in *Donkey Kong Country 2: Diddy Kong's Quest*, having Mario, Link, and Yoshi exhibits in Cranky's Video Game Heroes museum. Sonic's shoes were next to a trash can, labeled "no-hopers.") *Donkey Kong Land* was a fun game despite the poison pen intro, sold well (though not as well as *Yoshi's Island*), and prompted some sequels.

NINTENDO AVOIDED ENTERING THE 32-BIT GAME WITH THE two-step of boosting its 16-bit games' graphics and continually talking up the Ultra 64, a system that basic arithmetic proved was better than anything 32-bit. (And since bits were exponential, not geometric, 2^{64} was vastly bigger than 2^{32}.) The Ultra 64 was supposed to come out in 1995, but it wasn't ready. However, Nintendo stunned the gaming world by announcing it had a successor to the blockbuster Game Boy ready instead for 1995: a 32-bit handheld system . . . in full 3-D.

The Virtual Boy was credited to Gunpei Yokoi, Nintendo's ace designer. But Yokoi was merely a smart shopper. He had been shown a device of start-up company Reflections Technology, a new headset console they called "Red World." It used oscillating mirrors, red LED lights, and a 32-bit processor to create a 3-D environment inside the pilot-style helmet. This was Nintendo's bailiwick, Yokoi felt: a new technology that changed the very idea of games.

3-D wasn't a new idea for Nintendo. In 1987 it tried out a pair of 3-D goggles for the Famicon Disk System, using the same LCD shutter technology used in some 3-D glasses today. The add-on system only had a few games, and as a peripheral to a peripheral was quickly forgotten. Sega's 3-D glasses for the Master System received a similarly dour debut.

Yokoi spent four years with his R&D team developing Red World, renamed Virtual Boy, never getting it right. The Virtual Boy was stuck displaying only red and black, for instance, because the green and blue LED lights needed for color combinations weren't affordable. (They wouldn't be until 1996, a year after launch.) It gobbled up batteries, even using just red, the most efficient and inexpensive color of LED. It was too heavy to wear. This was solved by giving it a stand: so much for being portable. But even without neck strain, even without head-tracking technology, it still gave people headaches.

All forced-perspective 3-D does, or at least should. It's called *sho-boshobo* in Japanese, or "bleary eyes." Humans' eyes have had a lifetime to verge and accommodate in symphony with each other—to track an object and to change focus on it at the same time. With a forced-3-D image projected onto a flat surface, vergance is separated from accommodation: viewers only need to verge, since things become blurry when one tries to accommodate as well. That was as new and counterintuitive as trying to breathe underwater: a body's reflexes often refuse to do it. There were findings that playing too long could cause headaches, and Yokoi added a mandatory pause feature every twenty minutes or so to each cartridge.

The final product looked like a toolbox, not a pair of goggles, and arrived with an avalanche of bad press. It launched with the pack-in game *Mario's Tennis*, a decent game whose obvious selling point was that the returned ball would be flying right in Mario's (read: your) face. Other launch games were the *Star Fox*-y flight combat game *Red Alarm*, *Galactic Pinball*, and a *Bomberman* title. But a game of tennis, for $180? Didn't seem like much of a bargain. Perhaps the Virtual Boy's greatest failure wasn't its red graphics or eyestrain or rush to market but poor launch games. Why buy one if there's nothing worth playing for it yet, or even in the pipeline?

The closest thing to a hit was *Mario Clash*, a reimagining of the original *Mario Bros.* Mario had to throw red turtle shells across a series of red 3-D sewers to hit the invading (and red) sewer critters. The dimensional view was impressive, for those who didn't lose their lunch. But the game itself wasn't that deep. Once players got used to Mario both near and far, they were left with a game from 1982 that cost a whole lot more than a quarter to play.

Yokoi did not want the Virtual Boy released when it was, in 1995: he preferred to wait until a full-color version was feasible. (But even then, early testers said the colors made for double vision, not 3-D.) Yamauchi had wanted the project out early, at a reasonable price point that still brought in money for every unit sold. Wanting something, though, as he had learned about the Nintendo Network, was not the same as achieving it.

The Virtual Boy flopped like a koi. Nintendo experienced first-hand what it had taken such schadenfreude in witnessing in others: the price fell down and down and down, third-party game developers disappeared like the cool kids from a lame party, the industry went from making fun of it to honestly forgetting it was still on sale. Like an ER doc calling the time of death, Nintendo halted development on first-party games like *Mario Kart: Virtual Cup* and a side-scrolling *Super Mario* adaptation.

Perhaps if Yokoi had had another year, he could at least have introduced color, and one or two decent games. But he was rushed to market, and the console died because of it. To rub salt in the wound, the suits in Kyoto started blaming Yokoi, not themselves, for developing an expensive system people didn't want to play. Yokoi entered into the peculiar Japanese tradition of the window-seat tribe, the *madogiwazoku*. This is when exiled employees are put as far away as possible from the group—the windows. At some point, the errant *madogiwazoku's* penance would be complete, and they'd be allowed to sit at the cool lunch table again.

Yokoi, perhaps with some window glare in his eyes, went to work on a new Game Boy variant, a smaller one with a black-and-white display instead of green. It was more battery efficient as well. But around the time of release (when it made Nintendo more millions), one of Mario's two fathers decided he had had enough of Nintendo. Anywhere else, Yokoi would have been already poached away, fired, or left on his own. But Japanese culture is loyal to the company, and vice versa, making resignation an even more painful break. (Miyamoto has said that he stays at Nintendo for the money: not the yen they pay him, but the yen they let him develop with.)

Yokoi retired from Nintendo, and founded his own game company, Koto. One of its first clients was Nintendo (the blood wasn't that bad between them), who hired him as a consultant. Yokoi also worked with Bandai, where he developed a new handheld console: it would at last have a color screen, but no 3-D. It was called the WonderSwan, and it became a cult hit in Japan.

It was his last invention. On October 4, 1997, Yokoi was a passenger in a car that was involved in a minor accident on an Ishikawa Prefecture expressway, north of Tokyo. He left the car to examine the damage, and was sideswiped by traffic. Gunpei Yokoi died two hours later of his injuries, at age fifty-six.

Yokoi's ideas, though, live on. Nintendo's heritage and success could be summed up in five awkward words: "lateral thinking of sea-soned technology." All of its successes come from its inventiveness, not its state-of-the-art chips. His protégé Shigeru Miyamoto had taken that to heart; now Miyamoto was the world's greatest game designer. Even the Virtual Boy, for all its flaws, gave the world a con-troller with two directional pads, one per thumb, which became indus-try standard.

And, as a festschrift to Yokoi, the first in a successful new series of *Mario* Game Boy games was released that year. *Game & Watch Gal-lery* repurposed Yokoi's classic designs of *Octopus*, *Manhole*, *Oil*, and others, except with the Super Mario gang as the characters. The series has sold a few million copies: quite the lateral thinking. And since they started coming out in 1994, Gunpei Yokoi lived to see it: beloved char-acters he helped bring forth, placed in games he designed, ported onto a console he designed as well.

PART 4

THIRD PRIZE IS YOU'RE FIRED

16 - MARIO'S WORLD

THE N64

ne of the reasons Nintendo kept confusing video game consoles with computers was that they were both new inventions. It seemed egregious that a household would willingly have two expensive machines in two different rooms that were essentially the same. Why not use that NES as a modem? Why not play games on the PC? Nintendo was still licensing Mario to PC game makers, seemingly under the instruction that no creative thought go into the games. The last two Mario PC games were a collection of checkers, dominoes, and card games where you played against Mario, and a port of the *Mario's FUNdementals* learning franchise. Not exactly *Myst*.

Computers were always pitched as multiplatform devices, so playing games on one went hand in hand with word processing, spreadsheets, and online access. But game consoles, despite being comparable to computers, often get punished when they try to get uppity and think they're as good as a tower or a laptop. Look at the wide array of failed keyboards for consoles: no one wanted something that reeked of *work* in his living room after hours. But without a decent interface—no keyboard, no mouse—the modem project was in the Nintendoldrums.

While Nintendo was allured by the modem, Sega loved the idea of peripheral support. The Sega-CD attachment for the Genesis sold well despite a small selection of games. Now it introduced a second add-on, the 32X, which boosted the Genesis into a 32-bit system. This would require a new shelf of Sega games, besides the Genesis games and the Sega-CD games. Plus, there were a fourth group of games, CD32X games, which required both attachments to run. Oh, and Sega also released a kids' version of the Genesis called the Pico, with its own games. Oh, and Sega was going to smoosh the 32X into the Genesis, and rerelease it as the Neptune. And of course there was Sega's portable console, the Game Gear. And its portable Genesis, called the Nomad.

And one more thing: none of these were Sega's actual new console. The new console, the Saturn, was a true 32-bit system, with a strong pipeline of 3-D arcade hits—*Virtua Fighter, Daytona USA, Pebble Beach Golf.* Unlike the 32X, the Saturn had a Sonic game, *Sonic R*, a footracer—or is that paw racer? It was released with the high price of $399. To make up for it, one spring day at a trade show Sega officials (who were dazed trying to keep track of all these consoles) decided to scuttle their "Saturnday" launch of September 2, 1995. Instead, on May 11, they announced they were releasing it to select stores right then and there!

Sega did not think through this strategy. Most all of the Saturn's games wouldn't be ready until September, the original launch date. So early adopters had precious little to play or buy. Stores that didn't receive the Saturn were angry, and those that did receive them sold out immediately, with no second shipment for six months. The original release date had been demoted to a mere footnote. Sony shrewdly stole Sega's thunder by cutting its quoted PlayStation price by $100 to $299 the following day, giving gamers a solid reason to wait out the Saturn launch. Sega's Saturn would be a distant third in the console wars, behind the PlayStation, and Nintendo's Ultra 64, if the Ultra 64 was ever released.

The Ultra 64 would never be released. At least, not under that name, a tribute to Nintendo's Ultra devices from the 1970s. Konami had trademarked the name Ultra for a shell company (fittingly enough, one of its first releases was a *Teenage Mutant Ninja Turtles* title) to release extra NES games back in the day. Nintendo backed off using the adjective for its new system, hastily redubbing it the Nintendo 64.

And what a console! The N64 was designed around a Silicon Graphics CPU designed especially for low costs and 3-D graphics. Its 64-bit CPU was attached to a 32-bit system bus, which was the reverse of the feeble Atari Jaguar, which had a few 64-bit chips (and one 32-bit chip) all pushing data through a bottlenecking 16-bit CPU. The Silicon Graphics chip turned out to be almost too powerful: some developers only used 32-bit processing to make their 3-D characters and environs.

Even the controller was amazing, shaped like a trident head—room for three hands! Gamers could hold it one way to use the analog control stick, which the N64 popularized for the modern gaming age. If they preferred the direction pad, they could hold it another way to access that. Four yellow "C" buttons in a diamond on the right would work as a third control mechanism, or let players swerve a floating camera around. There was an expansion port for a memory card (not that many games would ever use it, thanks to saves available in each cartridge). That slot could also be used for a "Rumble Pak" to force feedback into the controller, which soon became a mandatory feature of every game controller. The entire thing was designed around the launch game *Super Mario 64*.

So what was holding up this marvelous console's release? *Super Mario 64*. After spending a whole year on *Yoshi's Island*, and producing a quickie puzzle game called *Mole Mania* for Game Boy, Shigeru Miyamoto was ready to tackle Mario's first outing on the N64. His never-finished *Mario FX* game could be reborn on the N64: A 3-D Mario in a 3-D world. For a while he considered not even having a game, just an environment for Mario to explore.

The move to 3-D would be the biggest single design change games had ever seen. Every game franchise would have to figure out how to upgrade its look without losing the core gameplay and enjoyment that made it distinct. Racing games wouldn't have to rely on Mode 7 fudging anymore. Sports games, stuck with replicating the flat camera movements of sports broadcasting, would see armies of polygons crashing into each other—and often waving hands and arms through each other. First-person shooters would thrive like rabbits in Australia. Everyone would learn about the uncanny valley, which posits that the more realistic an illustration is to its source, the more noticeable the errors. Larry Bird as a pile of peach and green pixels looks fine, but a photorealistic Allen Iverson looks like a zombie, despite being a thousand times more realistic.

Miyamoto had a tough decision to make for *Super Mario 64*, an adventure game: what to do with the camera? It could stay in a fixed position, and thus make an isometric game like *Populous* or *Q*Bert*. It could move according to a set program, making for an on-rails adventure. Or it could move all around, and thus cause chaos and confusion and people zooming the camera on Mario's knee and then wondering why they couldn't see anything but knee. Was there a way to solve this as elegantly as in *Super Mario Bros.*, where Miyamoto designed a larger Mario and then came up with a brilliantly fungal bit of gameplay to make the Super Mario part of the fun?

What would make everyone happy would be a SNES 3-D Mario game that Miyamoto could merely supervise, so he could focus on *Mario 64* another year or so. He had already shelved one completed game—*Star Fox 2*—for the counterintuitive reason that it *was* in 3-D. Miyamoto wanted the N64 and 3-D to be linked in people's minds, and releasing too many 3-D SNES titles would diminish that mental connection. He made an exception for a *Mario* RPG made by Square, the geniuses behind the *Final Fantasy* franchise, who had an office in the same Redmond office park as Nintendo.

The plot (yes, a real plot!) turned on new villain Smithy attacking the Mushroom Kingdom, forcing Mario and Bowser to ally against him. It would feature turn-based combat (the hallmark of RPGs) but with new action elements. For instance, selecting "jump" from a battle menu makes Mario jump on an enemy, but a well-timed button press during the jump animation will earn extra damage. The SNES, boosted by the Super FX chip, would display everything isometrically, as if the whole game were seen from a corner-mounted security camera. Square would prerender every element of the game in 3-D: characters from all angles, backgrounds, items, walls, coins. They'd even handle special lighting effects, which helped sell the illusion that this was a real place.

Super Mario RPG: Legend of the Seven Stars would be Mario's final outing on the SNES, and one of Square's last on SNES too. Early SNESes had been around so long they were literally yellowing with age. Everyone was migrating to the N64: Square was already developing the seventh installments of *Dragon Warrior* and *Final Fantasy* for it. Square, based in the busy port city of Yokohama, had been exclusive to Nintendo for a decade. But it had a problem with one of Nintendo's recent decisions: cartridges.

Despite Nintendo's and Sega's debacles with their CD-based add-ons, storing game information on a cheap, capacious CD-ROM still seemed like a no-brainer. Certainly it would allow games such as *Final Fantasy VII* to create novelistic depths to its story and characters. There were some pluses to cartridges: they loaded information faster than CD-ROMs, they were harder to pirate, and they could be upgraded from game to game. But they held less than a tenth of the data a CD-ROM did, with little room for full-motion video or rich textures. And they were much more expensive, heavy, and tougher to manufacture. Yamauchi's choice to yoke the N64 to cartridges was like an artist finding all the paint and canvas in the world, but still being told to sketch on napkins with a pencil.

One way to avoid the texture-shading problem of too little data was to use something called Gouraud shading, which results in a bouncy, cartoonish look. That was perfect for Miyamoto, who used it well in *Super Mario 64*, and in the other 3-D launch game he was working on, a sequel to *Pilotwings*. But it would be tough for a game to *not* have a cartoony look on the N64, though, without serious blurriness. This continued the impression that Nintendo was just for kids.

While *Super Mario RPG* used the isometric camera, Miyamoto could go freeform with the camera for *Super Mario 64*. But first he had to get Mario's movement right. His team worked for months moving around Mario and a sleepy bunny nicknamed Mips (which stood for Microprocessor without Interlocked Pipeline Stages, the N64's flavor of CPU). The plumber gained a variety of new moves—backflips, wall jumps, double and triple jumps. To demonstrate how he wanted Mario's swimming to look in 3-D, Miyamoto even stretched out on a

desk and mimed it. Once Mario could move, and was done paying tribute to Lewis Carroll by chasing a rabbit around, the team settled on
how the camera should move.

The *Super Mario 64* plot hinges on a winningly awful MacGuffin:
cake. Bowser takes over Princess Peach's castle, full of paintings that
are portals to other worlds. Mario, who stopped by because Princess
Peach offered him some cake, has to defeat Bowser's minions in each
painting, get the star pieces, and beat Bowser. Only then will Princess
Peach bake him a cake. (Perhaps in tribute, the action-puzzle game
Portal opens with the same promise of cake: midway through the
adventure graffiti proclaims "the cake is a lie.")

Miyamoto knew gamers would go nuts exploring the 3-D world,
so he made such exploration integral to winning. Each world had a
hundred coins in it; finding all hundred earned one of the seven stars
needed to complete a level. The other six stars come from tasks, which
often could only be performed in a certain order. So Mario would find,
say, a star piece high on a cliff, and not be able to get there until he
acquired a Wing Cap. Exploration, action, plus the greater puzzle of
figuring out what had to be done in what order.

Miyamoto had his team focus on designing fun environments to
run around in, and only afterward come up with challenges to fit into
them. This helps make *Super Mario 64* one of the first sandbox-style
games, where there's no time limit or oppressive enemy, but a series of
optional side quests. Do them, or just play around in a virtual world.
Such exploration just wasn't possible in a 2-D Mario game, where
everything was encountered in sequence: here, you could choose any
path you wanted, or backflip off the beaten path.

Miyamoto wanted forty different levels, each chockablock with
puzzles and assignments. But *Super Mario 64* was penciled in as a
launch game, and there was no way Nintendo would pull a Sega and

release the console without its star. The whole system would be delayed if Miyamoto was late. And he was late: the N64 was supposed to come out in 1995. Even months behind schedule, accounting for hundreds of millions in delayed and possibly lost profits, not to mention shelving perfectly good titles like *Star Fox 2*, with Yamauchi breathing down his neck, Miyamoto was still trying to shoehorn in new boards. But the big problem was the cartridge format: there just wasn't enough room. The same back-and-forth from the original *Super Mario Bros.* repeated itself: it's good enough! No, it's not! Yes, it is!

Eventually, Miyamoto accepted that thirteen levels of this degree of excellence would have to be enough. It was still an amazingly deep and polished launch title. Plus, he was working on a 3-D *Zelda* at the same time, so many of his unused Mario ideas migrated over to *Legend of Zelda: Ocarina of Time*. (The N64 *Mario* and *Zelda* games feel similar because of this, both mixing puzzle-based exploration and 3-D platforming.) The N64 arrived in Japan on June 23, 1996, and three months later hit American shores, selling for $199. Games were an unconscionable sixty-nine dollars each at first. (Some SNES games, such as *Super Mario RPG*, were an even steeper seventy-five dollars.)

Super Mario 64 was the best-selling N64 game ever, with 11.8 million copies, so fans seemed to like it. (*Super Mario RPG* sold more than two million units as well, no mean feat.) The 3-D Mario was featured in a Got Milk ad, escaping from the TV to chug some cow juice, which worked as a power-up. Taco Bell featured Mario's 64-bit adventures in a series of kids' meal giveaways. Nintendo also had a "one in 64 wins!" contest on Kellogg's cereals, giving away more than 1.4 million prizes. It even pulled an about-face with Blockbuster, with which it was feuding over rentals. By 1996, Blockbuster was Nintendo's "Official Rental Station," offering new titles to rent as well as consoles, for seventeen dollars for three days.

Its happiness was short-lived. Square, one of Nintendo's aces in the hole, announced it was leaving Nintendo. *Dragon Warrior VII* and *Final Fantasy VII* were going to become PlayStation games, for Sony. The reason? Cartridges. Despite being 64-bit, the N64's cartridges didn't have the memory Square needed to produce a top-quality game.

Square led the exodus of third-party developers to the promised land of the PlayStation. It could manufacture CD-based games cheaper, make more money off them, and have them be easier to program: a trifecta. Each defection was a vote of no confidence in Nintendo's hardware, in Nintendo's sales future, in Nintendo itself. For all the talk of Sega's poor decisions thumping it out of business, Nintendo's Sony dalliance now loomed like an iceberg over the *Titanic*.

The three rivals' new systems were on the shelves. Sega's Saturn was a decent enough console, but hampered by years of bad management. The PlayStation was a marvel, seemingly designed to entice developers to make great games for it. No cumbersome legacy problems, no bad blood. And Nintendo's new console? Compared to the Saturn and PlayStation, it seemed obvious that the Nintendo 64 was designed for Nintendo's benefit—more profits, no piracy, great Mario games—more than anyone else.

17 – MARIO'S COMMUNICATION KIT

THE NINTENDO 64DD

When the NES was the only game in town, Nintendo thrived, and kept its third-party developers kissing plumber posterior for approval. It arrived late to the 16-bit party with the SNES, allowing the Genesis to gain equal footing in the industry. Strong innovation helped Nintendo essentially wait out the 32-bit console cycle (not counting the Virtual Boy), so it could skip ahead and be first out the gate with a 64-bit system.

But it could no longer rely on the developers it had treated like peasants. Sony's 32-bit PlayStation was a developer's paradise, without having to learn the odd particulars of Nintendo architecture. Plus, a PlayStation game made more money for a developer per unit than a N64 game. One by one, Nintendo's best Japanese developers started to make PlayStation games: first Konami and Namco, then Taito, Data East, and Capcom. American companies also joined:

Midway, Acclaim, and EA. By the time Square defected, Nintendo was in panic mode: how to stop everyone from leaving?

Well, if a disc-based game system was so important to them, Nintendo would promote one. Nintendo's 64DD, which sounds like a matronly foundation garment, would be an expansion disc drive (hence the DD) that attached underneath the N64. It would double the storage capacity of a typical N64 cartridge. A wild new DD program called Creator would add rich new textures, characters, and entire levels into games. It would have rewritable proprietary disks, and let gamers download updates to games and preview new ones. With it the N64 would be as invincible as Mario with a Starman.

Certainly that was the sales pitch for it. But from the time it was announced way back in 1994 (when it was still paired with the Ultra 64), it just seemed like the latest attempt to keep Yamauchi's dream of a Nintendo network alive. Certainly the time seemed ripe. The "World Wide Web" had gone from some text-only bulletin boards to a series of walled-off networks by Compuserve, Prodigy, and America Online. Each offered a wealth of magazines, games, chat, and "community." You could read sports scores, follow the stock market, look up recipes, read the news—everything the Nintendo Network had offered in Japan a decade ago.

But by 1996 there were even more players. Directory sites such as Yahoo and Alta Vista let people leave the walled-off compound and explore the Internet—as the information superhighway was becoming known. Newspapers and magazines started independently posting their content. Businesses began making "home pages," along with individuals at GeoCities.com. Online stores even popped up: Amazon.com sold books, eToys sold toys, E-Trade sold stocks.

Yamauchi's dream was coming true. Society had finally started using its computing devices as communications tools. Whole new media forms had developed: the web page, the e-mail, the instant message. Yet the various Nintendo networks had been only modest hits. Yamauchi could get people online for a fraction of the cost of a Compaq or Packard Bell "PC clone," but they weren't interested. Arakawa wasn't even interested!

Mario was to blame. Mario was the de facto mission statement of Nintendo. He promised family friendly fun to kids of all ages. Nintendo would always be able to print money as long as Miyamoto and his ilk kept on cranking out quality games for its consoles. But Mario was also a jail sentence, dooming Nintendo to be seen as an entertainment company and not a communications company. Sony's list of products included PlayStations, DVD and CD players, Walkmans, VCRs, cameras, and stereos. Yet it handily bought CBS Records and Columbia Pictures without dimming its brand recognition as "electronics." Why couldn't Nintendo even get its customers to use its cheap machine for a purpose everyone seemed to want: going online?

Stupid Mario, and his stupid, cherubic, mustached grin. As long as Nintendo pushed Mario as its mascot, it would be shackled to the game business with golden handcuffs. A business of which it had less market share every year. The whole game industry was receding, Yamauchi could see with his unequalled erudition. It would take a decade or more, he knew, but the "Internet" would provide the primary entertainment for a new generation, the way television had threatened the hegemony of the film studios. The numbers of people walking away from gaming were rising.

Well, if Nintendo was stuck with Mario, he'd work for his daily bread. With all the game companies moving to greener pastures, Nintendo's first-party games would be more crucial than ever. It was in quite good shape for this sort of expensive development: for decades the big N had marketed and developed each major game like it was a blockbuster summer film. The game industry had revenue similar to movies: a few games were huge hits that everyone bought, and the curve rapidly dropped after that. There was no equivalent of a midlist novel or a cult TV show: either a nineties game sold a million copies and was all that and a bag of chips, or it was whack.

With enough great games, Nintendo would be able to ride out the lack of third-party developers. Who cared if the shelf was mostly Nintendo for the first few years? Most of the other games merely gave the illusion of choice. In reality, they sold as well as the dusty cake mix and pinto beans in the center aisle of a 7-Eleven. N64 gamers, like SNES and NES gamers before them, wanted Nintendo games. They wanted Mario, and Link, and little else.

So the grand dimensionalization project began, at Nintendo and everywhere else in the game world. Every 2-D franchise would, via trial and error, see what it would play like when placed in a virtual world. Just about every game franchise would have a stumble or two making this move. They were fundamentally different types of game play, and therefore resulted in different types of games. *Tomb Raider* may just be *Pitfall* with a supermodel, but the game play is quite different. Identical plots, but the Atari game was an obstacle course, and the 3-D game was a mix of puzzle-solving and action-adventure.

Castlevania, after one iffy switch to 3-D, went back to 2-D game play. *Mega Man* and *Mortal Kombat* did the same thing: both were thrown off-balance when characters wandered around instead of being corralled on a flat stage to confront opponents or obstacles. The look could change, but the content remained the same.

Mario had made the jump already, but he was holding down way more than one franchise. Besides the classic title, he had racked up the *Donkey Kong, Super Mario Land, Mario's Tennis, Mario Kart, Game &*

Watch Gallery, Yoshi's Island, Super Mario RPG, and Dr. Mario franchises. For the N64 to seem robust in game selection, they'd all have to make the move to 3-D—and soon.

Some were easy: the original Super Mario Kart had practically herniated itself trying to mimic three dimensions, so its upgrade was a natural fit. ("Kick Asphalt," went the tagline.) Donkey Kong got Donkey Kong 64, which was another natural fit—no more prerendering! A new sports title, Mario Golf (made with a Sega Saturn developer Nintendo stole, Camelot Software Planning), found a sweet spot between minigolf's fun and actual golf's skill requirement.

Miyamoto used his Super Mario 64 experience to chart true 3-D sequels for other Nintendo stars: Star Fox, F-Zero, and Wave Race. (Names for most of these were easy: just throw a "64" on the tail end.) He also created an original title: 1080° Snowboarding, predating the definitive action-sports title Tony Hawk Pro Skater (and his signature move, a mere seven-hundred-degree spin) by a year.

While Miyamoto was ginning up original games, why not some original Mario games? (Making a Zelda character, the lazy rancher Talon, resemble Mario was cute, but didn't count.) Mario Party was a board game, with Mario and company acting out the game pieces. A kaleidoscopic phantasmagoria of minigames determined who went first in each subsequent round, and so on. It was so true to the board game conceit, though, that it was no fun to play single-person against the computer. The N64 had ports for four controllers, and the variety of minigames made this an ideal game for families, siblings, anyone without six hours of spare time a day to devote to freeing Hyrule or collecting all hundred coins.

Yet another new Mario franchise, Super Smash Bros., served as a greatest-hits retrospective. It was a simplistic fighting game—games could be won by unskilled button-mashing, a cardinal sin in the world of fighting games. But the characters went beyond the *Mario Kart/ Party* assortment: you could also choose Kirby, Link, *Metroid*'s Samus, or Fox from *Star Fox*. And there were more unlockable characters, including Captain Falcon from *F-Zero*, Ness from *Earthbound*, and Luigi. The music and scenery were all tributes to Nintendo games, and power objects rained down from the sky like Coke bottles in *The Gods Must Be Crazy*. Ever seen Mario with a sword, or Yoshi with a gun? Overall, the game treated the Nintendo canon like *Wicked* treated *The Wizard of Oz*: with a dollop of sass and irreverence.

Both of these games were made by HAL Laboratories, a Nintendo developer that had been behind the *Adventures of Lolo* and *Kirby* titles, as well as porting over *Sim City*. (HAL had inserted the gag that Sim cities erect a Mario statue at half a million residents.) One of its lead developers, Satoru Iwata, had been programming Nintendo games since the early days of the NES, and worked part-time for HAL while he was still in college. HAL was contracted to develop a N64 version of a recent Game Boy hit, about collecting cute little monsters and arranging playdatelike "battles" for them. It was called *Pocket Monsters*—or *Pokémon*.

Pokémon was in development for years, and was assumed (upon its 1996 release in Japan) to be a strictly Japanese game. It was role-playing, with minimal graphics, battles that ended with one fighter "fainting" instead of dying, and an obsessive-compulsive goal of finding 150 critters wandering in the woods. Its developer, Satoshi Tajiri, had collected bugs as a child, and found joy in their variety and abilities. He studied under Miyamoto to design the game, and the illusory simplicity of the game was straight from Doc Miyamoto. Since the idea was to play against a friend using the Game Boy's link cable, there were two different colored cartridges, red and blue. *Pokémon Red* had Satoshi (changed to Ash Ketchum for America), and *Pokémon Blue* had Shigeru (Gary Oak in America). Other than that, they were just about identical.

The game was a bigger hit than anyone in Japan could have predicted. It tapped into the gaming zeitgeist of completion by having completion itself be the goal, instead of any nobler cause. When it became a card game, "gotta catch 'em all!" basically translated to "gotta *buy* them all!" Focus testing showed kids didn't care about trainers Ash or Gary: they wanted to be the trainers themselves, and the game allowed for just that experience. That in turn prompted a top-rated anime show. (The first most Americans heard of *Pokémon* was a 1997 episode of the show that caused seven hundred Japanese children to have seizures.) It was released in America mere weeks before the Game Boy Color's launch—and it was black and white. Clearly Nintendo didn't think this game would go over much better than *Earthbound* or *Mario Picross*, both flops. Only Minoru Arakawa believed in its crossover potential—and then only if the complicated gameplay and minimal graphics were brought over unchanged.

Nintendo had nothing to worry about. The two *Pokémons* were enormous hits, helping keep the Game Boy dominant for years. *Pokémon* games for other consoles followed, beginning with *Pokémon Stadium* for the N64. (One *Pokémon* game featured a Mario cameo, a HAL calling card: Iwata also snuck Mario and friends into the crowd of a *Kirby Super Star* game.) The original's graphical simplicity was part of the draw, forcing players to focus on strategy. *Pokémon* was a new type of chess: Charmander is a fire Pokémon and is great when attacking ice Pokémon, but not other fire types, or water types. Every Pokémon has a type, and each type is weak or strong against other types. How you stack your "deck" of six Pokémon, what order you play them, when is it time to waste a turn to retire an old one: this was the game. The boundless creativity of the punny edition's names (Charmander, a fiery lizard, is a mix of charcoal and salamander) would make J. K. Rowling jealous.

Pokémon would soon become the world's second-biggest gaming franchise, selling two hundred million copies, mostly to eight-year-olds. (A covetous Miyamoto, who joked about fans sending him loose change because Nintendo didn't pay him any royalties, reportedly said that *Pokémon* would only be a hit until his next Mario game was finished.) The pocket monsters' various games would all sell well—save for *Hey You, Pikachu!*, a microphone game where players told a Pokémon to go pick up a carrot and other humdrum tasks. They even showed up in *Super Smash Bros.* They'd be that many more nails in the coffin for the idea of Nintendo being seen as more than an entertainment company. Mario was *Crime and Punishment* compared to *Pokémon*, whose appeal surged among the younger set, and diminished with puberty. For crying out loud, a plastic Pikachu was being hot glued to special editions of the N64: who would accept it as a computer with a cartoon gerbil (or mouse, or whatever he is) on it?

The rumors of the 64DD continued for years, much like how the N64 rumors spread soon after the SNES's launch. In both cases, the crafty result was to keep gamers (and developers) from flocking to other consoles. But it wasn't to be: after five years of talks, Nintendo quietly snuck out the 64DD in Japan in December 1999, releasing it exclusively through a mail-order subsidiary. The online service was shuttered after two years, due to low usage.

The biggest success of the 64DD, if such a term can be used, was the *Mario Paint* sequel *Mario Artist*. The first title in the series, *Paint Studio*, was a reworked version of the painting and stamp-making tool: Mario wore a beret on the cover. Then *Talent Studio*, which let artists add 2-D faces onto prerendered 3-D bodies and animate them *South Park*–style. After that was *Polygon Studio*, to allow users to experiments with three dimensions. Finally *Communication Kit* let users share their creations with others in the microscopic 64DD fan base. If it hadn't been shut down, future *Mario Artist* titles would have included *Game Maker*, *Graphical Message Maker*, *Sound Maker*, and *Video Jockey Maker*.

Of the dozens of rumored and halfway developed games, only nine eventually saw release. The most notable was *Sim City 64*. Many others, such as sequels for *Earthbound*, *Kirby*, a platformer called *Banjo-Kazooie*, and two *Zelda* games, were reworked as regular N64 games (or in one case, stripped down for a portable edition.) Most were canceled, giving its various developers further proof to stay far, far away from Nintendo for its original projects.

Not many company presidents would have pushed for the 64DD, after the Satellaview and the NES modem both went belly-up due to lack of interest. But Hiroshi's neuroses had driven the company for decades into some odd choices, and they were rarely wrong. It might be several decades ahead of the curve, but Nintendo had geologic patience. Perhaps Yamauchi was secretly a rock Pokémon.

18 - MARIO'S MELEE

THE GAMECUBE

There are no Mario amusement park rides. It's a bit surprising, considering the huge marketability he has, and Nintendo's willingness to slap his face on everything from underwear to life-size replicas. Every new hit Disney movie—and even the misses—prompt new park rides. Universal Studios had gotten in the act, making rides out of hot properties Disney didn't have the rights to: *Terminator 2*, *Jaws*, and *Back to the Future*.

There have been rides based on *Song of the South*, on *Wind in the Willows*, on *Murder, She Wrote*, and on *Swamp Thing*. In Minnesota, the Trix Rabbit and the Lucky Charms leprechaun have their own theme park. Dolly Parton has her own, Dollywood. But no Super Mario Park. What gives? Nintendo's stable of characters seems custom made for a massive amusement park, with themed regions based on game series. A 3-D show where pipes squirt water at you. Princess Peach's pretty castle. The high-tech Sector Z for *Star Fox*, *Metroid*, and *F-Zero*. Kirby the toddler zone, with lots of soft bouncy foam. Hyrule for older kids, with Zelda roller coasters and a Link dungeon-crawl ride. A *Pokémon* petting zoo.

That these are easily dreamed ideas is exactly why they haven't been implemented, Kokatu.com reports. Nintendo's specialty isn't in big Disney-style entertainments, and no one has yet approached them with a dynamic new idea that wouldn't just palette-swap a Disney park with Mario and Luigi. Nintendo learned its lesson from educational games, and PC games, and movies, and Internet services, all the way back to rice and love hotels. Stick with what you do best.

Nintendo might also recall SegaWorld. In 1996, right around the time Sega was in talks with Bandai about a possible merger, Sega opened up SegaWorld London, an indoor amusement park/arcade/gift shop selling Sega swag. In Canada, a series of Sega City Playdiums followed. A year later it premiered Sega World Sydney, right in the shopping mecca Darling Harbor. Its building was a giant red cube with an enormous glass pyramid reaching up out of it. It was billed as Australia's DisneyWorld. Sega's plan was to build hype for four years, then steal the show when the 2000 Summer Olympics came to town.

But not even Disney could open up EuroDisney without years of poor attendance. Not even Spielberg could make GameWorks work as anything other than, ultimately, Chuck E. Cheese with beer. The Sega World Sydney rides weren't based on *Sonic* or Sega's other game heroes, like *Shinobi* or *Virtua Fighter*. They were just unbranded rides, with the Sega brand promising a speedy, "rad," interactive style that wasn't delivered. The only thing truly Sega was Sonic Live in Sydney, a children's stage show based on the popular *Sonic* cartoon.

The park lost money four years straight, even after the hundred-plus games were all turned free-play. (That might have cost Sega more in lost quarters than it gained them in attendance.) Sega World Sydney held on until the Olympics, but not even that attendance boost helped. Nintendo stole Sega's thunder on the cheap by having a Pokémon World Championship at Sydney University, paralleling the Olympics. The entire Darling Harbor economy (IMAX theater, restaurants, trendy shops) plunged like a high-diver following the Olympics. Sega World Sydney closed for good two months after the Olympics concluded. The stunning cube-and-pyramid architecture became a furniture warehouse, then was demolished in 2008.

Nintendo did try out a traveling Pokémon Park for a few months starting in 2005, which drew more than four million visitors. The closest Mario has gotten to a permanent home, though, is in block form. A Lego version of a certain plumber wearing blue overalls and a red shirt is on display at California's Legoland, quite appropriate enough for a character who was first constructed from square pixels. This plumber, though, is carrying an accessory we've never seen in any Mario games in all his years of adventure through pipes: a toilet.

Recently, students at New York University's "Big Games" class—who previously made a live-action Pac-Man through the streets of midtown called Pac-Manhattan—came up with the Nintendo Amusement Park. It's a fancy name for a military-grade haptic winch, which allows users to jump fifteen feet in the air and be safely lowered down. Students dress up like Mario or Luigi (complete with hats and fake mustaches) and jump on a papier-mâché Goombah and around a Bob-omb. They're hoping Nintendo takes them up on the theme-park ride idea: who wouldn't want to hop around in the Mushroom Kingdom?

ONE OF NINTENDO'S SECRET WEAPONS OVER THE YEARS was trepidation. Gamers were scared they'd plunk down money for Console X, only to see their friends all buy Console Y games so they could trade with each other. Only diehards had the discretionary income to buy both. Most bought one new game every few months, the exact rate Nintendo released big first-party titles.

Sega had experienced a one-two punch of this hesitancy. First, people stopped buying 1996's Saturn, which upon release had cut the legs out from all of Sega's various other Genesis-based consoles. Sega had foolishly announced a new console (what would be the Dreamcast) right when it should have been hyping the brand-new Saturn. People passed by the Saturn, the way bakery customers will wait for fresh bread and ignore the loaf sitting in front of them.

The Dreamcast, hot out of the oven, arrived in Japan on November 27, 1998. It sold out in the United States when it arrived a year later, with more than three hundred thousand preorders, and quickly hit a million units sold worldwide. Sega designed a fleet of exemplary "2K" Sega Sports titles, to make up for EA wanting nothing to do with Sega. It brought out a strong *Sonic* game, *Sonic Adventure*. It included a modem with every Dreamcast, which let gamers play RPGs like *Phantasy Star Online* with friends from around the world. It easily had the best graphics of any system so far.

The second-part of Sega's one-two punch was a clock-cleaning haymaker, not from Nintendo but Sony. Sony announced the PlayStation's successor, the PlayStation 2, would be available in spring 2000 in Japan, and six months later in America. The PS2 would have a DVD player built in: this alone went for three hundred dollars, so buying a PS2 practically gave away a video game system for free. Developers working on Dreamcast games put their fingers up, felt the wind, and decided to make PS2 games instead.

There was a theory among video game intelligensia that three video game consoles might not be sustainable. One certainly was sustainable: the 2600 and the NES had their unchallenged heydays. Two, yes: the SNES and Genesis both did well. But three might be pushing it. Like brands of soda, like political parties, like nuclear superpowers, you could have two working to spur each other on to greatness, but a third was the odd man out. Sega looked to be this third wheel, neither the family favorite (clearly Nintendo) nor the cool kids' choice (PlayStation).

This would have been fine for Nintendo, save for Nintendo being uncomfortably close to Sega's position. Both had lost third-party developers to Sony, and relied heavily (if not almost exclusively) on first-party content. Both had more powerful machines than Sony. Both had quickly followed up Sony's great idea of re-releasing top-selling games for a reduced price in a Greatest Hits brand: Nintendo's was called Player's Choice and Sega's was All Stars. Both had been around the block long enough, like Marvel and DC, to feel comfy in their rivalry. Mario and Sonic were opposites joined at the hip.

Sega's Dreamcast had beaten Nintendo's new console to market. Nintendo's new console, nicknamed the Dolphin (later Gamecube), would be out in 2001. It was still cranking out above-average games for the N64 until just a few months before launch. An upside to Nintendo's when-it's-done philosophy was that it released games all the time, not just in October when they'd sell best. A downside? Some games' graphics stunk, because they were so behind the times.

Paper Mario was an interesting example of both: it was a sequel to *Super Mario RPG*, yet it couldn't use that title (or any new characters in it, or its isometric look) due to Square's co-ownership rights. To protect themselves, the developers (it was Gunpei Yokoi's old R&D team, now renamed Intelligent Systems) designed a game that was a parody of the Mode 7 SNES style, with 3-D backgrounds and two-dimensional cutouts walking around like paper dolls. The turn-based timed combat was intact, with new sidekicks given to Mario over the long adventure. The plot was inventive too—Bowser kidnapped not only the Princess but her entire castle.

Learning from their mistakes was what Nintendo's new console was supposed to be all about. The Gamecube would have no more heavy expensive cartridges, for instance: Nintendo was finally going with discs. Yamauchi, ever in love with proprietary formats, had Matsushita design a special smaller disc, measuring eight centimeters across, not twelve. A smaller disc allowed for an overall smaller machine. The missing circumference meant that a few games would have to be dual-disc affairs, and many more would have to compress their audio and video.

It also meant that unlike the PS2, the Gamecube couldn't play CDs or DVDs. This kept its retail price down to $249, and stymied pirates, but made it seem like a lesser console. It also included a port for a modem (Yamauchi could never give up the modem idea), but only one or two unpopular games ever allowed for online play.

The wing-grip controller was designed to discreetly house lots of buttons: there was a big green "A" button that fit above the thumb, promoting the idea of simple one-button games. A smaller red "B" button, two eyebrowlike gray bottoms around the green A, and three shoulder buttons gave plenty of options for designers who needed lots of inputs. The controller also had two control sticks (one gray, one yellow) and a gray D-pad.

The Gamecube's insides were powered by a special IBM chip called Gekko, designed at a billion-dollar price tag to do everything the N64 could, but better. The N128? Not quite: the numerical nomenclature began to break down because the chips' design matters more than sheer horsepower. The 485-MHz Gekko only had a 32-bit integer unit, but a 64-bit bus, a 64-kilobyte cache, and a 64-bit floating-bit unit, which was often used as two 32-bit vector instruction units. What was that, 128 plus 32 in total? In any case, the Dreamcast had a Hitachi 200-MHz processor, and the PS2's "emotion engine" was 64-bit bus clocked at close to 300 MHz. There were no apples-to-apples comparisons anymore.

The look of the machine, a compact purple cube, wasn't anything like previous Nintendo consoles. Purple was a new color, one Nintendo promoted heavily for the next few years. Color theory links purple to feelings of royalty: hail to the King, baby. Dreamcast had chosen white with neon orange highlights: orange was the color of happiness. Sony's PlayStation was gray, but its PS2 was black with distinctive blue piping: blue is the color of intelligence. These weren't accidental choices.

Miyamoto had had two launch games lined up for the new console, and two more for the weeks after. *Wave Race: Blue Storm* showcased sloshing, sloppy water in sun-soaked tropical locales. A companion title, the snowboarding sequel *1080: White Storm* (featuring a golden calf–ish Mario ice sculpture), was delayed for years, and ended up being quietly released as *1080° Avalanche*. As with previous launch games, *Blue Storm* was a showoff of the Gamecube's physics engine first and a racing game second.

Also on tap was *Pikmin*, which had started out life as a trade-show demo called *Super Mario 128*. The demo, now an urban legend due to Miyamoto's insistence that it was a game and not a demo, showed Mario, who divided into two Marios, then divided again and again. The Mario army stood on a sphere so small they filled the whole globe. It showed off two new Gamecube developments: the ability to have lots of different characters on screen (128, as promised) and the planetary gravity system to allow some Marios to stick upside down.

Super Mario 128 would never come out, but its two key ideas were salvaged. The multiple-character trick was used in *Pikmin*, about a tiny stranded spaceman collecting pieces of his broken spaceship to return to the planet Hocotate (named after Nintendo's Kyoto address). For help, he plucks homunculi plantmen from the ground, who obey his command. The player controls both Captain Olimar (whose name ana-grams to Mario L) and the dozens of picked Pikmin. It was a real-time strategy game, done the Miyamoto way, which is to say like no one had ever done before.

Third on Miyamoto's Gamecube launch list was *Super Smash Bros. Melee*. The updated fighting game crammed in a dizzying array of music, characters, and weapons. The sequel added a hundred different winnable trophies, each one a mounted piece of Nintendo history. It would have been unbearably in-jokey and obscure, if millions of fans weren't winningly enthusiastic about being able to, say, have the Ice Climbers attack Mr. Game N Watch with Ness's home run bat in the Pokémon Stadium, to win a Super Scope.

And then there was the haunted house game, with a ghostbusting character who stunned ghosts with a flashlight, then twirled a control stick to wring the hit points out of them. His weapon of choice, a vac-uum, prompted one game rival to scrap plans for a Hoover-powered character. It featured wonderful light sourcing and a creepy feel: Nin-tendo's version of a survival horror game like *Resident Evil*. Add one Luigi searching for the ghostnapped Mario, and the game found its title: *Luigi's Mansion*. It sold well (more than 2.5 million copies), but it was not a sign of confidence in the new system. All previous consoles became hits with their long, captivating Mario games . . . but a Luigi game? The Frank Stallone of the Mushroom Kingdom? (Trivia: Frank Stallone played a Mario brother in *Hudson Hawk*.) There was a full-on Mario game in the works, but the Luigi game was a bad omen that the Gamecube wasn't as comparatively worthy as previous Nintendo consoles.

If Sega had chosen to go the Nintendo route by foregoing third-party developers on the Dreamcast, Nintendo went the Sony route by trying to woo them back for the Gamecube. Its eleven launch titles were from eight different companies, including heavy hitters like EA, Activision, and LucasArts. It locked in some exclusive titles, and made porting games developed for the PS2 over to Gamecube as simple as it could. Developers were more than happy to be wooed by Nintendo: it beat being bullied by them.

One of Nintendo's wooed developers delivered two arcade hits, *Crazy Taxi* and *Super Monkey Ball*, as launch titles. *Super Monkey Ball* was even a Gamecube exclusive. Its initials, *SMB*, were the same as the legendary *Super Mario Bros.* but the simians in this *SMB* looked more like Sega's aborted mascot Alex Kidd than Mario. Which made sense: *Super Monkey Ball* was a Sega game.

Seeing the writing on the wall, Sega had bailed on the Dreamcast, announcing in early 2001 (not even two years since its U.S. release) that *NHL 2002* would be its funeral cortege, its final game. All other games would be converted to more popular systems. It was a smart move. Sega's great strength was in developers like *Sonic*'s Yuki Naka and *Virtua Fighter*'s Yu Suzuki, and studios such as Visual Concepts, which created Sega's brilliant *2K* sports lineup. Now regardless of what console gamers voted for with their MasterCards, they could play *NFL 2K2*, or a *Sonic* game. *Sonic the Hedgehog* became a Gamecube exclusive. Sega's console and arcade games would still sell, but years of debt racked up trying to compete with Nintendo had hobbled the company's books.

Nintendo had played a very good hand leading up to the Gamecube release. And if its opponents had been ascending Sony and descending Sega, it would have been in a solid contest for the gold. But a fourth company had thrown its hat into the video game ring. That company, with its superb console, finger-of-God marketing power, and literally billions of dollars in ready-cash, had been what really scared Sega out of the console business. Hell, it scared Sony so much the PS2 started paying for big games like *Grand Theft Auto III* and *Metal Gear Solid II* to be PS2 exclusives.

The new company in gaming was Nintendo's neighbor from Redmond, Washington: Microsoft. Microsoft, the only American company of the four, launched its Xbox three days before the Gamecube. It had bought up a cadre of fine developers for first-party games, most notably Bungie, who delivered the outstanding shooter *Halo: Combat Evolved*. It convinced many of the big developers (EA, Konami, Midway, Tecmo) to sign up for third-party launches. Nintendo and Sony helped sign them up, too, in a way: Nintendo was late in sending out Gamecube software development kits and Sony had a shortage of PS2s. Both setbacks made the Xbox a more viable option. The Xbox launched in the United States first, a canny move, since American tech never did as well in the land of the rising sun.

Microsoft was so committed to its new console, according to Dean Takahasi's book *Opening the Xbox*, it even inquired about buying Nintendo outright as a developer. Arakawa brought the idea to Yamauchi, who quashed it. Microsoft also weighed buying Sega and Square, but decided in the end to buy smaller developers for its first-party content instead of an industry big boy. It wasn't ever a money issue; internal estimates said Microsoft was willing to sink $5 billion or $6 billion into the endeavor before expecting a profit.

This was the PlayStation all over again: a new rich kid in town with the best toys becomes the most popular. And what toys: the Xbox had a 733 MHz Intel processor, a DVD drive, and enough standard parts from PCs that it looked like a tower inside its large black case. (The black came with hints of green: green is the color of renewal.) It had an 8 GB hard drive, which cost a pretty penny, and a meaty controller that had breakaway cords for safety. Biggest of all was the Xbox Live service, letting players throw on a headset and chat with friends or strangers as they joined multiplayer games. (Coming full circle, one of Xbox Live's data centers is in Tukwila, Washington, Nintendo's one-time home.)

For all the innovations Nintendo has pushed for its modems over the years, online game playing was not one of them. Its games focused on single-player campaigns (see: Mario), with a multiplayer option (see: Luigi). But Microsoft came from the computer world, of *Counter-Strike* LAN parties and *Quake* and *Unreal* death matches. Multiplayer came first for them, so every Xbox had a free Ethernet card installed. Later games would be required to have an online component for Microsoft to release them. Xbox Live was a one-stop shop for a football match, a game of capture the flag, some boxing, racing, whatever you and your friends list wanted.

This was just Nintendo's luck: it spends decades flailing at one idea over and over like a jar that won't open, and tosses it aside just in time for Microsoft to claim hero status for opening it. Hey, Nintendo loosened the lid! The PS2 launched a modem as well, but it was a separate (and sometimes damnably difficult) process to connect for each new game. The Dreamcast's modem was a big hit, but only until the PS2 and Xbox showed up. As millions more got online every year, the time was finally right for online play.

Nintendo did try to get some skin in the online game. But it cost money and took disc space to develop online content, and on a mere 1.5 GB disc (compared to 8.5 GB discs for the PS2 and Xbox) there wasn't much room for it. Third parties weren't stepping up to the plate either. The same vicious circle that felled Sega started to churn around Nintendo: companies leave because third-party games didn't sell, which meant fewer third-party games, which lowered overall sales. If you wanted online play, you went to Xbox. If you wanted a variety of games, you went PS2. Only if you wanted Nintendo games did you go Gamecube.

Most gamers chose either Xbox (24 million sold), or PS2 (a staggering 141 million, still the all-time record). Gamecube (approaching 22 million) was third overall. Nintendo's games remained solid, but if an outside company had a new game to break—especially a gritty M-rated game—they turned to Microsoft or Sony. Speculation began that Microsoft's rise, combined with the second market-leading console in a row by Sony, would be Nintendo's doom. The Big N should follow Sega's footsteps into third-party developer territory, the feeling went. Make *Super Mario* games for the PlayStation 2, *Legend of Zelda* games for Xbox. The profits would be smaller, true, and the loss of face immense, but the company would survive. The economy was cramping after the double damage of the tech bubble popping and then the 9/11 panic. People didn't want a whole console just to play cute fun games. They want blood and guts, shooting and scaring, death and destruction. Nintendo wasn't a synonym for gaming anymore. It wasn't even a genre. It was a niche.

19 – MARIO'S TIME MACHINE

THE GAME BOY ADVANCE

There had been several enhancements to the Game Boy over the years. It gained a different colored case—the Play It Loud edition. It got smaller—the Game Boy Pocket. It gained a backlight—the Game Boy Light, and a color screen—the Game Boy Color. Nintendo put out accessories like a camera and a printer, toyed with a 16-bit version in 1995, and considered a touch pad adapter in 1998. But through it all it was still essentially an 8-bit machine, making graphics in 1999 and 2000 that were only fresh by 1983 standards.

Like moths to a bug zapper, company after company tried its hand making a handheld that could compete with the *Mork & Mindy*–era visuals. Sega's Game Gear, Atari's Lynx, Bandai's Wonderswan, NEC's TurboExpress, and a Chinese system called the Gamate were all robust game systems with hardly any games or support, which could never claim double-digit market share. Tiger even released Game.com, which downloaded games from the Internet and included a touch screen and stylus. Good ideas, but (as Yamauchi knew, fresh from the 64DD disaster) the timing was wrong. They were all losing to a system whose biggest hit was *Super Mario Bros. Deluxe*, a barely retinkered fourteen-year-old game.

The Neo Geo Pocket Color, released in 1999, had the best chance of them all. It was inexpensive (under seventy dollars), came in a variety of colors (a tactic Nintendo borrowed to sell to collectors), and after an exclusive launch with eToys made its way into all the big retailers' showrooms. It could communicate with the Sega Dreamcast, then a hot new console. Nintendo squashed it, thanks to advanced marketing buzz of a fully updated Game Boy. Customers knew that Nintendo was worth waiting for, and kept their debit cards in their wallets.

Twelve years—a cat's lifetime—was apparently the right amount of time to wait for a true upgrade. The word "withered" was more and more apt for the Game Boy Color: eight bits? It was a legacy machine, surviving (and thriving) because few wanted to discard all the *Dr. Mario* and *Pokémon* cartridges they had amassed over the years.

Legacy, then, would be what the next edition would embrace. Codenamed Project Atlantis, it would include a Z80 coprocessor, which would allow it to be fully compatible with all the previous Game Boy cartridges. The screen would be wider, and the whole thing would be rounded, like a junk-food fruit pie. It would add on a pair of shoulder buttons, to allow for double the game-playing complexity while still keeping the aesthetics minimal. Gamers got a robust fifteen hours per pair of AA batteries. It would have a 32-bit CPU, which would be able to easily whip up near-perfect 16-bit graphics. Think "portable SNES."

This, in fact, was exactly what Nintendo wanted third-party game developers to think. They had all made bundles with great SNES games a decade ago, before moving onto slick polygons and control sticks. All those games needed was a little retooling, and they'd be ready for the matte-black cartridge the size of a perforated graham cracker segment. Every game from 1990 on could have a second life, a paperback release, on the Game Boy Advance.

To prove it, Nintendo pulled a stunt that would have been called slothful and small-minded if it had failed. Its biggest launch games would be ports of previous games. *F-Zero: Maximum Velocity* was Miyamoto's Mode 7 SNES launch game, with a little polish. *Super Mario Advance*, even more egregiously, was a port of a mere NES game, *Super Mario Bros. 2*! Technically it was a port of the *SMB2* upgrade in *Super Mario All-Stars*—which made things worse, because *All-Stars* was four or five refurbished games. Now just one of them was being split off to stand on its own. As a salve, a fresh upgrade of the original *Mario Bros.* was included as a bonus.

A dozen other games launched with the Game Boy Advance on June 11, 2001, a great showing. Many of them were SNES ports, with loads more (*Mario Kart: Super Circuit*) in the pipeline. Even if the reheated leftovers didn't sell well, they didn't cost much. And expectations were low: the fans only wanted to talk about the three-way Thunderdome fight between the Xbox, PS2, and Gamecube. With no challengers, the GBA was a forfeit from the horse-race perspective.

It was a great horse race for anyone with money on the filly, though. The Game Boy Advance would go on to sell over 81 million copies in its lifetime. This could be attributable to the *Candy Land* syndrome: Hasbro realized that the birth rate three years ago was an almost exact predictor of how many *Candy Land* games would be sold that year.

Every toddler got one of his or her own. Same with the Game Boy series: every few years, a new generation would be getting it as a gift.

And, of course, that generation had never played any of the old Mario games: they were brand-new! Republishing existing works was standard in every other industry, but it represented a bold new chapter for Nintendo and video games. Its omnibus experiment with *Super Mario Advance* was now a whole new revenue stream for every developer. *Super Mario World* and its sequel *Yoshi's Island* (the fourth and fifth *Super Mario* games) were rereleased as *Super Mario Advance 2* and *3*, beginning a which-came-first confusion rivaled only by the Narnia books being rearranged chronologically. Realizing it had forgotten its best game at a rest stop, the series doubled back and released *Super Mario Bros. 3* as *Super Mario Advance 4*.

There were new games, of course. *Mario & Luigi: Superstar Saga* was a spiritual sequel to the *Super Mario RPG/Paper Mario* series. *Mario & Luigi* relied more on quick timing and clever gameplay than fancy graphics. Mario sticks by Luigi's side in this game, and the two of them have combo moves critical both for fighting and for exploration. The brothers venture to the Beanbean Kingdom to fight Cackletta the witch. Bowser's lack of villainy is explained by amnesia: he's forgotten he's Mario's enemy.

The nostalgia kick continued for Nintendo with the release of the e-Reader card, a nifty device that attached into the GBA cartridge slot. It was sold with five-packs of numbered trading cards, for early games such as *Excitebike*, *Donkey Kong*, and *Ice Climbers*. Each card had a strip of gray that was really binary dots in black or white. Sliding all five cards through the reader booted up a game. Nintendo had essentially brought back the punch card. And a cute town-exploration game, *Animal Crossing*, offered players one of nineteen different NES games as rewards, including seven *Mario* games, to be found or traded. Players could even collect real-world e-Reader cards and import them to the Gamecube via a special cable.

The quick-and-fun game play of early Nintendo games was brought back as well, thanks to the minigame action of the *Mario Party* and *WarioWare, Inc.: Mega Microgame$* franchises. Konami, Namco, and Tecmo were among companies that followed in Nintendo's footsteps by releasing its old-school eighties hits in collections. Other Jurassic franchises such as *Pac-Man* and *Frogger* were given 3-D reimaginings. Nintendo shoved four previous *Zelda* games into one Gamecube package. *Madden* started to add entire previous *Madden* games, complete with the vintage roster, as a bonus. *Doom 3* came with free *Doom* and *Doom II*. Atari joysticks were sold sans Ataris: ten classic games were on a chip in the controller. History class was in session.

This was playing Nintendo's game Nintendo's way, of course. Sony couldn't rerelease its 1990 games; it didn't have any. Neither did Microsoft. The argument for respecting the past continuum of games was another way of keeping customers thinking Mario. But looked at another way, it was Nintendo's admittance that the best it had to offer were reruns.

Nintendo freshened up the GBA's look in 2003, because they realized it looked like a Game Boy. The Game Boy Advance SP (for "special") resembled a wee laptop, moving the screen to the top flap and the controls to the base. It was squarish, and looked like the world's smallest multimedia player, or maybe a PDA. Anything but a Game Boy. Which was exactly the point: don't make it look like a game, and adults will come calling. Sales doubled.

Ironically, the GBA SP's design aped the two-screen Game & Watch design from 1980. This was taken to the nth degree with the limited Game Boy Micro, which carried over Game & Watch design elements down to the gold-on-maroon color. Nintendo also released a series of

NES games on GBA to celebrate the Famicon's 20th anniversary. Such naval gazing would make Narcissus proud—well, prouder. But where were the new ideas?

The apotheosis of this self-promotion was *Mario vs. Donkey Kong*, an original Game Boy Advance game that paid tribute to everything from Mario's ubiquitous marketing to *Donkey Kong* to Miyamoto's 1994 *Donkey Kong* tribute. (When an entire game is an homage to a game that was itself a homage, you're low on gas.) The plot had a jealous Donkey Kong steal Mario dolls, and Mario run around Donkey Kong–esque boards to get the Nintendolls back.

Games like this shouldn't have been passing muster. Where were the innovators? Shigeru Miyamoto didn't have an original game for the GBA until the *Mario & Luigi RPG* game, three years into the system's release. He had better things to do with the Gamecube, and so popped his greatest hits into the microwave every few months to satisfy the GBA audience. Other developers agreed: this was a portable SNES, and they had designed plenty of SNES games back in 1993. They'd rerelease those hits, and crank out subpar licensed dreck to tie in with new movies or cartoon shows. But write new games? No way. Despite huge sales, the GBA was fourth on most people's console-priority list.

20 - MARIO'S SAGA

SUNSHINE AND DARKNESS

The word "opera" calls up great Italian names: Monteverdi, *Pagliacci*, *Tosca*, Caruso, Pavarotti. Opera's mix of song and theater doesn't necessarily require a classical protagonist such as Salome or Don Giovanni. California Institute of the Arts grad student Jonathan Mann, for instance, aimed his sights so low for a star that he found him in a sewer.

Plotwise, every Mario game is already an opera. We know the what of the plot—big surprise, Bowser has kidnapped the Princess—but not the hows. We are the show's performers, though, not divas in Viking outfits. We act out the life-and-death struggle, we experience the ever-so-slightly modified emotions of each repeat performance.

The Mario Opera begins where many operas end: a wedding. Mario crawls through a pipe, finds Princess Peach, they fall in love and get married. Then Bowser arrives and steals the princess. After being taunted by a Goomba, Mario stomps him to death, and is horrified by how good it felt to end another's life. He rushes forward, transformed from Figaro to Sweeney Todd, killing all in sight in a berserker frenzy.

Then it gets weird. In a metafictional twist, first Bowser and then Mario become aware that this is not their first, or second, or even millionth time reenacting this conflict. They're pawns being controlled by us the gamers, and have no free will of their own. What sort of hero is Mario, then? What sort of villain is Bowser? The first acts ends with Mario dead at the hands of MagiKoopa (called Lizard Wizard, for rhyming purposes), sure to be resurrected to try again. (Mann never finished the opera, but currently writes and posts a new song every day at songatron.com, so he's kept busy.)

Mario shows up in harmonious form again and again: most recently in 2010's *Super Claudio Bros.* parody musical in Washington, D.C. Nintendo always delivered great music for Mario's games, from Miyamoto's *Donkey Kong* ditties to Kōji Kondō's hummable theme songs. These have been regularly released, both as music-from-the-video-game albums and remixed in the 1993 *Super Mario Compact Disco* album, whose title is the best thing about it. (The teen R&B singer Mario Barrett, who's billed as just "Mario," isn't connected to Nintendo.)

Mario pops up often in the variously branded gamer-friend subsets of music known as nerdcore (geek-referencing hip-hip), geek rock, and marching band music, which often uses disposable pop ditties (TV theme songs, ad jingles) to draw a reaction from a halftime crowd. The University of Maryland at College Park even has a hundred-strong Gamer Symphony Orchestra. The 14-Year-Old Girls—who have songs like "Castlevania Punk," "Run Lolo Run," and "1-800-255-3700" (Nintendo's customer service number)—depict themselves as the rocking cast of *Super Mario Bros. 2* on the cover of their album *Zombies In, Robots Out*. Another band calls itself the Minibosses, and has a song called "Super Mario Bros. 2." Rapper Benefit, in the song "Super Mario Bros.," starts off his reimagining of the game plot with "It's 1986 I'm in the first grade / I'm workin' really hard to get Mario laid." Other Mario-named bands include the Lost Levels, Stage 3-1, and Tanooki Rebirth.

It's not a recent trend. In the early nineties, reggae singer Shinehead recorded "The World of the Video Game," sampling the *Super Mario Bros.* music. Nintendo capitalized on the love of Kondō's music, via *Super Mario Bros.* sheet music and even a Mario & Yoshi Music Center synthesizer. Perhaps some of these modern musicians got their start via Mario. Or maybe musicians and gamers have a rebellious connection. "Video games are bad for you?" a well-known Miyamoto quote goes. "That what they said about rock and roll."

MIYAMOTO'S WORK ON THE GAMECUBE WAS AKIN TO A political aide in the last days of a failing campaign. He flew around the world to talk up the Gamecube hardware, software, and pipeline. He challenged his team of designers to explore territory they never thought they'd encounter as Nintendo employees. He took Mario places he'd never been before. All in a futile rush to keep the ever-sinking balloon of Nintendo's PR campaign up in the air, one mad swipe at a time.

It had all started a few years ago, with Conker. Conker was a cute squirrel designed by Rare, who made his first appearance in 1997's *Diddy Kong Racing*. (His name comes from a British game of swinging horse chestnuts at each other, to smash them open.) He got his own Game Boy Color game, *Conker's Pocket Tales*, two years later. Work began on a N64 game for a 2001 release, one of Nintendo's final offerings before switching gears to the Gamecube.

What was eventually released as *Conker's Bad Fur Day* goes up there with *Super KKK Bros.* for video-game infamy. In one puzzle, Conker reaches a switch by filling up a huge vault with cow diarrhea and swimming through it. He jumps to a hard-to-access area by bouncing on a female character's enormous breasts. Characters curse, and they're English so they curse well. The evil teddy bear characters are Nazis, and explode into stuffing when shot. One character is a talking pile of dung. Conker can urinate on others for extra damage, one of his powers when drunk. The game opens with a tribute to *A Clockwork Orange*.

Unlike most other infamous games, *Conker's Bad Fur Day* was also amazingly good. Technically, it was the N64's flat-out best game. The designers were inspired by *South Park*, a show that could play on the disgust of viewers the way Yo-Yo Ma could bow a cello. There were vast rolling hills of lip-synched dialogue, great textures, and no load times. It was a spitball thrown at the blackboard by Randy Johnson. Rare had gone the offensive route so the game wouldn't be lost in the crowd of fuzzy-animal platform games, like its own *Banjo-Kazooie* series. (Which did edge into *Conker* territory by featuring Loggo, the talking toilet: at one point he's clogged and asks someone to call you-know-who.) *Conker* didn't sell well, but it certainly was noticed inside the company.

Post-*Conker*, the rules were changed for Nintendo. Conker was vulgar, but Miyamoto knew that its real enticements were graphics and game play. Every other franchise needed to have a new personality for the Gamecube. If it couldn't promise the best graphics or sound, then it would scrape together enough sheer moxie to draw attention. Miyamoto sometimes told staffers, when they had an unworkable idea, to put it in a drawer, because one day the technology would be around the fix the problem. It was time to root through that drawer.

First up was *Metroid*, which had never received a N64 game and had been forgotten. It was in development as a 3-D sci-fi exploration, through cramped dark spaceships and distant planets teeming with hostile life. Exploring around in ball form would be a game in itself. A new *Star Fox* flight-combat game was also in the works, as well as a new *Zelda* title.

That was fine, but Miyamoto pushed for more. A twist, something no one expected. *Metroid*, he announced halfway through development, would be a first-person shooter. *Star Fox* would keep the flight-combat angle, but Fox himself would get out of his vehicle and explore around as well. *Zelda* was going to use a new rendering tool called cel-shading to make Link and Ganon look like hand-drawn 3-D cartoons.

For the *new F-Zero* game *GX*, there weren't many changes other than increasing speed and challenges. There is no such thing as a racer that's too difficult, so Miyamoto and company were free to reach for insanely difficult levels, while showcasing the neon explosions that made *GX* comparable to the best PS2 or Xbox experiences. The biggest change was behind the scenes: Miyamoto's team codesigned the game with Amusement Vision, one of Sega's game-making divisions. Perhaps to take himself down a notch, Miyamoto included a fat mustached android, with a Starman on his belt, designed by a "Shiggs Mopone," called Mr. EAD. (EAD was the name of Miyamoto's R&D division.) Shiggs' favorite food? Italian, of course.

And then there was *Eternal Darkness*, Nintendo's foray into survival horror, and Shigeru Miyamoto's first M-rated video game. It was about Alexandra Roivas, who finds an ancient evil book that attracts monsters and makes the possessor go insane. She gets flashbacks to previous generations who possessed the book, and the player has to survive the flashbacks to find out what happens to Alexandra and the Tome. The game had a sanity meter; see too much weirdness and hallucinatory monsters start surrounding you. Get scared enough and the Gamecube will even start acting like it's possessed, spitting out illusory error messages.

All of this was great, of course, but none of it was a new Miyamoto Mario game. He hadn't made a true Mario game since *Super Mario 64* way back in 1996. Now everyone and his brother had 3-D platformers. Developers had learned to program in 3-D. Mario, like a rich movie star who flirts with retirement every picture, had more to lose than gain from a new game.

Certainly Mario titles were attempted: *Super Mario 64 2* was announced for the 64DD, then failed to materialize. Then *Super Mario 128*, which had turned into *Pikmin*. Mario needed something new, something distinct. At the same time, one of Miyamoto's many protégées, Yoshiaki Koizumi, was working on a water-gun game. The Gamecube allowed for great water effects, as *Wave Race: Blue Storm* showed, and Koizumi had game-play ideas for how to use a power washer—to clean graffiti, propel around like a jetpack, hover, and batter down doors.

There was enough there for a *Super Mario*–type game: instead of getting new suits, Mario would get new nozzles. Years of 3-D experience would make the challenges a mix of exploration and action. The tropical-isle setting (Isle Delfino, a wink to the Gamecube's development name of Dolphin) would be kept, which would also make this look very different than *Super Mario 64*'s digital Mushroom Kingdom. The new villain was Shadow Mario, very much like Sonic's adversary, an evil hedgehog also called Shadow. Of course, Shadow Mario would kidnap the Princess and ended up one being of Bowser's Koopa Kids. *Plus ça change . . .*

Miyamoto had worked closely with Koizumi on many Zelda and Link games, and knew and trusted the younger man's vision. Miyamoto had reached the management stage where so long as he knew the project was successful, he'd let developers follow their muse without too much interference. He let Koizumi sneak story elements into the *Zelda* games, for instance. But Miyamoto had always come back as director for the *Super Mario* franchise. For *Super Mario Sunshine*, though, he handed the baton to Koizumi. Miyamoto would still produce, but he had been making Mario adventures for twenty-two years. It was time for a successor. This retirement possibly prompted an industry rumor that Miyamoto had died of a heart attack.

Nintendo publicized *Super Mario Sunshine* by cooking a Guinness World Record-winning 3,265 pounds of spaghetti in San Francisco's Little Italy, dubbed "Pasta a la Mario." Prizes were hidden in it, and six fans dressed as Mario dove in *Double Dare*–style to find them. The game sold 5.5 million copies, beaten only by *Super Smash Bros.* and *Mario Kart* (both sold seven million copies) in Gamecube popularity. But the hit games from Xbox and PS2—*Halo*, the *Gran Turismo* and *Final Fantasy* franchises—all outsold Gamecube's best. All three *Grand Theft Auto* PS2 games outsold Mario as well, a sign of the times.

The year 2002 was a transition for Hiroshi Yamauchi as well. For more than a decade he had been hinting at retirement, and had considered various different leaders to take over his business. The natural choice would be Minoru Arakawa, Nintendo of America's president— he was family, he was Japanese, he had strong American ties, no one knew the business better than him. And the seventy-three-year-old billionaire had once had his eye on the son-in-law, true.

But Arakawa and Yamauchi had had a strained couple of years. Yamauchi, whose top showing as Japan's richest man on the yearly *Forbes* billionaire list was no longer a lock, refused to visit his daughter, son-in-law, and grandkids in Seattle—or even meet them halfway in their shared Hawaii home. Arakawa wasn't grooming himself to be the attack dog Nintendo would need to survive, Yamauchi felt. In one infamous moment, Arakawa had fallen asleep in front of clients, almost dooming a partnership. Yamauchi's zori were too big to be filled by just any feet.

Since the early nineties, Yamauchi took glee in saying that whomever he picked as successor, it would not be his son-in-law. Arakawa, perhaps saving face, began stating that Yamauchi was the only good choice for Nintendo president, and publicly agreed with Pop's decision to look elsewhere. In fact, in early 2002 Arakawa announced his retirement from Nintendo of America at age fifty-five, beating the old man to the punch.

Banker Tatsumi Kimishima, who had been hired to run the *Pokémon* division as CFO and then president, was promoted to Nintendo of America's president. He was the sort of mature, buttoned-down person who seemed to have been born an old man, and he was now running Nintendo's biggest division. Perhaps, though, a money man was too conservative a choice.

Four years later, Kimishima would be replaced by the boisterous Reggie Fils-Aime (pronounced *Fee-*a-*me*), who opened a press conference by claiming, "I'm about kickin' ass, I'm about takin' names, and *we're* about makin' games." Fils-Aime, quickly nicknamed the Regginator, was not only American but black. Nintendo of America's leadership went from Grandpa Ojiisan to Will Smith. Fils-Aime's broad features and goofy, energetic manner made him seem like a character escaped from one of Nintendo's own games.

But who could sit behind Yamauchi's desk in Kyoto? It couldn't be anyone new to the industry, since he'd just feel that Nintendo needed to get some skin in the hardware arms race of Sony and Microsoft. Nintendo's corporate philosophy of creativity being king must not change. Did anyone else have the decades of experience, the variety of backgrounds, the ability to win holding Nintendo's cards?

Yes, it turned out. The choice of successor revealed Yamauchi's skill at management, and at go. Go is a devilishly complex game, in which an opponent's all-black board can be turned snow white with just a few perfectly placed white stones. Yamauchi was a famous fan: the first NES game he ever bothered to play was a game of go. He hardly ever lost. It's just about impossible to become a billionaire without gamesmanship, not mere money, driving you. Yamauchi was placing some of his last pieces, and they were going to turn the dark board white as rice.

He picked Satoru Iwata, forty-three, the HAL Laboratories developer who was one of Nintendo's second-party vendors. Iwata had been president of HAL since 1993, when he helped bring it back from the brink of bankruptcy. (Yamauchi bailed HAL out on the promise that Iwata become HAL's president.) Before that he was a designer, working on the *Kirby* games. In 2000 Yamauchi had brought him into Nintendo's fold proper, as head of corporate planning. In retrospect, it was a try-out job, to see what Iwata would do with the throne.

Iwata was aligned with Nintendo's (and Yamauchi's) belief that bigger wasn't better. His *Kirby* games were designed for beginning players, yet were still fun. The *Pokémon* games certainly weren't breaking new graphical ground, but they were a hit too. This was when developers were cranking out violent epics that cost tens of millions of dollars. That was great for hard-core gamers, but there was a whole world out there besides young males at 2 A.M. online sessions. Gameplay innovations could lead to cheaper, quickly designed quality games that could outsell behemoths such as *True Crime: Streets of LA* and *Battlefield: 1942*.

Hiroshi Yamauchi stayed on as head of the board of directors, an honorary (read: rubber-stamp) position in Japan. He turned down his pension, letting Nintendo reinvest it. "Hiroshi" does mean "generous,"

but as a billionaire, he could afford to turn down about $10 million—
or he was canny enough to know it would net him more in Nintendo's
hands than in his own. He also started dishing out collateral-free
loans to Gamecube developers, to entice them. After three years heading the board, he left at age seventy-five, passing the chairman/CEO
baton for the Seattle Mariners to Howard Lincoln. He currently holds
a 10 percent share of Nintendo stock, and due to Japan's rebounded
economy is no longer in the top five of *Forbes*'s richest-in-Japan list.
The Yamauchi shogunate would continue, with a new shogun.

Within months of each other, Miyamoto, Arakawa, and Yamauchi
all took steps back from Nintendo. Miyamoto was busy trying to
come up with ways of making each new Gamecube game have a special connectivity feature with the Game Boy Advance, which had a
rearranging-deck-chairs futility to it. Yamauchi had to adjust to not
walking through the front doors of 11-1 Kamitoba-Hokodatecho like
he owned the place. And Arakawa was free of Yamauchi's taunts, professionally if not as his son-in-law.

This was the end of an era for Nintendo, and the years that followed certainly seemed like they were on a sort of gotta-make-the-
donuts autopilot. *Mario Partys* 4, 5, 6, and 7 came out, with many
shared minigames. *Mario Golf* was upgraded, with the GC-GBA connectivity between *Toadstool Tour* (GC) and *Advance Tour* (GBA). A similar arrangement was made for *Mario Power Tennis* (GC) and *Mario
Tennis: Power Tour* (GBA), which features the *Mario Kart* items for a
dodgeball feel. *Dr. Mario* was repackaged a few more times. A Gamecube *Mario Kart* came out, and another *Paper Mario*. One of the *Mario
Partys* was turned into an arcade game, then one of the *Mario Karts*.
To paraphrase Jan Brady, it was Mario Mario Mario.

Many of these were solid games, but they didn't expand the Mario brand as much as continue it. With not much game-play difference between the Gamecube and the Nintendo 64, the new versions were like the yearly *Madden* updates: incrementally slicker and improved versions of the previous year's game.

Some games did try to push Mario into new territory, but met with resistance. *Mario Pinball Land* had Mario become the pinball to stop Bowser. The mix of adventure and rolling worked better with *Super Monkey Ball*. A *Mario Mix* version of *Dance Dance Revolution* came out, with Mario music and classical tunes to dance to. The attempt to lure in sports gamers with arcadey action continued with *Mario Superstar Baseball* (Mario knows baseball) and *Super Mario Strikers* (Mario knows soccer too).

Meanwhile, the PS2 and the Xbox were trying to be all things to all people. Continent-sized games routinely came out for both systems: *God of War, Star Wars: Knights of the Old Republic*, the *Grand Theft Auto 3* series. In addition, Sony, Microsoft, and numerous third-party developers tried to make their own Mario-type platforming collection game. *Jak and Daxter, Blinx, Ratchet and Clank, Sly Cooper, Ty the Tasmanian Tiger, Tak*. They were added to the previous list of Mario wannabes—*Spyro, Crash Bandicoot, Rayman, Bubsy, Gex*, and of course *Sonic*. Only a few of these—*Crash, Jak, Spyro, Ratchet, Sonic*—stuck around.

Which meant, of course, that there was a big, gaping Mario-size hole in the lineups of the PlayStation 2 and Xbox. Both systems had even more tremendous upgrades arriving soon: the PlayStation 3 and the Xbox 360. Gamecube games that weren't Nintendo-made were becoming more and more scarce. The user base for both systems was enormous, and growing. Sega had done very well making its *2K* sports games, now rebranded *ESPN*, available for all three consoles. It was faltering with recent *Sonic* games, which were Gamecube exclusives. Was this the view from the top of the death spiral?

To an outsider, going multiconsole looked like Nintendo's best bet. It'd receive a big increase in sales. Everyone loved the Mario franchise: it was parodied in everything from the Xbox sci-fi game *Advent Rising* (a secret room with three pipes) to Blizzard's *World of Warcraft* (with feuding friends Larion and Muigin, who complain about plants coming alive) to *Assassin's Creed II* (with its Uncle Mario character). The Kyoto company would stay in business, and change with the times. Let other manufacturers make the razor blades—and at a loss. Nintendo could sell the blades. It'd be a step down, but it would keep them alive. If Yamauchi's data about the gaming audience shrinking was true, how else could they survive?

Nintendo's ship was being steered by Satori Iwata's uncalloused hands now. When Yamauchi called Iwata into his office to promote him to president—Iwata has said he thought he was going to be fired—Yamauchi almost certainly demanded that Iwata not leave the hardware business. Nintendo made money selling its software, but also its hardware, a trick no one else in gaming had ever done long-term. It kept pushing gameplay innovations, but all the hardware was necessary for its premier software to be properly viewed. That was Nintendo's essence: not Mario but Miyamoto, and Yokoi. (And Genyo Takeda and Masayuki Uemura, the underrecognized daimyos.) Bigger did not mean better, and quality of play was not related to quantity of megahertz.

Iwata had no plans for putting Nintendo games on anything other than Nintendo consoles. He and Fils-Aime were firm believers in Yokoi's maxim. This belief had been recently reiterated in business guru Clayton Christenson's "disruptive technology" theory, which said that new inventions—think of digital photography—could topple giants like Kodak. Nintendo was huge, but still David in the contest against the twin Goliaths Sony and Microsoft. But what could that disruptor be? Iwata and Fils-Aime started talking about disruptors all the time. Others might think them touched for believing this. But touching can be good.

PART 5

WII ARE THE CHAMPIONS

21 – MARIO'S REVOLUTION

THE DS

n the final months before the Game Boy Advance came out in 2001, HAL Laboratories designed a Game Boy Color game called *Kirby Tilt 'n' Tumble*. The nifty twist was that instead of moving Kirby around with the D-pad, players tilted the Game Boy Color itself around to roll the puffball like a marble though a labyrinth.

It received little notice: Kirby games, aimed at kids, never did. But each translucent pink Kirby cartridge had an accelerometer in it, a cost-effective type called a micro-electromechanical system, or MEMS. The MEMS chip was basically a tiny spring with a weight on it: move it, and the spring registers the movement and translates it to Kirby. Accelerometers are used everywhere, in bridges and cars and medical devices.

It wasn't a perfect fit. Game Boy users were accustomed to holding their machine in any number of slouchy ways: now that Kirby was as volatile as a blob of mercury, they had to keep things balanced—and pray there was sufficient light to see. The only practical way to make it work, Iwata concluded, would be to have a special console controller with built-in accelerometers. Players could tilt that however they wanted, and still see their TV screen. No, it wouldn't do for a handheld device. And Nintendo's upcoming handheld, the DS, had enough hooks. "[Gamers have] given up on video games," Iwata said at a trade show. "[W]e have to call them back in."

Iwata, following through on Yamauchi's vision, was introducing a new portable console in 2004. This was two years after his ascendancy to the top post, and only three years since the Game Boy Advance was released. It would be his first real test. He wasn't running things the same way as Yamauchi; he encouraged the daimyos to cooperate and share staff, instead of feud. He talked nonstop to the staff, using reams of charts to back up his statements. Anything to measure up to the shogun and his inerrant instinct.

While he didn't glower at people like Yamauchi did, Iwata lived and breathed Nintendo philosophy as much as the employees who had logged in decades of dedication. He larded vast hoards of cash, kept staff low, and refused to branch out beyond games. Yamauchi, still a board member, backed up Iwata in print . . . to a degree. "If we are unsuccessful with the Nintendo DS, we may not go bankrupt, but we will be crushed," he told the *Nihon Keizai Shimbun*. "The next two years will be a really crucial time for Nintendo." In other words: let's see if he screws this up.

The Nintendo DS built off of the success of the GBA's mature-looking edition. DS stood for Dual Screen, and each unit had two three-inch LCD screens. Mario could explore in a fold-out world with double the sky, jumping up into the second screen's territory when faced with a high obstacle. Or, he could keep a constant map of his travels on one screen, along with possessions and various power meters. Or, turning the DS sideways, Mario could explore a portrait-oriented world instead of a landscape. The possibilities were untapped. Which young blood thought up the idea of reusing Gunpei Yokoi's ancient Game and Watch two-screen idea? Yamauchi, who passed Iwata the idea just before retirement.

Even better than two screens was the touch screen. The base screen had a resistive panel, which turns the whole image into a digital button. Wherever pressure was applied, the two resistive layers connected, sending an electrical impulse, no different than when the A or B button was pressed. ATMs used the same technology. "Touching is good," went the naughty advertising campaign slogan. All DSes shipped with a stylus as well, so people didn't smudge the screen.

The DS was backward-compatible with the GBA games, but designers didn't kill themselves trying to accommodate Game Boy and Game Boy Color games, which had slightly larger cartridges. That 1989 version of *Tetris*, alas, wasn't playable anymore. Twin speakers allowed for true stereo sound. Puzzlingly, there wasn't room for a headphone jack: anyone who wanted to listen on a train had to buy an adaptor. The screen resolution was also anemic compared to high-end cell phones. A small mike in one corner allowed for talking games—some *Pokémon* games were already planned using the mike.

The DS's guts featured a 67 MHz CPU designed for 3-D rendering, as well as a less powerful 33 MHz chip to display the 2-D graphics on half of the screen, and to emulate the GBA. What this meant was, despite the measly megahertz, the DS was capable of running a Nintendo 64 game. And what better way of showing this off than by repeating the GBA trick of launching with a Mario port?

Wisely, the launch team chose a more fondly remembered game than *Super Mario Bros. 2* to port over: the 3-D marvel *Super Mario 64*.

Miyamoto had the chance to add in all the extras he couldn't cram into the N64 game's original release. Most of those ideas had been incorporated into *Zelda* or *Star Fox* projects, though, so he made new changes. The DS CPU could crank out more polygons, and didn't have to rely on compression techniques. The gameplay was altered as well; instead of Mario getting different hats and exploring solo, he, Luigi, Yoshi, and frenemy Wario took turns exploring. Each character had distinct abilities, so what once required Mario's Metal Hat now required switching to Wario.

The top of the screen was the 3-D game: on the bottom was a 2-D map, along with icons showing where all four characters were in relation to each other. Using the stylus while playing took some getting used to: some preferred greasy fingertips. The touch screen was also used for a series of *Mario Party*–esque minigames, which could be "won" by chasing after in-game rabbits. A modest multiplayer battle mode was helped out by an essential new option, "Download Play." This let up to four DSes link up not only without a cable, but without four copies of the game.

The DS used a digital D-pad, which many disliked. Digital controls either send a 0 or 1, but couldn't capture any fractional shades of gray in between. Analog control sticks, on the other hand, could slice a thumb press into 256 gradations. Just about every 3-D game was moved by an analog stick, so reverting to digital made the controls "sticky." Hence Mario was tough to move around.

The most radical addition to the handheld might not have been the double screen, or even the touch screen. Keeping with the if-at-first (and second, third, fourth)-you-don't-succeed ethos, the DS included a way to get Nintendo gamers online. Technology and society had finally caught up with Yamauchi's vision. People didn't just dial up to AOL on a 14.4K modem, or access a swift T1 cable line: they bought new gadgets every year based on what they looked like, how small they were, and what they could do. Wireless communication was a key feature. A three-inch touch screen that collapsed to the size of a sunglasses case, with Wi-Fi access? That played Nintendo games? For $150? Sold.

Interestingly, Iwata's first console was released in the United States first, on November 21, then Japan on December 2. The Japan-first philosophy had changed, but only for this one console. Japanese tech buyers can be a fickle lot. Odds are Nintendo wanted its first launch site to be a big success. It spoke to Iwata's nervousness about the DS that he changed the normal release schedule to front-load it with more positive press. The DS did turn out to be a slow initial seller in Japan, where portable doodads have to weather a much more acidic litmus test than in the States. This is, after all, a culture that recently spawned the *keitai shousetsu* literary genre, novels written on cell phones as epistolary text messages. Its standards might be insulted by Nintendo trying to cram Internet access into a gussied-up Game Boy.

The DS wasn't aimed at kids who wanted to play *Pokémon*, though they were certainly welcome. It was aimed at adults, with their Black-Berrys, and cell phones, and MP3 players. Adults had loads of money to drop for accessories like a Bluetooth headset or a chromium skin. They would be into brief games: no long adventure campaigns, just something to kill five or ten minutes between appointments. They wouldn't consider themselves "gamers," but would routinely spend an hour sweeping mines or shuffling through *Spider Solitaire*.

In addition to *Super Mario 64 DS* (the original title was even worse: *Super Mario 64 x 4*), the DS launched with a healthy spread of older-skewing titles. There was *Sonic* creator Yuki Naka's *Feel the Magic: XX/*

XY, a minigame collection. There was *The Urbs*, an achingly hip *Sims* spinoff about building up "rep." There was a *Madden*, a *Spider-Man*, and a driving game called *Asphalt Urban GT*—sense an "urban" theme?

Trying to attract another underserved audience group—females— brought *Super Princess Peach*, a game where Peach finally avoids being princess-napped. Bowser kidnaps Mario and Luigi instead, and it's up to her for once to save them. The second-wave feminism lasts as long as it takes Peach to acquire a magical talking parasol. Peach's powers manifest through her emotional states. When she is calm she can heal herself, when happy she can fly, when glum she can water plants with her tears, and when angry she literally catches on fire. Using emotions as part of basic game play is a daring concept, and feel free to sub in "insulting" or "outrageous" or "awesome" for "daring." The concept might have been taken more seriously if not for touches like the pink umbrella, and Peach having unlimited lives—core gamers hate being unable to die.

Another game that showed off the new controls was *Yoshi Touch & Go*. It was essentially a Game & Watch title, with Yoshi running to get Baby Mario to the end of the crayon-drawn level in time. Players controlled neither Yoshi nor Baby Mario but used their styluses to draw clouds that Yoshi walked on, letting him lemming his way to the level's end. To get rid of a cloud, players blew into the microphone. It was almost pure game play, an Aristotelian demonstration of how the DS changed how people could play games. But the cartoonish look and kid-friendly vibe made anyone older than eight—aka the target audience—stay away.

Miyamoto wasn't involved in producing *Super Princess Peach* or *Yoshi Touch & Go*. He was too busy walking the dog. His family had gotten a new pet a few years ago, a breed called a Shetland sheepdog that looks like a collie without shins. Miyamoto named his family's Sheltie

Pikku, after banjo picks. Games were fun, but dogs were responsibilities. Dogs could play with you in unexpected ways. They had their own lives, likes, and interactions. It got Miyamoto thinking. The virtual-pet idea was not new: Tamigotchis were a big hit in 1996. But that was simple button-pushing: give it food every X hours, water every Y hours.

Dogs needed more than kibble and walkies. They needed to be petted: hey, look, a touch screen. You could teach dogs to understand your commands: hey, a microphone. You could take them to the dog park: hello, Download Play. You could choose what type of dog you adopted: therefore the simulation would come in one of four cover breeds, Chihuahua, Dalmatian, Dachshund, and Labrador Retriever. You could unlock up to fifteen breeds total, plus a hidden characters named "Shiggy" and his Sheltie Pikku. It would be a simulation, not a game. That was okay, since the people Nintendo was luring to the DS weren't gamers, but casual fans. After decades of making *shonen* games for boys, Nintendo finally hit upon making a true *shōjo* game for girls.

Thus did the distaff Nintendogs launch, going on to rack up over twenty-one million copies worldwide. It won awards from places expected (GameSpot, IGN) and unexpected (People for the Ethical Treatment of Animals, the Associated Press). Such was the power of the girl gamer. One strange consequence of the game's success was a company ban on Miyamoto talking too much about his personal life. He thought of *Pikmin* while gardening, and Nintendogs while playing with a pet. If the world knew he, say, liked to hang-glide, or swim, imagine the industrial sabotage . . . ! Unfortunately for Nintendo, it was already well known that he was a fan of music, tilting their hand of an eventual music game.

One thing everyone already knew that Miyamoto loved was his alter ego, Mario. His Mario game, *New Super Mario Bros.*, certainly seemed as if it was yet another shovelful of 1989 into a new handheld.

But this was a different beast. There were new levels. There were new items, including the Blue Koopa Shell, which made him hide like a frightened turtle, a Mega-Mushroom to Godzilla him up to supersize, and as a yang to that yin, a Mini-Mushroom to bring him down to ant level. The camera zoomed in and out on the action, the bottom screen displayed a DVR-like display of how far was left in each level, and modern physics engines allowed Mario to interact in a pliable, mutable world. It was the big-budget remake of a classic TV show.

For the first time since 1992, Mario was in a side-scroller. Credit producer Takashi Tezuka for doing what music producers Rick Rubin and Dae Bennett did for Johnny Cash and Tony Bennett, respectively: revitalized their long careers by cutting away artifice and showing them doing what made them great. In Tezuka's case, it was injecting a breath of fresh air into supervising producer Shigeru Miyamoto's original side-scrolling style of game play.

Don't believe, though, that this meant Mario wasn't getting more exposure than a Speedo wearer in the desert. Just about every Mario game you can think of—*Mario Kart*, *Mario & Luigi RPG*, *Yoshi's Island*, even *Mario Vs Donkey Kong*—received a sequel or two. He showed up in original titles as well: *Taiko Drum Master*, a mah-jong game called *Yakuman DS*. And *Mario Hoops 3-on-3* added yet another sport to Mario's Thorpe-ian letterman's jacket, basketball—he also cameoed his rock skills in *NBA Street V3*, and snowboarded his way into *SSX on Tour*.

In March 2005, Shigeru Miyamoto, who let so many millions chase after stars, received one of his own. He was one of two video game creators to be given the first stars in the new Walk of Game in San Francisco's Metreon mall: Atari's Nolan Bushnell was the other. Bushnell's picture shows his large frame in a gray silk shirt, no tie or jacket, top button undone: the portrait of a software pioneer.

Miyamoto's is covered with stuffed animals: Mario, Wario, Yoshi, Donkey Kong, a hidden Bowser over his shoulder. He wears a blue blazer and cream ribbed turtleneck that, combined with his unkempt hair, makes him seem to have walked off the Regal Beagle set from a *Three's Company* taping. Four game franchises were inducted. Two of them were Miyamoto's: *Zelda* and *Mario*. *Halo* and *Sonic* rounded out the list. Miyamoto did not attend, but sent a foam-headed mustached emissary in his place. The Metreon stopped giving the award out the year after, but Miyamoto's steel star remains. He left his mark in San Francisco.

A short stroll from that star is a Sony-branded PlayStation store, selling nothing but PS2 this and PS2 that. Starting in 2005, it and every other video game store in the United States started stocking the PlayStation Portable, the biggest-ever threat to Nintendo's handheld hegemony.

Sony didn't seem to have many weak spots in its frontal assault on the DS. The PSP had a big screen: a whopping 4.3 inches wide. Its capacity was big; it used optical discs for its storage, and could play entire films on special Universal Media Discs. Its memory was big: it had 16 GB of flash storage. Its controls were big: it had a modified PS2 controller hidden around the wide screen, including a nub of a joystick. Its games were big: it played note-perfect PlayStation ports, and launched with some of the best initial games ever: *Spider-Man*, *Need for Speed*, *Tony Hawk*, *Tiger Woods*, *NBA Street*, *Metal Gear*, *Twisted Metal*. Its extras were big: it had Wi-Fi access. Aha, Nintendo maniacs countered, but its energy drain was big: players had four to six hours on a charge. And that $250 price tag? Big.

The PSP roared in popularity in 2005. Its promised connectivity with the PS3, its widescreen movies, its software-running abilities, its hit game franchises: the PSP could do no wrong. Then, as if living up to the PlayStation heritage, a wave of piracy began, aided by Internet access and capacious memory sticks. Despite regular security patches, scofflaw gamers could still download just about any game they wanted, including PlayStation titles never released on the PSP in the first place. This led to third-party makers ceasing production, and Sony overcompensating by announcing that it didn't want their games in the first place. Within a year, you'd be forgiven if you thought the PSP was a media-watching device, based on how few people were ever seen in public playing a game on it.

Almost double the 25 million who bought a PSP (many in Japan, where it remains very popular) went for a DS, which (stop me if you've heard this before) wasn't as technically powerful or robust but had a longer battery life and offered more distinctive gaming choices. In response to the PSP, Nintendo released the redesigned DS Lite, and sales almost doubled again. PSP countered with its own redesigns, the thinner PSP Slim & Lite and then the PSP Go, which hid its controls the way texting phones hide their keyboards. Nintendo countered with the DSi, which has a pair of cameras, then the supersized DSX. The PSP remains a legitimate gaming system that makes Sony a lot of money every year. But it's living the life of Napoleon in Elba, a conquered conqueror waiting for the next chance to strike.

22 – MARIO'S PRINCESS

THE WII

V ideo games get compared to movies quite often. Certainly game makers themselves have helped bolster this parallel. They bill themselves as directors and producers, hire actors as voice talent, feature long full-motion video sequences, and frame their shots for maximum cinematic impact. But maybe films aren't the best metaphor. They're both audiovisual experiences, yes, but films are passive. Games aren't. Gamers' imagination and resources determine what happens, and how much enjoyment they get out of it.

Perhaps the better media comparison is with books. Think of a big-box bookstore, two stories high with titles of every stripe. Most every video game ever made would go into one of a paltry few stacks: science fiction, fantasy, young adult. Indeed, these are where the novelizations of many of these games, the *Mario* novels included, are found. But the majority of the sections would be almost barren of video games. Business and finance? Cookbooks? Reference?

Biographies? Address books? Calendars? Whatever people enjoy doing, shouldn't there be an audience who wants to do that in a game? Most games were escapist adventures: but not everyone wants or needs to escape from his or her life.

Video games were a specific stripe of genre fiction, in other words. Even the puzzle games were given a story: players couldn't just play a tile-matching game, they had to pretend to be feuding pirates who fight via pseudo *Tetris*. Putting the yoke of such a story on an experience was limiting. Adding insult to injury, often it was a terrible story, with derivative plots, wooden characters, and rank dialogue. All those empty shelves represented a massive untapped market.

NINTENDO'S GAMECUBE SUCCESSOR, WITH THE WORKING name of Revolution, promised to be exactly that: a revolution. It would have to be, going up against both the PS3 and the Xbox 360. Its biggest weapon was a man, with the initials SM, who was the worldwide symbol of excellence in games. And he was not an Italian plumber. Whatever the new system would be, credit would go to Shigeru Miyamoto, who on March 13, 2006, was honored as a knight of arts and literature by the French minister of culture. His appointment book was now peppered with lifetime achievement awards receptions.

The PS3, out in 2006, was going to be the most powerful game system yet, and came standard with a Blu-ray player. (Which helped eliminate its rival HD-DVD: both systems cost hundreds of dollars, but only one shipped with a free video game system.) The Xbox 360, which would be first to market in November 2005, was outputting frame rates and picture quality so precise that only flat-screen televisions were sophisticated enough to show its details. Microsoft and Sony had thrown themselves into the megahertz measuring contest with full force. Both systems produced a quality of output that was often comparable to the special effects of summer blockbusters.

The Revolution, by contrast, was not trying to be the biggest or the baddest. In fact, its modest abilities led to one frustrated developer saying it was just a pair of Gamecubes duct-taped together. It used Intel's Broadway chip, successor to its Gecko Gamecube chip that used 20 percent less power and ran 50 percent faster. Great for Nintendo, maybe not so great for someone who expected a 2006 console (running at 729 MHz) to be more powerful than a 2001 Xbox (733 MHz). It was designed to be small and sleek, no bigger than three DVD cases, and so efficient it didn't need a cooling fan. This frustrated Nintendo's third-party developers: the spectacular graphics that they made for the 360 and the PS3 had to be severely dumbed down to be ported to Nintendo's new console. The end result was like watching a long R-rated movie on network television: time-compressed, edited for broadcast, pan-and-scanned, replete with cuts. Why bother?

Nintendo's seasoned-technology mindset had never been so evident—or so daring. It was purposefully taking itself out of the arms race driving its competitors. Making money from selling hardware was part of Nintendo's success story. Let the others price the bare-bones Xbox 360 at $300 and PS3 at $499—with gamers having to fork over another C-note if they want to actually get online with either. Nintendo would compete on price—$250. Saying good-bye to an easy couple of hundred million dollars each year, it announced that all online play would be free.

The entire console was Satoru Iwata's *Radar Scope*, the one big decision that would decide his company's fate. But this wasn't a brash moment of putting the life savings on the number-four horse. First off, zigging where others zagged was Nintendo's consistent strategy.

If anything, the watered-down Gamecube was when Nintendo tried—and failed—to join the slam-dunk club. Once Iwata and Miyamoto saw the success of the DS, specifically its new operating system, they felt their new paradigm would find favor when it was released.

For this new paradigm they could thank the same man who Yamauchi had once cursed: Mario. Mario stopped Nintendo from being anything more than an entertainment company. But amusing people was now the mission statement, the decree of the new shogun. Not being the biggest or fastest, but having the best games. Invention is needed for new amusements, and while this year's inventions would be copied by the rest of the industry, Nintendo would continually invent new ones for next year.

It took work to find the revolutionary for the new console. Nintendo had considered making the Revolution's controller a touch pad. That would copy the DS, though. Motion-control, via a camera? Too complicated. One authentic-looking fake ad was for a Virtual Boy–ish helmet called the Nintendo On. The On was not that far from the truth.

The reveal—of the official name, at least—came on April 26, 2006, a few months before release. Nintendo's new console was the . . . Wii. Huh? The letter "W" was an emoticon meaning "smile" in Japan, and the two lowercase "i"s represented two players standing next to each other. And "we" implied family gaming. The initial ad campaign would feature two friendly Japanese men traveling through America, Johnny Appleseeding Wii systems across the fifty states.

History repeated itself. Just as *Donkey Kong* was saddled with a name that was just too easy to mock, Nintendo picked a name that was a synonym for urine. It was small, underpowered, and came after the weak Gamecube. It was being released in America on November 19, two weeks before Japan (December 2). It smelled like not screening a movie for critics.

One final nail in the Wii's coffin? Just like the Gamecube, the Wii was launching without a Mario game. (*Super Smash Bros. Brawl*, which had Mario in it, wasn't ready.) Instead it had a forgettable string of tie-in movie games—*Barnyard, Cars, Open Season*. There were a lot of minigame collections as well, such as *Rayman Raving Rabbids* and *WarioWario: Smooth Moves*.

Miyamoto had a guiding principle when designing the console: make moms happy. Moms had an uneasy relationship with the game machines that sucked the sand out of their kids' hourglasses—and lured away the dads as well. Mom was the person who had to buy this stupid expensive time waster, and purchase new games every Christmas and birthday, writing down these ridiculously precise titles—not just *Star Wars* but *Star Wars Jedi Knight II: Jedi Outcast* for Xbox—for fear of buying the wrong one.

One way to make moms happy was to give their console a simple, happy name: Wii. Another was a low(er) price. And there were the games: family friendly stuff younger brothers could stay in the room to watch. To further prep moms for this shift, McDonalds and Nintendo put out Mario Happy Meal toys aimed at encouraging healthy, active lifestyles. (Make your own jokes about that.) One huge mom advantage? Every Wii would have a pack-in game.

Wii Sports would contain five different games—tennis, bowling, boxing, golf, and baseball. Combined, they were a steal. Another game, *Wii Play*, took a similar format to activities like skeet shooting, air hockey, pool, and fishing. When it was bundled for no extra cost with a second controller, which alone retailed for forty dollars, *Wii Play* sold itself.

And that Wii controller . . . It may have started with the desire to not have long wires uglying up the living room. Nintendo had had success with the wireless Wavebird controller for the Gamecube. All of the Xbox 360 and PS3's controllers, remarkably, were wireless. Their controllers had traditional setups: control stick on the left, lots of buttons on the right, index-finger triggers, plus more buttons and more control sticks. Mom was scared she would shoot off a nuke if she handled it the wrong way.

Finding a way to friendly it up challenged many of the long-held assumptions about gaming. Players moved with their left hand, and performed actions with their right hand. It synced up with clumsy pop neurology: the left brain was great with logic and spatial relations (such as where to move) and the right brain was for art (which creative method to dispatch the guard?). This basis more or less defined games as being Mario-ish third-person adventures, since that's what it was designed to do. The games that tried to mix up controls were rare, and often counterintuitive to play at first.

Miyamoto went back to the drawing board, back to the beginning of games themselves. They were ways to pass the time, to have fun, to duplicate tasks your body would normally do. They were tools: tools for fun. Fun was much broader than controlling a character.

Years before *Donkey Kong*, Nintendo had marketed a light-gun game. Players held a toy gun and shot imaginary bullets. Games since then had lost that generality of play. Play was something everyone did. What had happened to the industry so a typical mom would say she wasn't a "gamer"? This is someone who deals herself rounds of *Freecell*, actually enjoys *Sorry* and *Chutes and Ladders*, pretends to be a princess for a tea party, and helps her kids with batting practice. The same woman might tear through a Nora Roberts book, yet claim to not "read" because Nora isn't Virginia Woolf. Well, she *does* read, and she *does* plays games. Nintendo just had to let her feel good about that.

Miyamoto and company looked at lots of different devices with buttons—not just game controllers but cell phones and channel changers. They wanted to see what felt right. After trying a cell phone–derived controller, they went with a remote-control shape. Unlike most remotes, this one would have only a few white-on-white buttons: their size and location denoted their relative importance. One-handed, no control stick, simple as a garage door opener. When the Wii's name was released, the device—officially the Wii remote— got the inevitable nickname of Wiimote.

Building on the accelerometer research HAL did a few years previous, the Wiimote could sense movement. Three accelerometers controlled the horizontal, the vertical, and the yaw. A sensor strip along the top or bottom of the TV shone infrared LEDs, which the Wii used to constantly orient itself via triangulation. A small speaker built into the Wiimote, combined with a Rumble Pak, let force feedback and sound emit from the controller, two ways that made it easier to believe waving in the air was having a palpable effect.

It took years to get the controls right: for a while, any room with an incandescent bulb (or even a candle) would make the Wiimote act wonky. But once its bugs were squashed, the Wii offered not just a new interface but a new way of thinking about games, appealing to a vast audience who'd stayed away from consoles before this. There was consideration of releasing it as an accessory for the ailing Gamecube. But that system's time was at an end. The current gaming market, to use another business-book analogy, was a red ocean, awash with blood and sharks. Nintendo had spent too many years being bitten by those sharks: time to take their more deserving Wii console into the blue ocean of an untapped market.

The Wii, though, was not exactly a more deserving console. It did do several things right: backward compatibility with Gamecube discs and controllers, standard-size twelve-centimeter optical discs, 512 MB of internal flash memory. The Wii's expansion storage uses standard SD memory cards, the breath-strip-size flash cards found in digital cameras, and the Wiimotes have storage space as well. But what was going to sell the Wii was the presentation. When the game started up, players were shown the Wii menu, with a choice of screens to click on. There was whatever game was inserted. There was a News Channel— those hooked up to the Internet could see headlines, local weather, and sports. Wanna get online? You can.

The Wii menu was strongly influenced by Apple, beyond its soothing white color scheme. Apple's MP3 players were very expensive, and hampered with digital rights issues. But they saw huge popularity thanks to an intuitive, simple interface: a click-wheel, a minimum of confusing buttons, a system that automatically finds each album's cover art for you. Nintendo would do the same, and offer it at bargain prices. Take that, Steve Jobs.

The iStore equivalent, the place where people could painlessly browse and buy great tracks they never knew they needed, was the Wii Shop Channel. It sold older games playable on emulators of the NES, SNES, and even the Nintendo 64. *Mario Bros.* was a Wii Store launch game, and Mario fare both well known and obscure soon followed— from *Donkey Kong* and *Super Mario Bros.* to *Mario's Super Picross*. The Wii Shop offered WiiWare, original games not sold in stores, such as *Dr. Mario Online Rx* and *Dr. Mario Express* for the Wii and DS, and *WarioWare: Snapped*! for the DS. All of these were managed by Wii Points, digital tokens equivalent to a penny. Most NES games cost five bucks.

Nintendo was in no way unique at this point in selling downloadable content for its console, despite pioneering it decades ago. Xbox Live's menu gave gamers a richer online experience than the Wii did. And the PS3's PlayStation Network offered downloads of older hits, too. One true standout of the Wii Menu, though, was the Mii Channel. Clicking on it brought the user to a face-creation program, intuitively designed with an emphasis on eyebrows. There are strange omissions—no red hair? No dark skin tones? No body customizations other than height and width? But most any face can be created with a shocking degree of accuracy. (A regular contest for Wii users gives them famous people to design—Don Quixote, or Mario.) They were based on the Japanese art of *kokeshi*, armless wooden dolls.

The Miis weren't just for *Mario Paint*–ish fun. Each family member would design his or her own Mii, which would be his or her avatar. The Miis showed up as spectators in other games, such as *Mario Kart Wii*. Character customization was once a true burden to use. The Mii Creator's depths and ease made it a game to design a custom face. After all, game designers had fun designing characters: why not share that fun? Mario had been the default Nintendo face since 1981. The Wii offered a better option: us. (Or, we.)

The Wii's popularity became a self-feeding fire, generating more attention and exposure, which prompted more sell-outs. Most consoles sell out for the first few weeks, or maybe until Christmas. The Wii sold out every month for three years straight. Retailers didn't bother stocking them: shoppers would sniff them out in the supply room. Assisted-living facilities and nursing homes now have Wiis as a mainstay, right alongside the History Channel and stool softeners. Cruise ships have them. Malls and theme parks have Wii zones, where tourists can try out some archery with Link or racing with Princess Peach. Hard-core gamers sneer at the Wii the way they would a family film. But guess who tops at the box office, time and again? Steve Martin. Tim Allen. Robin Williams. More than eighty-four million Wiis have been sold at record speed.

Mario games still came out for the Wii, and on a regular basis. *Mario Party 8* finally had a new reason to live: despite subpar graphics and the same warmed-over content as before, the minigame board-game format was a hit with the Wiimote. (That same year, the virtual became real when the Mario characters showed up in a branded *Monopoly* game.) *Super Smash Bros. Brawl* finally came out, after years of development, and has become a top-selling game. A half dozen Mario games were released for the Virtual Console in 2007, with more every year since.

A Wii sports game tied into the 2008 Beijing Olympics was the digital equivalent of Ragnarok, matter and antimatter colliding, cats and dogs living together. The title? *Mario & Sonic at the Olympic Games*. Developed by Sega Sports, but supervised by Shigeru Miyamoto, it added double the star power to the minigame Olympic format. The *Sonic* canon (Amy Rose, Knuckles, Tails, etc.) and Mario's klatch go oversized-head-to-oversized-head in a wealth of Olympic events. The game's ads neutered Sonic by having him be the straight man, trying to give an interview while Mario foils it in slapstick fashion. *Mario & Sonic at the Olympic Winter Games* followed.

Super Paper Mario was a spiritual kin to *New Super Mario Bros.*, plunking Mario down in a sedate side-scroller, then turning that world topsy-turvy. *Super Paper Mario* did so by letting Mario swivel the camera around to show the three-dimensional world hidden by forced perspective and overlapping images of 2-D. Clever. But the years of development (it was going to be a Gamecube game way back when) had a price: for a Wii game, there was next to no motion sensing. Also clever was the premise for the newest *Mario & Luigi RPG* game for the DS, called *Bowser's Inside Story*. Mario and Luigi have to defeat a giant-size Bowser by traveling through him, fighting his cells.

Finally, there was the Mario game that everyone had been waiting for: Miyamoto's true Mario sequel, which arrived once per console. *Super Mario Galaxy* did not disappoint. It took the unused gravity-field idea from the *128 Marios* concept and applied it to an outer space setting. Mario blasted off from world to world, each a tiny sphere circumnavigable in seconds. Miyamoto, perhaps feeling his French oats, had followed up becoming a chevalier by essentially making *Le Petit Prince* as a video game.

Whatever dissatisfaction there was for *Super Mario Sunshine* disappeared with *Super Mario Galaxy*, which has sold nine million copies to date. Mario gains a new primary attack: spinning, performed with a satisfying shake of the Wiimote. The camera somehow never gets lost. Kōji Kondō wrote orchestral music for the game, to suit the bombastic sci-fi feel. There are new power suits (ghost suit, spring suit, bee suit), and even a modest two-player cooperative mode: one person is Mario, and the second is his star buddy, who mouses around the screen gobbling up valuable star pieces.

Miyamoto, who had serious involvement with the project, even agreed to put out *Super Mario Galaxy 2* a few years later, filled with all the gameplay they couldn't cram into the first game. Plus, he helped whip up a whole new side-scroller, *New Super Mario Bros. Wii*, which rocketed to ten million sales in its first two months after release.

Shigeru Miyamoto ended 2006 being profiled in *Time* magazine's list of Asian heroes. He was not put on the Artists & Thinkers list, alongside Akira Kurosawa, Hayao Miyazaki, and Salman Rushdie. Instead, he was added to the Business Leaders section, alongside microloan pioneer Mohammad Yunus, Yahoo's Jerry Yang, and ramen noodle creator Momofuku Ando. True to form, Miyamoto is a goofball in the photo, holding out his arms so a squad of Pikmin can stand on them. The following year, the goofball was given the Innovation Award for Consumer Goods by *The Economist*.

23 – MARIO'S PARTY

THREE DAYS IN THE LIFE OF NINTENDO

To properly demonstrate the scope of Mariolatry, let's look at one slice of it: cake. Mario and friend show up on a lot of cake. Groom cakes, birthday cakes, sheet cakes, multilayer cakes, cakes with Mario's face, cakes with Mario leaping out like a stripper, cakes of Peach's castle, cakes shaped like particular consoles, cakes so vast they replicate an entire level of the game. He's even prolific in the handheld console of baking, the cupcake: clever bakers have arranged colored cupcakes or brownies to make Mario out of delicious pixels. (An all-brown version was also done in the medium of burned toast.) Other artists draw different characters and icons on each circular spread of icing. A search for "Mario cake" in Google images returned 1,490,000 results.

And then there's statuary. Michaelangelo's *Pieta* has been parodied, life size, with Princess Peach cradling fallen Mario. Another Mario statue, six feet tall, was made out of thousands of Lego blocks.

It is far from the only Mario Lego sculpture. A life-size piranha plant out of *papier-mâché*. Mario on a red hydrant. Mario on a bowling pin. A wiener dog as Mario. Mario out of four thousand cans of food. A SMB mushroom out of ice.

Mario's pixilated origins, and his variety of designs over the years, affords him the ability to be re-created in media that wouldn't be able to show, say, Sonic. A Mario cross-stitch? No problem. Mario out of poker chips? Line 'em up! Pushpins? Push away! Bullets? Ready, aim, fire! Crocheted squares? It's hip to be square! Floppy discs? Boot it up! Bottle caps? Let's twist! Rubik's Cube squares, broken off and rearranged? Pivot away! A supermarket display of a thousand twelve-packs of soda? It'll take all weekend but it'll be worth it.

Novelty T-shirts? There's a new one every week. A piranha plant in a green pipe, underneath Magritte's famous phrase *"Ceci n'est pas une pipe."* An impressionistic painting of Donkey Kong's first screen. A gray shirt that emulates the NES cartridge design. A winged Mario: WING MAN. A red mushroom: GROW UP. A green one: GET A LIFE. A gold coin: OLD SCHOOL GOLD FARMER. A question block: I'D HIT THAT. A gold coin, a star, and Princess Peach: FIRST YOU GET THE MONEY, THEN YOU GET THE POWER, THEN YOU GET THE WOMAN.

Want to, say, decorate your car to look like it drove out of the Mushroom Kingdom? It's been done. Trick out a bass guitar to look like Bullet Bill? Done. Mock up condom wrappers with names like Donkey Schlong and Sextris? Rerecord "It's a Wonderful World" with a Louie Armstrong impersonator singing about *Super Mario World*? Play the *SMB* theme using half-filled beer bottles or wineglasses? Put on a Mario-themed burlesque? Paint your nails with Mario designs? Sketch what Wario would have looked like as a baby? Pornography, of all Mario-inspired manners? Make Luigi a robot? Freeze him in carbonite? Mario, King Koopa, and Yoshi in a samurai-style Japanese print?

Mario dissected? Princess Peach as the Virgin Mary? Mario and Luigi as zombies? Propose in-game? Make Super Mario Little Pony Bros.? Imagine Mario as a gay hustler? Design Mario furniture? Mario Russian nesting dolls? Mario graffiti? Raise a hundred thousand dollars by playing a marathon Mario session for charity? Done, done, done. Well, surely no one is dedicated enough to a video-game character to tattoo him on his or her skin permanently? Tell that to the half a million results on Google Images.

An ongoing discussion among critics had tackled the question of whether games can be art. Film critic Roger Ebert says no, that the freedom games give you overrules any possible message a creator could hope to deliver. (Miyamoto agrees with the decision, if not the rationale: he says games are entertaining and challenging, but claims no art status for them.) On the other hand, Tom Bissell in *Extra Lives* says yes, they can be, but only if they move away from aping films and give the player alternate worlds in which to make choices and accept consequences you could never do in real life. The debate continues, but the key objection is interactivity: I watch a Kurosawa film, and observe a Dalí painting, but I take part in a Miyamoto game.

That interactivity is the rub: what the best art strives to accomplish—connection—even the most shoddy games get automatically. In one sense, then, games are superior to any other art form: if connectivity to the audience is the goal. But the art of, uh, art is forging that connection through passive observation. It's almost not fair to compare a painting with a painting you can jump into. All parties can agree on one thing, though: if not art himself, Mario is a very reliable muse for other artists.

GAME DEVELOPERS LOVE AND LOATHE LOS ANGELES THE third week of June, for the yearly Electronic Entertainment Expo, or

E3, trade show. Whatever they're working on, no matter the release date, needs to have a playable demo plus a kickass trailer ready for mid-June. Time your production schedule wrong, and a full month of your development time can go to creating a very fancy ad for a select few people, who will scoff at anything other than a fully finished product. This is one of Miyamoto's grievances as well: people who spend hours and hours on a simple presentation to him, instead of devoting that time to the game and sending him a memo.

Yet skipping E3 is a forfeit, so everyone in gaming attends, and makes his big promises, and spends the rest of the year trying to live up to those lofty words. It's gotten better over the years, scaled down to keep the Comic-Con crowd of fans away. But E3 remains a place where no one eats steak but everyone orders the sizzle.

Microsoft's ascent into gaming had been very successful. The Xbox 360 was a tremendous gaming instrument, and its superlative Xbox Live infrastructure recreated a vital multiplayer world. There were people out there who had played a hundred hours of *Halo 3*, and hadn't once played it single-player—or ever played with an actual second person sitting next to them. Like Sega and Sony before it, it had defined itself as the base camp for the core gamer. *BusinessWeek* estimated Xbox Live's subscription costs alone were bringing in a billion dollars for Microsoft a year. It spent money by the forklift to enter the gaming world, and now forklifts were bringing that money back home. There was only one problem: Microsoft was losing.

Sony was in a very close race with Microsoft. Both were trying to claim the same territory of core gamers. Sony's PS3 architecture was arguably superior to the 360's, but a developer could do just about anything with either machine. Many of Sony's wounds were self-inflicted, going back to launch where its blustery president claimed it was sold out in every store, an easily disproven claim. Some outstanding games made all forgiven with the geek crowd: titles like *Uncharted*, *Resistance*, *LittleBigPlanet*, and *Assassin's Creed* were epics. There was only one problem: Sony was in third place.

Microsoft and Sony had the same problem the book industry had during J. K. Rowling's *Harry Potter* opus. Bestseller lists started excluding them from the "adult" bestseller lists, saying they were for children and thus didn't count. This conveniently freed up the number-one spot for other authors. This strategy was a sound one, so Microsoft and Sony had for five years said they were duking it out for first in sales, not second, because they didn't consider the mere Wii as a competitor.

It wasn't working: sales figures of the three consoles side by side by side looked like pencil marks of a child's height at age five, six, and nineteen. Nintendo, whose plebian console wasn't even HD, had been the one to redefine terms, really: coming up with a whole new marketplace with new preferences. Its console sales bested Microsoft and Sony combined. If Nintendo had just stayed on the same playing field it would be in third, where it belonged!

For Nintendo execs, the E3 challenge was to have as much spring in their step as possible. They were coming off a lackluster year: few exciting games, a wounded stock price, and increased competition. Execs that year lowered sales estimates by more than a billion dollars, mostly due to the strong yen, which strangled export profits. They were still winning, but the profits weren't miraculously growing every year. Nintendo had learned from past success stories (notably Microsoft in the nineties) to always feel the underdog, never rest on your laurels. They weren't even taking the easy out of blaming low sales on piracy or the yen: Iwata stated that Nintendo's job was to "increase the number of our consumers who are willing to shell out their money to purchase our products."

So they started setting up "Nintendo Zone" Wi-Fi hot spots in Tokyo McDonalds. They gave out baseball stats to folk who brought their DSes to Mariners games. They arranged for the best game designers in the world to fall over themselves praising *Super Mario Bros.* for its twenty-fifth anniversary. Miyamoto had the month before E3 earned global applause for *Super Mario Galaxy 2*. Even the NASCAR car GameSpot sponsored, which was painted with Mario and Yoshi, won its first race: a good omen.

Nintendo had perfected the art of attracting casual fans with one hand, while luring over the core fans with the other. It has taken years for third parties to figure out how to make decent Wii games, but now they were cranking out hits like *EA Sports Active* and Tecmo's *We Ski*. But the casual fans had deep pockets: they would buy the Wii, a Wii Board, Wii Fit, and even the Wii toys given away at Wendy's, and then never use them. They also picked up an ever-growing pile of one-game-only peripherals: billiard sticks, cooking gear, crossbows, helmets, steering wheels, paintbrushes. All three consoles were guilty of this for instruments, thanks to *Guitar Hero* and *Rock Band*, selling hundred-dollar plastic axes. The cash of the fair-weather fans who try out video games like a hobby was just as green as the fanboy's.

The Wii's new stated goal, Satoru Iwata said, was to break the PS2's record to become the world's most popular console. That was a steep cliff. The Wii already had eighty-four million units after five years, spurred on by a 2009 price drop. That number looks great—it's more than twice as many Atari 2600s sold—except when measured next to the PS2's 143 million (and counting). In 2009 the PS2 was still outselling the PS3 certain months. There are more PS2s than there are residents of Japan. Could Wii sales still be practically doubled? No one could tell Iwata he wasn't setting his ambition as high as Yamauchi.

The yearly product demos of the three console makers, as well as A-list publishers like EA and Ubisoft, are true stage shows. Microsoft brought out Cirque du Soleil. Sony had rising comic Joel McHale host for them. Nintendo was not averse to playing this game either: it had sent a Mario mascot into zero gravity with Buzz Aldrin to promote the first *Galaxy* game. For E3, Nintendo used not celebrities or performers but its own in-house celebrities. No, not Mario and Link.

Nintendo president Satoru Iwata walks on the stage, introduces himself, then lets a white screen drop down. Iwata (wearing the same suit) appears on screen, picks up a DS console, and sees Mario's hand sticking out. Mario slaps a fake mustache on him, and then Iwata is sucked into the machine like it's a *Ghostbusters* floor trap. Shigeru Miyamoto (recently voted the most influential person in the world in a 2008 *Time* magazine poll) enters, has a Nintendog jump out of the screen into his arms, then is sucked in as well. Finally, NOA president and COO Reggie Fils-Aims comes out, and chuckles at what he sees on the screen: Bowser in a lava dungeon chasing the two Nintendo creatives. Then Bowser sticks his head out through the DS and breathes cartoony fire all over Fils-Aims. The screen goes up, and the Regginator stands there for real, dressed in a burned suit. Cue applause for Nintendo's yearly company play.

What they demonstrated was the 3DS, a new iteration of its venerable DS system. (Fils-Amie jetted to New York to show it off on talk shows later that week. Miyamoto raved about it in L.A., but kept to his rule to not appear on Japanese television: he doesn't want to start getting mobbed for autographs when he's walking his dog.) The DS had miraculously eclipsed the Game Boy's total sales, become popular with boys and girls, adults and kids, all around the world. The 3DS, as the name suggests, delivered 3-D images (the bottom screen remained 2-D, but touch sensitive). Its big launch game was a new franchise that

Nintendo was dusting off: *Kid Icarus*, last seen (in anything more than a cameo in a *Smash Bros.* game) in 1991. The 3DS didn't require glasses, a trick that Nintendo guarded like the Coca-Cola formula but would be found out soon enough. The main suspect was parallax barrier LCD, which no one had used for a film because it only worked from one seat in the house, dead ahead. Sony's PlayStation 3, in perpetual third place, could show 3-D games, but only with glasses—and an expensive 3-D-capable flat screen.

The 3DS also allowed Nintendo to cash in on a new media stream: 3-D movies. There had been a sharp increase in 3-D films, which theater owners loved because of the higher ticket prices. Studios fell over themselves to convert 2-D movies into 3-D. But there was no easy way to replicate the experience of watching a hit like *Avatar* at home: despite the fifty-two-inch plasma display and the six-speaker sound, it was flat as a pancake.

Nintendo's comparative tiny screen, smaller than a YouTube window (but with better resolution), had the movie theater beat. Players could take a break from *Paper Mario* (one of the first wave of 3-D games, along with *Nintendogs + Cats*, *Pilotwings* and *Star Fox* flight titles, and of course *Mario Kart*) to try Nintendo's deep third-party support (*DJ Hero*, *Resident Evil*, and *Kingdom Hearts*) or watch a hit 3-D film like *How to Train Your Dragon*. Being Nintendo, they dragged their feet for six months after E3 before mentioning that Miyamoto was working on not one but two 3-D Mario games. One would be an old-fashioned side-scroller, and the other would be a 3-D Mario game in, uh, the other kind of 3-D. Miyamoto said working on the games was bringing back Virtual Boy memories, which might not be the best thing to bring up.

The 3DS was also an MP3 player, could get you online, and even let you chat in 3-D. There was enough to it so that even if you didn't play games, you could want one. This was a pyrrhic defeat for Nintendo, which had purposefully kept the peanut butter of other applications out of the chocolate of their game system: witness no DVD player on the Wii. The big N was caving to nongame interests: it had recently let Netflix stream movies via the Wii, years after the 360 and PS3 were serving them to millions of viewers. Nintendo's consistency defense was that all the bells and whistles were just ways to keep the game system from being forgotten.

Nintendo's drift away from gaming could be called the "everything box" syndrome, named after the Holy Grail of electronic companies: a set-top box that provides broadband, music, movies, games, and all conceivable applications. There are few technical boundaries to making such a box anymore. But try lining up third-party developers for a satellite receiver with a game controller. Try getting movie studios to stream their new hits on your wireless router. Try getting people to make a phone call from their GPS. When convergence lets anything do everything, the mission-statement navel-gazing of what a company's actual purpose is, and what sets it apart, becomes critically important.

For instance, Microsoft's biggest 2010 gaming offering was the Kinect, a movement-based interface: basically, a Wii minus the Wiimote. (Sony's top in 2010 was the PlayStation Move, a kludgy combo of Kinect and Wii technologies.) If you wanted to steer in a racing game, turn an invisible wheel: to hit a tennis ball, wave your hand back and forth. It incorporated voice commands as well, just like on *Star Trek*. It offered game play that the Wii couldn't, which stole from the Nintendo playbook. In promoting the Kinect, one of the producers even said it was as innovative as *Super Mario Bros.* Microsoft saw the

future, and it was Marcel Marceau. The Nintendo-doesn't-count argument wasn't working, so Microsoft (and Sony) had about-faced and
were now trying to out-Nintendo Nintendo.

There were differences between their companies and Nintendo.
Microsoft and Sony wanted to gobble up every hour of your free time
however they could, for your life to become devoted to their games and
products. Which was a fine business model for companies with an
enviable record selling electronics and computer programs. Nintendo
had wanted that too, at one point, but not anymore. It had learned its
product wasn't hardware or software: it was amusement. With games
for staying in shape, training a pet, gardening, playing music, shooting pool, and fishing, its goal now was to reflect your life via games.
The Wii was an existence simulator.

Nintendo had researched a look-ma-just-hands interface when
designing the Wii, and decided against it. With no physical matter to
press or hold, players would have to learn the mimetics of how to play
a game all over again. And that was if the technology worked perfectly: Microsoft's version was plagued with rumors that the seeing
eye couldn't yet detect hand motion if players sat. And Sony had
already tried the motion-sensing controller gambit before, with its
Sixaxis controller, which had been phased out due to lack of use. Even
if it worked perfectly, was there an audience? Would anyone who
wanted a Wii drop double its price to play an imitation of it years
later? Such were the E3 rumors: not only were Kinect and Move car-
bon copies of Nintendo's idea, they were smudged copies. Nintendo,
for its part, lost millions later than year when it denied a rumor that
the 3DS would be in stores for Christmas: sorry, not until next year.

The everything-box syndrome was most in evidence for portable
devices. Nintendo's DS was now competing not only with Sony's

waning PSP, but also with Apple's waxing iPhone. iPhone models featured a touch screen, a high-speed 3G connection for phone and Internet access, and a nifty but small on-screen keyboard. Most notably, it featured a shockingly robust "App Store" with hundreds of thousands of programs, either for free or for a few bucks. This led to a cadre of other touch-screen phones, each one with its own geometrically increasing pile of apps and games. How they differed from the DS on paper was negligible. So if mobile devices were providing gaming, what could Nintendo do with the DS to compete?

Nintendo had copied Apple to a degree, opening its own minigame store for the DS. It branded many of its regular DS games "Touch Generations," calling them "Great games anyone can play." (Mario does not appear in any Touch Generation title, save for a *Tetris* cameo.) And, like a guidance counselor recommending a career as a guidance counselor, Nintendo offered for download a free title like *Flipnote Studio*, where gamers could make their own animated films, and *WarioWare D.I.Y.*, whose purpose is making and distributing hand-crafted games online, for free. A way to find the next Miyamoto? (Nintendo was so worried they'd lose Miyamoto the same way they lost Yokoi they recently forbid him from walking or biking to work.) Or a devious trick to outsource new Mario content? Maybe Nintendo can allow the best designers the chance to whitewash their fence.

Nintendo's twin concerns were losing market share and mind share. Would a DS unit play as sweet if a user had another device in her pocket that let her play games? But how much push could it give the Wi-Fi and cameras before forgetting those were features added so people would merely, in Nintendo's corporate walleye view, have it on hand more often to play games? That was the hail-Mary genius of the 3DS: a function ideal for gaming that no other device had, which introduced a whole new suite of activities, all exclusive to the 3DS. Suddenly the other everything boxes didn't have everything.

AS OF 2010, THE FIRST DECADE OF THE TWENTY-FIRST CEN- tury was over, with nine more to go. Every bit of technology, every way people lived, would be changed due to the new connectivity and speed of culture. Many of these changes have already happened: music fans who hear a new artist download the track (sometimes they even pay) instead of trekking to a music store to buy the whole album. No one visits the library when he can Google a subject in .00007 second. We accept that ads will infiltrate their way into every aspect of our life, a problem that can be alleviated with an ice-cold Coors Light. And the hallmark of this connectivity is interaction. All avenues of our lives, in other words, are turning into video games.

How will this affect games? In a lot of ways it already has. Xbox Live (and its Wii and PS3 counterparts) are online communities where you can compete with or against friends or strangers. Nintendo lags in this, stressing its own limited interactivity. Iwata and Miyamoto have both said that Nintendo is probably not doing enough when it comes to online gaming.

But there's more to connectivity than that. Facebook's low-res fare such as *Parking Wars* is a glorified game of mail chess, where each time you log on you see your friends' moves, and respond in turn. Others are old-school remixes: *Farmville* looks familiar to *Sim City* players, and *Mafia Wars* is an isometric beat-em-up: *Civilization* via the Cor- leones. Facebook, Twitter, and Xbox Live, it was announced around the time of E3, would soon share update threads. But Facebook's ubiq- uity, its platform, makes for a threat bigger than any rival peripheral. It wasn't much discussed, but during the show word got out that Google had invested up to $200 million in Zynga, the company behind many top Facebook games. OnLive, a cloud-computing service that let owners of run-of-the-mill laptops play A-list PC games such as *Assassins' Creed II*, had just launched. It was getting easier every year, every month, to imagine a world with so much bandwidth and processing oomph available that specialized machines just to play games wouldn't be needed.

Speaking of those specialized machines, what happened to the concept of new consoles? All three consoles are at least five years old by this time: E3 should have been rife with chatter about PS4 prices, or Xbox 720 release dates. Instead, Microsoft and Sony spun their Wii-clone add-ons as if they were whole new game platforms, not just accessories. Nintendo, in turn, kept making new console games as if the concept of a Wiiquel was inconceivable. This was because Microsoft and Sony were on ten-year plans, kicking the can of the console death spiral to 2015. Making the most of seasoned technology? Another page out of the Nintendo playbook.

24 – MARIO'S LEGEND

THE FUTURE OF NINTENDO

Mario, somewhat infamously, is stuck in a *Groundhog Day* of perpetually having to rescue the princess from Bowser. Even when the plot is new, the story stays old: Mario stops the big bad and saves the girl. Imagine Sherlock Holmes if every single Sherlock Holmes story had to involve Moriarty stealing the Crown Jewels from the Tower of London: it would get old fast. But we merely *read* Sherlock Holmes, and try to understand him via his actions and interactions. We *play* as Mario, and have a completely different relationship with him. We *are* him: his frustration at missing a jump is our own, his joy in grabbing a coin is ours as well. That's why his (or any other game character's) story-mandated in-game conflicts seldom ring true emotionally for us: they're breathers, a halftime show.

In fact, his lack of consequence has its definite advantages. No soap opera recasting: "The part of Mario will be played by Crash Bandicoot." No *Zelda*-style collective amnesia over what happened in previous games. No *Dune*-style flame-outs where later stories are hamstrung by the originals. Tell a story long enough, even one like James Bond or Batman where the actors keep swapping in and out, and soon enough it has to be rebooted. That consistency, Ralph Waldo Emerson's famous "hobgoblin of little minds," becomes an anchor weighing down new ideas.

Mario has no such consistency issues: all Miyamoto wants from the guy is a connection to gamers. He's at one end of a tug-of war, pulling for Mario to be recreational, away from the half-hour cut scenes of the storytellers on the other end of the rope. But Miyamoto is only one man, and thus some very clever story sometimes sneaks in under the portcullis.

For instance, the end of *Paper Mario: The Thousand-Year Door* reveals that the big treasure Bowser and Mario have been questing for the whole game is . . . a ruse. Mario has really been doing a demon's work, and his collected Crystal Stars will reassemble the Shadow Queen, an evil force who was banished a millennium ago. And the body she's coming back in is Peach's. Now Mario has to attack the princess he's been trying all game to save: very troubling. After Mario and company drop her hit points by seventy-five, the Queen becomes invincible. Round after round, she no-sells whatever he throws at her. The player undergoes a level of panic paralleling Mario's dilemma: there's no way to win.

Then, since this is Mario, things get better. In a cut scene, Peach fights back and escapes to safety, Mario gets his hit points maxed out, and the next round of the fight begins with the Peach-free Shadow Queen. Mario (and you at home) can without agita now finish the fight.

Most any other game would feature more realistic-looking

characters, proportioned not like giant toddlers but like adults. But the hydrocephalic Mario look ties in with cartoon academic Scott McCloud's theory of simplistic empathy; the more basic a drawing, the more human and relatable it is. We feel for good old Charlie Brown's heartbreak more than Funky Winkerbean's, because Charlie Brown is simpler. We feel more with Mario than with a more realistically proportioned hero like Master Chief or Lara Croft. (Not that the buxom Ms. Croft is the best example of realistic proportions.)

Most every other gaming hero that's come since has had the burden of creating a personality for its star. Crash is silly, Sonic is snarky, Jak is stoic. Mario has the freedom to have no personality at all: that's why Charles Martinet's Father Guido Sarducci voice seems so risible. When Mario opens his mouth he's a specific person. Mute, he's our eternal alter ego. To update Joseph Campbell's line, Mario is the face of a thousand heroes.

MARIO MAY NEVER FIGHT AN OPPONENT OTHER THAN Bowser, but Nintendo is seeing some new rivalries. Let's look global. Nintendo is at the very top of Greenpeace's yearly naughty list for electronics companies. Unlike every other hardware manufacturer, Nintendo has no recycling program to strip out harmful toxins and heavy metals in its old Gamecubes and Game Boys. Greenpeace is promoting a contest to see which company goes green first, but Nintendo is the only one not even trying. This despite the Wii using five times less energy than competitors.

It would be Nintendo style to have been working on such a solution for years, and not want to rush things to meet Greenpeace's deadline, and thus be branded the most irresponsible company in electronics. But it would also be Nintendo style not to have any such plan (because that's what the competition is doing), or to have even considered the matter. But maybe it's learning: all of its Wii releases now come in ecofriendly containers.

Part of Nintendo's reluctance to talk about manufacturing is because no industrial company wants to discuss the real engine behind its low-cost quality goods. That engine is China. The conundrum of the China Price is one where Nintendo has gone along with the herd. Workers in Shenzhen costs a lot less than those in Kyoto or Redmond, and can assemble the same products with the same precision. And Chinese subcontractors have perfected the cutting-their-own-throat negotiation tactic, slashing their costs however they can to offer better and better deals for Europe, the Americas, and Japan. Like a union in reverse, they offer more and ask for less.

But there's a price for the Price. Many of the world's Wiis, and much of world's tech products, are made at a single Foxconn plant in Shenzhen. The plant's size is about a hundred times larger than you can imagine: 350,000 workers. Imagine if all of Cincinnati or Pittsburgh were twenty-five-year-old men, and worked for just one company, a company run like a boot camp that encouraged long hours, low pay, and no complaints. That's Foxconn, where no one can afford anything they manufacture. Santa's village, run by Mr. Burns.

Foxconn does offer a few benefits: company housing and life insurance. But the life insurance is worth much more, about ten years' worth of salary, than the pittance its employees make. The Chinese workers are so uniformly desperate to support their rural families that a shocking number of them "fall" off the top of their dorms, suicides for the life insurance. That some of these workers made Mario games, about a jumping hero, is ugly to the point of disgust.

The factory has pledged to increase salaries by 20 percent. And Foxconn's other big clients—Hewlett-Packard, Dell, and Nintendo rival Sony—are in the same boat. Everyone wants this to go away. "This," unfortunately, is the attention, not the process of cutting a small check and receiving a large pallet of goods from someplace far away.

Another Foxconn client, Apple, is shaping up to be a heavyweight Nintendo contender. After decades of "Apple gaming" being a joke among the PC community, Apple is making a killing selling touch-based games on its portable media devices. Apple and Nintendo are quite similar; both are famously closed-system, both have devoted fan bases across many ages and both genders, both emphasize style and fun. The main difference between the 3DS and the iPod, philosophi-cally, is that only one has an off switch.

Apple, like Microsoft and Sony, is at heart an electronics company. It charges a lot more for the quality of its products. And then it comes up with subtle ways to make you unable to break the iHabit. If you have an iPod, why not use QuickTime, since Apple keeps asking to reinstall it alongside iTunes every two weeks? Why not keep iTunes running 24-7, since your podcasts won't download otherwise? Why not throw away your six-month-old iPod because Apple's new OS for some reason won't communicate with it? On the other hand, Iwata had considered installing governors into the 3DS, so no child could play it too long. Don't look for that as an app anytime soon.

Another new competitor is Wall Street, or rather Kabutocho, Japan's financial district. Nintendo's shares in the Tokyo Stock Exchange have been traditionally safe bets. But in early 2009, due to the cratering economy, Nintendo posted its first drop in profits since the handheld DS revitalized the company. This is bad if you play bridge—and the stock market is one giant continual round of contract bridge, trying to reward companies not only for high earnings but for correctly guessing in advance how well they thought they'd do.

Nintendo's stock crisis halved its $78 high down to $35. But Microsoft and Sony's stocks lost billions more, and their new-normal trading figures were about $16.

These are Nintendo's new rivals: Apple, Greenpeace, Foxconn, Wall Street. And of course, social media and its addictive casual games. Not to mention Microsoft and Sony. Biggest of all is the specter that's haunted Nintendo for two decades: the slow walk of young men growing up and putting away their childish things. Nintendo doesn't covet this core audience as much as before, thanks to the 360 and PS3 fighting over them like dogs with a hunk of meat. But the great land run is on to claim the world's lunch hours and puttering-around time of the casual audience.

All of Nintendo's plotting and fighting for the casual fan has one giant flaw: the casual fan. Nintendo can't get them if they're too casual, otherwise they'll drift to no-cost options like Facebook. (Iwata has forcefully denied that Nintendo would ever make a browser game or an app: no lateral software without paying for seasoned hardware first!) But they're also unable to use what for three decades has been their heavy artillery, Mario, for fear of scaring their new audience away. Nintendo's Touch Generations games don't feature Mario. Mario is core, not casual. He has to let Nintendo fight this fight without him.

Nintendo not letting itself make a browser Mario game has not stopped a flash flood of in-browser Mario games. *Super Mario Flash*, *New Super Mario Bros. Flash*, *Infinite Mario*, and the amazing *Super Mario Crossover*, which lets you play the original *SMB* games using characters from *Castlevania*, *Excitebike*, *Ninja Gaidan*, and more. (If you like that, try *Abobo's Big Adventure*.) There are free (and unlicensed) Mario games where he rides a motorbike, takes a shotgun to the Mushroom Kingdom, decides to fight with his fists, is replaced by Sonic, replaces Pac-Man in a maze game, and plays dress-up. They receive no admonition from Nintendo's once-ferocious legal department. Why not? Iwata's explanation is commonsensical: "[I]t would not be appropriate if we treated people who did something based on affection for Nintendo as criminals." This is also why no one has been told by lawyers to stop selling Wario-as-a-pimp T-shirts.

Nintendo's most recent successes have made it clear: Mario is no longer Nintendo's biggest draw. The Wii and the DS's lifestyle games sit in that throne now, and they try very hard to be unlike other video games. Mario's still the most popular man in the world, but despite his range he's a limited performer. Casual fans are fine with him in small doses—a race, a fight, a minigame. But they don't want any hint of story other than their own improvement, any more than Xbox 360 players want cute minigames. (Sorry, Kinect!) The closest he's gotten to these new gamers is cameoing in one picture on one matching game from *Big Brain Academy*. Five years ago, that game would have had his name on it.

Mario games, both platformer and spinoff, still sell very well. *Super Mario Galaxy 2* is one of the best-reviewed games in years, earning rare perfect tens left and right. And he'll always be a favorite for Halloween costumes. But he's not the king anymore, the perpetual emperor of physics engines. Take a look in the mirror to see the new face of Nintendo gaming: it's you. You—*Time* named "you" the person of the year in 2006, so don't be modest—have taken Mario's job away from him. He's still uniquely qualified to bounce around on Goombahs' heads, and will still sell millions of copies in even a bad game. But he belonged to the first wave of video games.

Current nomenclature says that there are seven video game "generations." The dominant consoles for the seven generations are: Atari Pong (first), Atari 2600 (second), the NES (third), the SNES (fourth), the PlayStation (fifth), the PlayStation 2 (sixth), and the Xbox 360 (seventh). This order assumes that the Wii shouldn't even be counted as a seventh-gen system, since what it does well is almost unrelated to the red-queen advancements in capabilities of the muscular Xbox 360 and PS3.

From the point of view of Mario, and Nintendo, though, there have only been three eras. One began with *Pong*, of course, and lasted through the video game crash of '83 and the early Famicon/NES years. Call this the joystick era. Games were totally original, written from scratch every time, all with dynamic (and often unique) control schemes. Often they were solid state: no computer, just dedicated circuits soldered into a pattern that made a paddle game. Many tried to simply duplicate a fun activity: sports, racing, target practice, mazes. There was little connection to storytelling: any "story" was the age-old man-versus-opponent conflict.

The second era flared up with the NES's popularity, especially with a certain overalled pipe fitter. This is Mario's generation, starting with *Donkey Kong*. Call this era the D-pad era. The new paradigm of third-person took hold, making most every video game a gussied-up puppet theater where the toy du jour finds treasure and stomps enemies. Phrased another way, they were hunter-gatherer simulations. Mario, Sonic, Master Chief, Niko Bellic—it's all playing atavistic caveman, rolling around in the basement of Maslow's hierarchy of need. The message of the D-pad medium was third-person play. Even when joysticks returned, they were small thumb-size affairs used just like the D-pad. Computer keyboards? D-pads with extra buttons.

This era is still going on, but it's overlapping with the third era. We now live in the first years of the motion era, started in 2004 with the Nintendo DS. (It had been nascent for decades, of course, in arcades and a garage sale's worth of one-game-only peripherals for consoles.) One by one, players started drifting toward video games, with simple new control schemes: press the screen, wave a wand, strum a guitar. Not *games* as much as *activities*. You can be sure all eighth-generation game systems will come standard with motion-control setups.

These activities are basically all joystick-era games in philosophy. More lively, with a nebula's improvement in graphics, but the same concepts: play at shooting, play sports, play with friends, basically just play. The character-driven D-pad ethos was too cumbersome: it was time to take a step back and perform activities without a fictional world being at stake.

As it stands now, the core gamers are loyal D-padders, and the casual gamers drift strongly to the motioners. There's overlap and crossing over, but most people, like most games, fit into one camp more than the other. You can be sure that Nintendo will have a load of Mario games for years to come, for both camps. Mario is uniquely suited for such transition: games such as *Mario Paint*, *Tennis*, and *Golf* establishing him as a Renaissance man.

Most all other game characters are, to their detriment, actual characters, with personalities and story lines specific for their game. They're often ramped up to absurd levels: look at any afro'ed character, ridiculous weapons like *Gears of War*'s chainsaw bayonet, or women who dress like strippers (this includes, sadly, almost all female characters). They try so hard to set themselves apart from Mario's blandness, by whatever means necessary. And all this screaming for attention had made them stuck in a single game genre.

The motion era's trademark is a return to the joystickers' style of game play. Like swing music and bell-bottoms, the base-level creativity of early game developers is returning. What is a minigame, after all, but a joystick era game, now economically repriced to come forty to a pack? Some stink, just as some games back then stunk. (Recall sci-fi author Theodore Sturgeon's valuable law: 90 percent of everything is crap.) But developers are learning how to design creative short games, sports simulations that aren't steroid fests, and innovative puzzle games.

Video games have changed the world in the forty years since *Pong* told us to "avoid missing ball for high score." A new medium exists, produced by a multibillion-dollar industry. Its rise paralleled computers' prominence: now many homes have one of each. It's changed how people behave: business gurus preach that gamers are more self-motivated employees if you give them tasks to accomplish instead of instructions to be obeyed. Games' geeky scenarios have propelled science fiction and fantasy into the mainstream. Entertainment went from being something we saw in crowds to something we experienced as single players, a trend that is now shifting back to group interaction. The global quality of life is undeniably raised by all this dedication to a new form of play. Games—whether joystick, D-pad, or motion—are at their root enjoyable. They make the world a happier place.

There will come a fourth era of video games, which I'll dub the unified era. This will blend the motion era's accessibility with the D-pad era's commitment to epic story and clever refinements of genre conventions. Perhaps it'll also mix in whatever is the new gaming trend as well: thought-controlled games, say. In TV this era would reflect a *Hill Street Blues*, which married the police procedural and the soap opera into a synthesis where viewers cared about both the cases being cracked and the personal lives of the officers on duty. In books it would be *Oliver Twist*, mixing up the bawdy fare of an ongoing narrative with shocking indictments against society's mistreatment of children: entertainment and information. In the theater it's Shakespeare, writing to noblemen and commoners using the same pen. In movies it would be none other than *Citizen Kane*, which merged the theater-perfected melodrama with a fleet of technical camera tricks that made clear this was no filmed teleplay but a motion picture.

The games of the unified era may not come around for another ten years: the societal obstacles are profound. But they will combine the addictiveness of D-pad era games with the accessibility of motion fare. Imagine a football simulation where your perspective doesn't shift from player to player but focuses on just one person: the running back always trying to get open, the quarterback constantly racing the clock, the linebacker stopping an unstoppable force every single play. (For that matter, imagine giving a hoot about characters in a sports game.) Or a fighting game where the damage you take doesn't easily heal, where every character is a limping, scarred map of stress points. Or a racing game where you care so much about the other players you watch online matches you're not in, to root for favorite drivers.

These almost certainly aren't going to be what the hit games of tomorrow are. I'm not a game designer, and perhaps it shows in these examples. But there are currently two warring tribes consuming video games, and there's no reason for them to be at war. It will take a few years, some olive-branch releases on both sides, before casual players accept a game with a story, and core players accept an activity without a game. And the first few games that try to bridge these camps may crash and burn, like Nintendo's 64DD.

But I would like to, cautiously, and with a book's worth of evidence as backup, make a claim about who will be the designers of the unified era's first blockbuster title. Shigeru Miyamoto, in one of his last great performances for Nintendo, will use the knowledge gleaned from his shuttle diplomacy missions between the core and casual camps. He'll understand what lizard-brain types of game play appeal to both groups, and what sort of structure that foundation would best support. Satoru Iwata, continuing a tradition, will premiere another new console like the Wii and the 3DS that makes up for in innovation what it lacks in horsepower. Reggie Fils-Aime will continue to merge the roles of hype man and president, tailoring his sales pitch to what people want to buy, not to what he wants to sell.

Nintendo will need a hook for this new console, a specific game that couldn't be played, or conceived, on any other platform, even with down-to-the-atom motion sensing or a Beowulf cluster of processing power. But they'll already have their star lined up. Miyamoto and Iwata and Fils-Aime will call up Nintendo's most famous character, propelling him once more unto the breach. Super Mario will be back. And he will be as big a star as ever, in this new game that will unite the great schism of gaming. It will take a few years, and maybe a few misfires, but the plumber will reclaim his throne.

THANKS, MARIO, BUT OUR NOTES AND ACKNOWLEDGMENTS ARE IN ANOTHER CASTLE

Just kidding.

I hope it doesn't come off as bragging when I say that this book could have been double in size. There's a lot of Mario out there, but not all of it moves the Nintendo story forward. Much of my editing work was in snipping out lines, paragraphs, and in two instances entire chapters that were tributaries that diverged too far from the stream. Those two chapters are available at www.supermariobook.com, if you want to learn more extensively about Nintendo's relationship to Japan in its early days, and about the fascinating and very secretive man Mario is named after, Mario Segale. Think of them as downloadable content, to use a gaming term.

I've listed most all of my book sources in the bibliography, but the list of Web sites I consulted would probably go on for half the length of the book itself. Just about any possible question I could ask myself, regarding facts or analysis about Nintendo, someone before me had asked and answered. Thanks to them, I had a true surplus of video game heritage and trivia to immerse myself in. The beginning of chapter 23, for instance, grew just about daily. Just because I found a hundred different types of Mario shirts doesn't mean all hundred have to be described.

There seems to be a pact among Wikipedia users: they'll use it but never actually cop to doing so. I will gladly cop not only to looking at but to printing out and reviewing (on an hourly basis) two Wikipedia pages: one on Mario's appearances ordered by year, and one of Miyamoto's games, arranged the same way. It's very difficult to find an error on Wikipedia: I became an expert on Mario and Nintendo, and I only found a few minor release-date discrepancies. The stigma persists, though, and thus I didn't use a Wikipedia source if I could get the same information any other way.

Other Web sites I visited for information include 1up.com, businessweek.com, slate.com, newyorker.com vintagecomputing .com, oxfordamericanmag.org, industrygamers.com, kokatu.com, and joystiq.com. Nintendo fan sites (miyamotoshrine.com, gonintendo .com, n-sider.com, zeldauniverse.net, among others) were great portal sites to find older, Google-ignored coverage of Nintendo moments. I'd like to especially call out GameSpot.com, which ran an exhaustive history-of-Mario series; VGChartz.com, from which I found most all of the sales figures in this book; and Nintendo's own Iwata Asks series, where I got to be a fly on the wall as Nintendo execs held candid postmortems about what went right and wrong during development.

People were often the best sources. Some lent books, others helped with translations, and others (well, just one) volunteered to put on a mustache and red overalls to make a promotional video. Thanks go to Justin Brennan, Philip Jan, John Merriman, Kristin Linsday, Benj Edwards, Deanna Talamantez, Alison Holt Brummelkamp, Candace

Smart, Mikkel Paige Mihlrad, Konstantin Karpenyuk, James Brennan, and Vinnie Nardiello. Jeannette Fee, Sean Ryan, and Cynthia Ryan were early readers, and offered edits so good I felt embarrassed I hadn't thought of them first. Also there was that one guy at the Gamestop in the mall, and that other guy at the other Gamestop in the same mall . . . People want to talk when they find out you're writing a Mario book.

My parents could have written off $200 from their 1987 taxes if they knew I'd write this book. Thanks to Kathleen Ryan and Dennis Ryan for resisting the urge to buy an Atari 5200 for Christmas, and thus starting me on my literary endeavor. And to Brendan Ryan, Bridgette Parker, and again Sean Ryan, three siblings I love more every year.

I've done my best to make the professionals at Portfolio and Penguin not regret their decision to publish a book about video games. Thanks to Emily Angell, Christy D'Agostini, Maureen Cole, Faren Bachelis, Linda Cowen, Daniel Lagin, Dan Donohue, Jennifer Tait, Eric Meyers, and my editor Courtney Young. Without all of you, the world would never know about *Hotel Mario*. And thanks to my agent Lynn Johnston, who set me up with my first interview, her fifth-grade daughter, soon after we sold the book.

I dedicated this book to Bill Rudowski. Who is he? He's who won the book dedication auction, with all proceeds going to Child's Play, which donates toys and games to children's hospitals. Thanks to him, Laura Whalen, Ed Byrne, Jimi Cullen, Andrew Melzinek, and everyone else who stopped by eBay for a bidding roller-coaster ride.

The various people I've met over the years at Nintendo—from the Redmond and Kyoto branches and their Golin Harris press office—have been very generous and helpful, arranging interviews, providing review copies of material, touring me around the facilities, even setting up an interview with Shigeru Miyamoto. But Nintendo is a particular company, and one of those particularities is not cooperating with the press when it comes to books. So most all of that access dried up when I told them I was working on something longer than a magazine article. My time spent embedded in the Mushroom Kingdom was thus unofficial.

I've thanked Cindy Ryan for her editing before, which she's done for my writing projects since before we were married. She's also responsible for buying me our Wii, defeating the Pit of 100 Trials, outracing me without the aid of any red shells, and winning several NES games in the *Animal Crossing* village of Qwerty. She's also brought two princesses into our lives, Sylvia and Holly, which makes her twice the hero Mario is. I would say more wonderful things about her, but I'm running out of ways to couch them in video-game argot. Here's one more: my life is super because of you.

BIBLIOGRAPHY

Ashcraft, Brian, with Jean Snow. *Arcade Mania: The Turbo-Charged World of Japan's Game Centers.* Tokyo: Kodansha International, Inc., 2008.

Beck, John C., and Mitchell Wade. *The Kids Are Alright: How the Gamer Generation Is Changing the Workplace.* Boston: Harvard Business Press, 2006.

Bender, Jonathon. *LEGO: A Love Story.* New York, Wiley, 2010.

Bissell, Tom. *Extra Lives: Why Video Games Matter.* New York: Pantheon Books, 2010.

Burnham, Van. *Supercade: A Visual History of the Video Game Era, 1971–1984.* Cambridge, MA: MIT Press, 2001.

Bloom, Steve. *Video Invaders.* New York: Arco, 1982.

Christensen, Clayton M. *The Innovator's Dilemma: The Revolutionary Book That Will Change the Way You Do Business.* New York, Harper Paperbacks, 2003.

Cohen, Scott. *Zap: The Rise and Fall of Atari.* New York: McGraw-Hill Company, 1984.

Compton, Shanna, ed. *Gamers: Writers, Artists & Programmers on the Pleasure of Pixels.* Brooklyn, NY: Soft Skull Press, 2004.

Dear, William. *The Dungeon Master.* New York: Houghton Mifflin, 1984.

DeMaria, Rusel, and Johnny L. Wilson. *High Score! The Illustrated History of Video Games.* New York: Osborne/McGraw-Hill, 2002.

Detweiler, Craig, ed. *Halos and Avatars: Playing Video Games with God.* Louisville, KY: Westminster John Knox Press, 2010.

Donovan, Tristan. *Replay: The History of Video Games.* London: Yellow Ant Media, 2010.

Friedman, Thomas L. *The World Is Flat 2.0: A Brief History of the Twenty-first Century.* New York: Farrar, Straus and Giroux, 2006.

Gilsdorf, Ethan. *Fantasy Freaks and Gaming Geeks: An Epic Quest for Reality Among Role Players, Online Gamers, and Other Dwellers of Imaginary Realms.* Guilford, CT: Lyons Press, 2009.

Grann, David. *The Lost City of Z: A Tale of Deadly Obsession in the Amazon.* New York: Doubleday, 2009.

Halberstam, David. *The Reckoning.* New York: Morrow, 1986.

Heath, Chip, and Dan Health. *Made to Stick: Why Some Ideas Survive and Others Die.* New York: Random House, 2007.

Herz, J. C. *Joystick Nation: How Videogames Ate Our Quarters, Won Our Hearts, and Rewired Our Minds.* Boston: Little, Brown, 1997.

Inoue, Osame. *Nintendo Magic: Winning the Videogame Wars.* Tokyo: Vertical, 2010.

Johnson, Steven. *Everything Bad Is Good for You: How Today's Popular Culture Is Actually Making Us Smarter.* New York: Riverhead Books, 2005.

Juul, Jesper. *A Casual Revolution: Reinventing Video Games and Their Players.* Cambridge, MA: MIT Press, 2010.

Kent, Steven. *The Ultimate History of Video Games: From Pong to Pokémon.* New York: Three Rivers Press, 2001.

Kim, Chan W., and Reneé Mauborgne. *Blue Ocean Strategy: How to Create Uncontested Market Space and Make the Competition Irrelevant.* Boston, Harvard Business Press, 2005.

Kohler, Chris. *Power-Up: How Japanese Video Games Gave the World an Extra Life.* New York: Brady Games, 2004.

Kidder, Tracy. *The Soul of a New Machine.* Boston: Little, Brown, 1981.

King, Brad, and John Borland. *Dungeons and Dreamers: The Rise of Computer Game Culture from Geek to Chic.* New York: McGraw-Hill, 2005.

Kushner, David. *Masters of Doom: How Two Guys Created an Empire and Transformed Pop Culture*. New York: Random House, 2003.

Klein, Naomi. *No Logo*. New York: Picador, 2000.

Leguizamo, John. *Pimps, Ho, Playa Hatas, and All the Rest of My Hollywood Friends*.New York: Ecco/Harper Collins, 2006.

Lewis, Michael. *Pacific Rift: Why Americans and Japanese Don't Understand Each Other*. New York: W.W. Norton Press, 1993.

Loftus, Geoffrey R., and Elizabeth F. Loftus. *Mind at Play: The Psychology of Video Games*. New York: Basic Books, 1983.

Mezrich, Ben. *The Accidental Billionaires: The Founding of Facebook: A Tale of Sex, Money, Genius, and Betrayal*. New York, Doubleday, 2009.

Miller, G. Wayne. *Toy Wars: The Epic Struggle Between G.I. Joe, Barbie, and the Companies That Make Them*. New York: Times House, 1998.

Oppenheimer, Jerry. *Toy Monster: The Big Bad World of Mattel*. New York: Wiley, 2009.

Poole, David. *Trigger Happy: Videogames and the Entertainment Revolution*. New York: Arcade Publishing. 2000.

Sheff, David. *Game Over: How Nintendo Zapped an American Industry, Captured Your Dollars, and Enslaved Your Children*. New York: Random House, 1993.

Stross, Randall. *Planet Google: One Company's Audacious Plan to Organize Everything We Know*. New York: Free Press, 2008.

Sullivan, George. *Screen Play: The Story of Video Games*. New York: Frederick Warne, 1983.

Takahasi, Dean. *Opening the Xbox Inside Microsoft's Plans to Unleash an Entertainment Revolution*. Roseville, CA: Prima Publishing, 2002.

INDEX